Good Housekeeping

ONE SHILLING NETT   FEBRUARY 1932

Why are we failing the dead? *by* Godfrey Winn

Lorna Rea ~ O.Douglas ~ Mabel Constanduros
L.A.G.Strong ~ A.Duff Cooper ~ Clemence Dane

Good Housekeeping

OCTOBER 1932   ONE SHILLING NETT

THE TECHNIQUE OF MARRIAGE
A New Series by Mary Borden

Martin Armstrong ~ Dame Ethel Smyth ~ Virginia Woolf
A S M Hutchinson ~ Lady Violet Bonham Carter

Good Housekeeping

December 1932

1.
NETT

CHRISTMAS NUMBER

D.K.Broster ~ Vicki Baum ~ Francis Brett Young
I.A.R.Wylie ~ Kate O'Brien ~ Walter de la Mare

Good Housekeeping

DECEMBER 1934

Christmas Number

1. NETT

New Novel by Joanna Cannan
Beverley Nichols ~ Susan Ertz ~ Warwick Deeping
Maude Royden ~ Kathleen Norris ~ Temple Bailey

Good Housekeeping

JANUARY 1935   ONE SHILLING NETT

Complete Story by
MARY PICKFORD

Doreen Wallace ~ Sylvia Thompson
Mary Roberts Rinehart ~ Naomi Mitchison
Articles of Special Appeal to All Who Love Children

Good Housekeeping

FEBRUARY 1935   ONE SHILLING NETT

Special Illustrated Supplement :
SUGGESTIONS FOR GARDEN PLANNING
New Complete Story by Dorothy Whipple
Clare Sheridan : Joanna Cannan : Virginia Pye
Ursula Parrott : Emma Lindsay Squier

Good Housekeeping

JULY 1935   ONE SHILLING NETT

NEW SHORT SERIAL by DOROTHY WHIPPLE
Sinclair Lewis : This Golden Half Century
Robert Bernays ~ Phyllis Duganne
Dr. W. Howard Hay ~ Sewell Stokes ~ Neil Bell

Good Housekeeping

SEPTEMBER. 1935 — ONE SHILLING

The Institute's Eleventh Birthday

Mary Roberts Rinehart • Naomi Mitchison
Noel Streatfeild • Countess of Oxford and Asquith
Christine Jope-Slade • Beverley Nichols

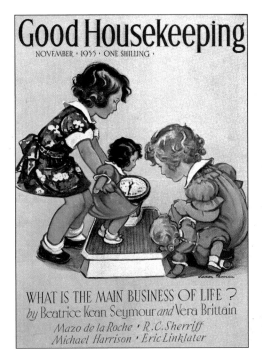

Good Housekeeping

NOVEMBER • 1935 • ONE SHILLING •

WHAT IS THE MAIN BUSINESS OF LIFE ?
by Beatrice Kean Seymour *and* Vera Brittain

Mazo de la Roche • R.C.Sherriff
Michael Harrison • Eric Linklater

HOME
sweet
HOME

HOW "GOOD HOUSEKEEPING" CAN SERVE YOUR NEEDS

The

Everlasting Problem
of Home Management

Shortening the Longest Job in the World

MEN get very little credit, as a rule, for the work they do during the day.

But women get still less !

Men, at least, are paid for their work. Women seldom secure even the reward of praise.

The Press delights in such questions as, Who are the most popular women ? Who are the most beautiful ? Who are the greatest ? But there is only one really great woman—the *home-maker.*

It is hardly necessary for us to point out to you how unselfishly, how unceasingly women work. The task of home-making is never done. Always there seems some task overlooked, some new duty which insists on attention, some routine obligation which cannot be neglected or postponed. Whether you have servants or not, the demands are equally persistent.

How, then, can you overcome them ?

You never can—completely. It is futile to hope for such a thing. But you can make your tasks lighter, your working hours shorter. How ? Good Housekeeping will help you. Good Housekeeping will help you as it is helping thousands of women. Good Housekeeping has the necessary facilities and services ; it is all a question of using them—when and as often as you need them.

You can do this in three ways. (1) Through the editorial pages of Good Housekeeping, (2) through its advertising pages, (3) through the correspondence services.

In the editorial pages of Good Housekeeping you will find the answers to most of your home-managing problems. You will find articles by staff experts and outside

authorities. These articles are written by practical workers, who understand the subject, and aim not to fill space, but to aid you.

Also through these pages you can do a large part of your shopping. Goods from the London Shops that are really excellent value for money are photographed and displayed in our pages. These can be had through Good Housekeeping on the receipt of the order and money. So although you live in the country the London Shops are not prohibited to you.

In the advertising pages you will find hundreds of guaranteed advertisements— advertisements of just the devices and household supplies you need to make work easier and of shorter duration. And *every one* of these advertisements is guaranteed. (You will find the guarantee on page 88 of this issue.)

Through the correspondence service you can have any question, not covered by the magazine, answered and discussed at length. Your case is specially considered, and the utmost care and thought is given in dealing with it. Until you have tried it, you cannot realise the enormous help that expert outside advice can bring to the solving of your problem.

The best way, perhaps, to understand how Good Housekeeping treats the problem of home management is to examine a few recent issues. Going over them we find detailed articles which discuss thoroughly the following problems among many :

Spring Cleaning, a special study by the Department of Home Management.

The Family Tool Chest.

Labour-savers that are Hygienic. Simple gadgets that can be installed in any home.

How to Repair Upholstered Furniture.

Laundrywork done at Home: the problem discussed in articles from time to time.

The working secrets of innumerable Housekeepers.

Cooking by Steam Pressure.

Solid Fuels, old and new.

How Gas can be saved.

Stepping Stones to Good Cookery.

Planning the £1,000 House.

Heating, Lighting, and Cooking by Oil.

Daily Maids in the Small Town House.

Vacuum Cleaners. How to choose the one most suitable for *you.*

House decorating with your own hands.

Labour-saving on the Staircase.

Running the Basement House without Servants.

Keeping House with Electricity.

When you use Anthracite.

Banishing Rust and Decay.

Typical Stains and their Removal.

We have selected from recent issues of Good Housekeeping only a few of the articles which deal directly and specifically with the problem of home managing. In addition, there were, of course, hundreds of articles dealing with fashions, cookery, child training, lessons in home dressmaking, lessons in interior decorating and home furnishing, articles on home building, together with plans and specifications by famous architects, articles on the professional and business woman, the social worker, as well as stories by the world's greatest authors.

The problems already dealt with will be dealt with again—discussed and elaborated along with many additional ideas, in the light of added experience and new discoveries, the result of endless experience, to make your tasks lighter.

Good Housekeeping is *your* magazine. Use it.

HOME
sweet
HOME

THE BEST OF GOOD HOUSEKEEPING 1922-1939

With contributions from:
Rebecca West, Lady Violet Bonham-Carter, E.F. Benson,
Vera Brittain & Evelyn Waugh

Compiled by
Brian Braithwaite & Noëlle Walsh

LEOPARD

This edition published in 1995 by Leopard Books
Random House, 20 Vauxhall Bridge Road, London SW1V 2SA

ISBN 0 7529 0033 1

Printed and bound in Great Britain by
Butler and Tanner Ltd, Frome and London

CONTENTS

6 Foreword

8 The Ideal House - *Herbert Jeans* (March 1922)

12 Under the Eaves - *Gertrude E Whinfield* (June 1922)

15 Living Together - *Mabel C Leigh* (July 1922)

16 Wireless for the Home - *John Ellacott Genner* (July 1922)

17 Wives, Mothers, and Homes - *Rebecca West* (October 1922)

20 The Ideal Home Part IV - *Herbert A Welch A.R.I.B.A.* (October 1922)

23 Bed as a Refuge - *J E Buckrose* (February 1923)

24 The One Thousand Pound House - *F J Watson Hart* (November 1923)

26 The Fifteen Hundred Pounds House - *H V M Emerson A.R.I.B.A.* (May 1923)

28 The Servantless House - *Dora J Moore* (June 1923)

31 Houses I Have Lived In - *Annie S Swan* (September 1923)

35 Daily Maids in the Small Town House - *Margaret Benn* (April 1923)

36 What is a Home? - *W L George* (July 1923)

40 A Home Beside the Sea - *H N M Emerson A.R.I.B.A.* (August 1923)

42 The Well-Mannered House - *C H James A.R.I.B.A.* (July 1924)

47 Adam at Home - *Clara Savage Littledale* (June 1924)

52 A Home in London or in the Country - *Lady Violet Bonham-Carter* (January 1926)

59 Anne Orr's Needlework (February 1927)

60 So This is Marriage! - *Clara Savage Littledale* (March 1926)

63 The Mending Basket - *Caroline Gray* (April 1926)

66 Cheap Living in Paris - *J D Beresford* (March 1927)

68 Desirable Residences - *E F Benson* (February 1929)

73 Are you a Good Housekeeper? - *Lady Violet Bonham-Carter* (November 1928)

76 Good Housekeeping Builds a House - *Herbert A Welch & D D Cottington Taylor* (June 1929)

83 A Song of Home - *Ethel R Fuller* (October 1929)

85 Beauty - *Margaret Marshall* (June 1929)

93 The Tale of a £900 Cottage - *The Owner* (February 1929)

94 Fiction: A House Needs a Husband - *Alice Booth* (September 1930)

108 Should we retire before working? - *Helena Normanton* (August 1931)

110 A Single-Handed Garden for Penelope - *Jane Farley* (August 1931)

114 One Roomitis - *Vera Brittain* (June 1932)

121 New Houses - *Grace Noll Crowell* (September 1927)

122 In Fact - Things Last Too Long - *F E Baily* (May 1933)

125 Prayer for a Bride's House - *Christie Lund* (January 1934)

126 How Others Live -VII: A Fifteen-Roomed House and an Income of £376 (April 1934)

134 Design in the Small Garden - *Annette Hoyt Flanders* (July 1934)

136 Training a General Maid (January 1934)

141 Our Readers and Ourselves (June 1934)

142 The Importance of Good Design in the Small House - *Joyce E Townsend A.R.I.B.A.* (September 1935)

144 Real-Life Budgets - *P L Garbutt* (January 1936)

148 A Convenient Country House - *Baseden Butt* (April 1936)

152 The Itch of Efficiency - *Helen Simpson* (August 1936)

156 Half-Time Home Life - *Irene Stiles* (April 1936)

159 The Cross-Word Garden - *Gerald Wynne Rushton* (May 1936)

161 Bedtime Boat - *M T* (November 1936)

162 Do You Know? - *P L Garbutt* (October 1937)

165 Furnishing & Decoration (May 1937)

169 Good Housekeeping Extends a Cordial Invitation to its Readers - *D D Cottington Taylor* (March 1931)

170 Anne Orr Needlework Designs (August 1937)

174 Home Planning at the Empire Exhibition - *Moray Macbeth* (June 1938)

176 Bachelors' Homes - *Winifred James* (July 1938)

182 Do you Know? - *P L Garbutt* (March 1938)

184 Fiction: An Englishman's Home - *Evelyn Waugh* (August 1939)

192 Prayer For a New Home - *Virginia Eaton* (July 1938)

FOREWORD

EDITORIAL VIEWPOINT

Plus ça change. That's the overwhelming impression looking back over 70 years of the home as seen through the pages of Good Housekeeping. Oh yes, the numbers may have altered - try and find the £1,000 house or the flat in London for £87 rent per year today - the size may have diminished and the servants may have fled. But the discussion about what makes a home and who should run it has vivid echoes in newspaper articles and dinner table discussions today.

Good Housekeeping, while offering serious solutions to the problems of home management, treated the subject with some degree of levity. "...the home is the organisation which changes slowest. Kings rise and fall, religions wax and wane, but boiled bacon is always the same." The author avers that "the making of homes is the curse of Eve".

For poor Eve, the task of home-making is never done. "Always there seems some task overlooked , some new duty which insists on attention, some routine obligation which cannot be neglected or postponed," says the author of one article, meaningfully subtitled "Shortening the Longest Job in the World". At first, she holds out little hope of overcoming the problems of home management. "It is futile to hope for such a thing. But you can make your task lighter, your working hours shorter. How? Good Housekeeping will help you ...(it) has the necessary facilities and services; it is all a question of using them..."

The Twenties saw a rebellion among young women towards the home. Deprived of the servants whose labours their mothers had enjoyed, they refused to tie themselves to uncompromising bricks and mortar, to old-fashioned kitchens and ranges, to the never-ending task of home management. Relieved of kitchen fodder in the form of servants or young daughters, old houses were carved up into flats, and vacuum cleaners, plate-washers and mechanical potato peelers were invented to lighten the load. These changes in the home made their impact on society as a whole. Smaller homes increased the tendency for the whole family to congregate together in the living-room rather than take their leisure apart, accentuating family tension. Smaller, more uncomfortable homes also increased the likelihood of its members leaving it to find their pleasure elsewhere - one of these new activities involved eating out at restaurants, hitherto considered rather a fast thing to do. And young mothers no longer being seen as born doctors, fashion designers and nutritionists meant the foundation of welfare centres, baby clinics and nursing organisations.

While Good Housekeeping chronicled the changes in women's attitude to running the home, it also relayed the practical commonsense facts of life about the costs involved . Whether it was bachelors' homes or a country vicarage, the Good Housekeeping Institute , set up in 1924 , was at hand with money-saving ideas, budget planners and down-to-earth advice. Those were the days when people took far more interest in the planning of their home. Thus when Good Housekeeping built its own house in Weybridge, Surrey, in 1929, the floor plan was just as important as the cost, finding the sight and choosing the building materials.

For some of you, the pages of this book will be like a journey into the past , a reminder of the concerns and mores of a generation for whom a house was a home, not just an investment. For others, brought up in the housing boom of the recent past, read its pages well, for history has a lot still to teach us.

NOËLLE WALSH

ADVERTISING VIEWPOINT

As always with our series of "nostalgia" books from the pre-war times of Good Housekeeping magazine, the advertisements present an endless social commentary through the years. This volume is dedicated to the home and the housekeeping life and the only problem in decorating the editorial pages with advertisements was the agony of selection - so much had to be omitted which we would have loved to have included. Those examples we have chosen follow the years faithfully and, although we have juxtapositioned advertisements which are germane to the general theme of the book we have often left the advertisements which were in situ to the original editorial, even if they are not directly applicable to the home. We felt that this gives the correct sense of chronological perspective as well as affording pleasant glimpses of commercial life between the wars.

Obviously appliances feature strongly throughout the advertising pages, from the Polliwashup machine on page 14 (which removed "the odious task of washing up" and cost only ten guineas for the larger model, suitable for families of ten persons) to the more recognisable and sophisticated electrical machinery of the late Thirties. Along the way we meet the opportunity of hot baths for one penny each and the universal geyser, familiar to us boys of the 1930's when a more senior member of the family usually seemed to claim priority to drain the hot water supply.

It was the new inventions which must have dazzled and excited our mothers or grandmothers, like the shift from messy coal fires to the new world of gas fires such as Radiation and Cannon and the efficient grates like Triplex (page 118) "a Christmas gift every good wife deserves". And the new methods of house cleaning with the constant blandishments from Hoover and Goblin. And the telephone! A whole new social world was opened up by the Telephone Development Association in 1926 (page 64) with the irresistible offer of a telephone in your own home for half-a-crown a week - with the charge of one penny for each local call (and nothing for the calls you received!).

The coming of the refrigerator must have revolutionised the average middle-class household with the whole concept of pure fresh food. The meat safe and the larder were overtaken by the appearance of the new brands like Frigidaire, Electrolux and Coldspot - yours for sixpence a day. Cold milk, ice cubes and crisp lettuce had arrived for the fortunate minority.

All the other commercial enticements on offer, by the department stores like Harvey Nichols, Gamages and Drages, to the new-fangled but logically argued devices like wall insulation (page 119) and the artistic range of Lloyd Loom furniture, must have caused much envious knuckle-gnawing by the sheer variety and temptations of this brave new world, designed to transmogrify the whole ambiance of household drudgery to a more pleasant utopian dream. Britain's advertisers were quick and eager to answer the call.

BRIAN BRAITHWAITE

A country cottage of the bungalow type with upper story, designed on entirely modern lines, which, at prevailing prices, it is estimated could be built for about £1,600, apart from the cost of the land

The Ideal House

For the Person of Moderate Means

By Herbert Jeans, *Editor of "The British Builder"*

A practical article, which describes how a house with four bedrooms and two or three reception-rooms, standing in its own grounds and containing all the necessary structural labour-saving features, may be built, at present-day prices, for the modest sum of from £1,450 to £1,600

GROUND FLOOR PLAN

FIRST FLOOR PLAN

Fig. 1

IN these days of reconstruction many an old family is reconstructing its house by de-molishing wings and attics which tend to make the building too costly in upkeep. It seems a paradoxical way of achieving the ideal house, but the practice is becoming so well estab-lished that one reads in a technical paper a serious suggestion that the art of remodelling by demolishing in this way may provide a new opening for the archi-tect. It is well known, even to the layman, that the profession has passed through very troublous times since the year 1914, and that a new opening of some sort is devoutly to be desired. But, hitherto, as the title itself implies, it has been the business of the architect to build up;

and the fact that he is willing now to exercise his art by pulling down—by scientifically knocking off a wing here and a story there—brings us to the con-clusion that the ideal house must necessarily be one that does not throw an unbearable strain on its owner's purse.

No wise person will dispute that contention. And since we are none of us (or very few of us) rich nowadays, I pro-pose to describe only the small house that can be built for from £1,450 to £1,600, plus the cost of the land, and to dis-cuss what may be ob-tained for a sum in the neighbourhood of those figures.

A glance at the illus-trations will show that a very presentable and fairly commodious house can be built for the amount indicated. In each instance a house or bungalow type of residence standing in its own grounds is represented. The lay-out of the garden would of course depend in a large measure on the extent of the land acquired; whilst a garage or stable, which would be a matter of extra expense, could be placed where the exigencies of the site allowed, and could be built to provide whatever accommodation the owner might require.

The houses illustrated in these pages have been designed for erection in almost any aspect. Site and soil are necessarily questions of locality, and as everyone knows that low-lying ground is less desirable than high ground, and that a clay soil, although it may be excellent for rose-growing, is not to be chosen for living on, it is not proposed to labour those points.

In planning the house itself, however, there are certain rules or principles that one must insist upon the architect's observing—such as the avoidance of long trots in the performance of essential household duties, and the provision of central heating and ample lavatory and cupboard accommodation.

It is the custom in planning nowadays, wherever possible, to place the dining-room and kitchen next to each other, with a serving-hatch communicating. This aperture, to be properly effective, should be a double hatch, so arranged that the opening of one closes the other, thus preventing the noises and odours of the kitchen from entering the dining-

Edward II, restrictions were imposed on the burning of soft coal, on account of the injury that resulted to the community. And yet the practice is continued to this day. It has been said very justly that those who are interested in the brighter London movement should concentrate first on the abolition of the open grate, which is responsible for so much fog. The Committee on Smoke Prevention recommended that the cottages built under the various Government housing schemes should be each provided with only one open grate; but, in deference to the general prejudice referred to, this recommendation has hardly ever been carried out. But, apart from questions of health, if labour saving is to be an essential feature of the ideal house, then the open fire must surely go. The labour involved in carrying coals about the house, laying and raking out fires, and the dust that re-

A detached two-story cottage, designed on labour-saving principles, for erection in an English garden city. At present-day prices it is estimated that this house could be built for about £1,450, apart from the cost of the land

sults are only too well known to every housewife and to every housemaid. It is for this reason that the houses here illustrated are fitted with radiators, which are intended to be worked on a simple system which combines cooking and heating. An installation of this description provides an excellent cooking-stove, which supplies ample hot water for the bath, lavatory, and sink, in addition to an adequate heating system for radiators, which can be shut off in the summer, leaving the domestic hot-water supply unaffected.

By placing a radiator in the hall and on the first-floor landing, a warm current of air may be assured throughout the house, if the bedroom doors are left open. Any further heating that may be required may be obtained by radiators or gas fires in the rooms, an open grate for burning coal or wood being provided in the chief living-room.

An additional economy could be attained by building gas flues in the walls, without the chimney-breasts that are needed for coal fires, and this would also afford so much extra space in the rooms.

If I have dwelt at some length upon this purification of the atmosphere and dispelling of unnecessary

work by the abolition of the smoky chimney, it is because I feel that the Government has neglected its duty in this vital matter; and the reform, which is one of the essentials of the ideal house, rests with the building owner.

The provision of a cupboard for coats and cloaks in the hall should not be overlooked. The hanging of coats and hats in the old-fashioned hall-stand gives an untidy appearance at the very entrance to the best kept of houses. No less necessary is adequate lavatory accommodation. In the examples herein illustrated, a lavatory with hot- and cold-water supply is shown in the hall. This is a convenience which overcomes the necessity of going upstairs whenever one wishes to wash one's hands.

This provision should be carried further, and the lavatory basin, with hot and cold water, should be installed in each bedroom. Plumbing considerations may in some cases make this difficult,

(Continued overleaf)

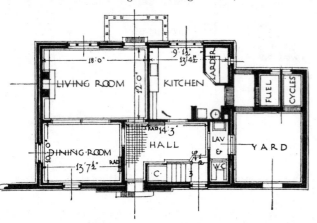

GROUND FLOOR PLAN

Fig. 2

room. In the plan (Fig. 2) of the ideal cottage it will be seen that these two rooms are not so arranged, but the kitchen in this case is effectively shut off from both sitting-rooms, and placed sufficiently close to the dining-room to make the few steps across the hall of but little account. But in the plans of the larger house this hatch is provided, and the larder has a window on the external wall. A hatch for tradesmen might with advantage also be provided in this wall, with an outside shelf in a porch to protect from the weather. The larder shelves themselves would be of marble or slate.

In advocating central heating for the private house one is up against the deeply rooted English prejudice in favour of the open grate. Those who read the really interesting report of the committee appointed by the Government to inquire into the matter of smoke abatement will be surprised to learn that, as long as 600 years ago, in the reign of

tory, and sink, in addition to an adequate

FIRST · FLOOR · PLAN

C. M. HENNELL · F·S·I · & · C·H · JAMES · A·R·I·B·A ·
ARCHITECTS · 19 · RUSSELL · SQ · LONDON · w·c·l

Fig. 3

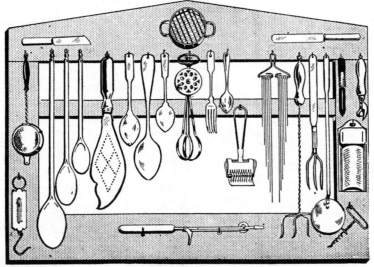
The Ideal House
(Continued)

as in the plan shown in Fig. 3. In this instance the occupier of No. 2 bedroom would use the lavatory basin in the bathroom across the landing, which, in view of the fittings in all the other bedrooms, should not be overmuch in demand. A better plan is to build the lavatory basin in a small washing annexe to the bedroom, but this is rather a costly affair, and we are discussing a house for people of moderate means.

The modern bath, although in itself an excellent fitting, is not usually cased in, as it was a generation or so ago. There is, therefore, liable to be, between the lower part of the bath and the wall, a space which it is difficult to clean. Mr. G. Berkeley Wills, A.R.I.B.A., one of the successful designers in the last *Daily Mail* Ideal House Competition, got over this difficulty by making his bathroom circular in plan, the bath itself projecting into the room, with the shower and taps end built into the angle of the outer wall. But, there again, your house would cost you more. A simpler plan is, where space permits, to place the side of the bath well away from the wall.

The need for cupboards in the upstairs rooms cannot be overstated. In addition to wardrobe cupboards in the rooms themselves, all available space between rooms should be utilised in this manner. A good example of the occupying of space in this way is shown in Fig. 3, where the cupboards built in between bedroom 3 and the bathroom are arranged to serve those two rooms and the landing respectively. All of the cupboards should be ventilated, and, where they are large enough, should be fitted with seats and lockers.

Each of the plans that we publish affords accommodation for fuel and bicycles outside the house. In each also is shown a loggia or pergola, which are both of course intended for open-air lounges in suitable weather. But to my mind the ideal house, however small it might be, would not be complete without a balcony, with access from a bedroom with a south or south-west aspect. The boon to a sick person, who could be wheeled out on to such a balcony during the sunny hours, is incalculable.

In the foregoing remarks I have touched lightly on the main points of a house that may be built, at the present time, for a round £1,500. I have dealt with the structure and essential fittings only, leaving equipment out of the question.

But equipment is a comprehensive item; it may include built-in furniture, such as buffets in the dining-room, tables for divers purposes, and cabinets in the kitchen, fitted wardrobes and chests of drawers and even built-in beds in the sleeping-apartments— all these things may be constructed by the builders whilst the house is being erected, but they would not come within the estimate that we set out with.

On the other hand, deep sinks, draining-boards, rounded angles to walls, curved skirtings, and a solid balustrade to the stairs in concrete or brick, to avoid the dust-harbouring balusters, may well be reckoned among the essentials of our ideal house. Doubtless enough has been said to prove that, with a well-kept garden without, and the latest appliances for cookery, cleaning, and labour-saving within, an ideal house is not necessarily the appanage of the rich only, but is quite within the reach of the man or woman of moderate means.

THE

20's

*The kitchen in the all-gas house showing gas cooker with
plate rack above, modern gas fire and gas-heated circulator.
In the adjoining scullery are fixed a gas fire, incinerator,
a gas copper, and an internally heated gas iron.*

No Small Achievement

TO warm a house comfortably, light
it pleasantly, ensure cooking that is
dependable, and hot water in plenty—
all without extravagance—is no small
achievement. Yet all this can be done
with perfect ease by using gas

*Write for Gas Economy Leaflet No. I
. . on the " All-Gas House " to . .*

THE BRITISH COMMERCIAL GAS ASSOCIATION

30 GROSVENOR GARDENS, S.W.1

Rambler rose trees " growing " in the corners of the bedroom make one think, on waking, one has slept in a garden

UNDER THE EAVES

How to Treat the Attic Rooms of a Bungalow House

By Gertrude E. Whinfield

THOSE dormer windows of the bungalow house look most attractive and " cottagey " viewed from the garden, and we do not always realise that dormers are generally the outlook from the room of sloping ceilings. I am not speaking in disparagement of this type of ceiling, as what some people might consider an eyesore can, with a little originality of treatment, be transformed into the most decorative feature of the room.

I was once besought to help make presentable what a friend described as ' a nasty, impossible attic with two ugly sloping roofs." Armed with a keg of washable distemper and the necessary stainers for graduating shades, I proceeded to paint the entire wall and ceiling surfaces in imitation of tightly drawn gathered muslin of a delicate shell-pink shade, and to emphasise the draped effect I painted a pale-blue ribbon two inches wide along the angles and above the skirtings as though holding the material in place, breaking the monotony of the line in places by simulating at intervals a tie in the ribbon, holding a posy of pink rambler roses.

The effect was that of the interior of a tent, softly lined, and was both uncommon and inexpensive. The walls were already clearcoled, and the whole

WITH this article the furnishing and decoration of "The Ideal House," described and illustrated by Herbert Jeans in our March number, is completed, and it remains only to find the land and set about the building of the bungalow house

scheme cost less than would have had to be expended on paper, whitewashing, and paperhanging. In the bungalow under discussion in this article we will use more everyday methods of decoration, which at the same time will show the possibilities of an attic room. By papering or distempering walls and slopes alike you increase the apparent height of a room, as an expanse of white ceiling extending to within a few feet of the floor acts somewhat as a lid in effect.

A pale primrose-yellow jaspé paper is chosen for the walls of the largest room. Along the angles above the skirting, and outlining the door and window, is pasted a two-inch black-and-gold key pattern border. This border is also placed in strips along the slope from wall to flat ceiling, forming panels as in illustration at top of page 13 A black carpet covers the floor, throwing up the colour of the painted yellow furniture on which bold lines of black give a

striking effect. The curtains are a black-and-gold shot-silk damask with round designs in gold. ·This is an excellent material, 50 inches wide, and as damasks go is very cheap—being procurable at 13*s*. 11*d*. per yard.

In all the rooms furniture has been chosen of low design, and plenty of breadth, the panelled beds especially giving this effect.

To anyone with artistic ability this plain furniture may be much enhanced by painted or lacquered panels, or stiff conventional borders to harmonise with the room's scheme of colour. Then there is the compo work, which can be applied and decorated in gold or colours.

The second room, facing west and north, is treated in lilac tones, and the leaf green of the lilac tree is used for the furniture relieved by lines in lilac and deep pansy purple. The same purple is chosen for the oval rug, and the floor itself is dyed with purple aniline (in size) and finished with two coats of hard varnish. The effect of this stain is delightful, throwing up the colours of the furniture excellently. Cretonne is used for the short curtains and loose covers, the predominating colours being purple and green, with touches of orange and cream. These

colours are repeated in the lampshade and bedspread.

The compo candle-bracket shows up well on the lilac background, and groups of compo fruit could be used on the bed panels, keeping to tones of gold, purple, and dull green. One more bedroom remains—illustrated at the top of page 12. This we have papered in softest grey, and colour is supplied in the form of rose trees laden with rambler pink roses growing, apparently, in the corners and around the window and door, and stretching long branches frieze-like along the sloping side and on the upright inner wall of the room.

In the bedroom at top of page painted yellow furniture has been used with excellent results. A black carpet covers the floor, and the walls rejoice in a pale primrose jaspé paper

When the bedroom contains plain furniture, as that to the left, the introduction of one or two cretonne-covered easy chairs adds an interesting decorative note and increases comfort

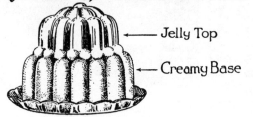

The 5 guinea model is suitable for a family of five.
The 10 guinea model, with gas-ring for applying heat, and automatic scrubber for saucepans, casseroles, etc., is suitable for larger f milies of, say, ten persons.

REST AFTER YOUR MEALS

Nothing is more disagreeable than to be confronted with the miserable task of washing-up after a good meal. The preparation of a meal is irksome enough, but this sequel is worse. It spoils the satisfaction of an appeased appetite and sets a culminating seal of fatigue to household labour.

No More Odious Washing-up

need ever worry you if you take advantage of this greatest household labour-saver of all Time.

THE
POLLIWASHUP
MACHINE

is a portable appliance, entirely free from mechanical complications, and requiring no attachments, which does this unpleasant work for you, perfectly, without breakages, mess, or extra cost.

It requires the simple addition of hot soapy water, a few turns of the handle, a second supply of water for sterile rinsing—and the work is done.

Perfectly safe to use and easy to operate. The apparatus is fool-proof, and considerate housewives will install one for lightening the maid's duties.

(Power-drawn models of any capacity for large catering institutions)

Write Now to—

The WASHING-UP MACHINE Co. Ltd.
34 Fulham Road, London, S.W.3

D.S.

'Phone: Kens. 5696

HONEYCOMB MOULD
Queen of Table Sweets

← Jelly Top

← Creamy Base

A most delicious dinner or supper sweet. It is easily made in one simple operation, turning out a beautiful jelly top on a rich, creamy base. No more nutritious or refreshing sweet can be put on the table. It is ideal for anyone at any time on any occasion. The delicate flavours please the most refined palate and the rich colours enhance the charms of the table.

HONEYCOMB MOULD will tempt and strengthen an invalid when nothing else can.

Made in five delicious flavours—original, chocolate, fruit salad, imperial and royal

All good Grocers sell HONEYCOMB MOULD.

STODDART & HANSFORD, Islington Green, LONDON, N.1.

MAKE YOUR OWN ICE-CREAM
Without Trouble, Turning or Mess
A NEW IDEA IN ICE-CREAM FREEZERS
Vacuum Process

With the Iceberg Ice-Cream Freezer all you have to do to make *Delicious, Luscious, Refreshing, Appetising Ice-Cream* is to pack the Freezing Compartment with Ice and Freezing Salt, close it down, and then fill the Central Chamber with the Creaming Mixture. In half an hour you have Ice-Cream fit to place before the best in the Land, including yourself, your family and your guests.

The tiresome task of more or less continuous turning a handle is entirely done away with.

YOU SIMPLY FILL—IT DOES THE REST

The "Iceberg" Rapid Freezer is made in three sizes to suit all requirements.

Size 1.	1 Imperial Quart	...	...	**21/-** Post Free
Size 2.	2 American Quarts	...	...	**27/6** ,, ,,
Size 3.	4 ,, ,,	...	...	**52/6** ,, ,,

AS SHOWN AT THE "IDEAL HOME EXHIBITION" WHERE THOUSANDS WERE SOLD

Send for an "Iceberg" Freezer to-day, and be prepared for one of the greatest pleasures of a Hot Summer's Day. Ideal for Picnics by Motor or by Boat.

COMMERCIAL MONOPOLIES LTD. (Dept. 90),
56 Ludgate Hill, E.C.4

14

The more business-like of the two partners should make herself responsible for all out-goings, and strict weekly accounts should be kept

LIVING TOGETHER

A successful partnership in home-making may be achieved by any two women blessed with tolerance and common sense

By Mabel C. Leigh

NOWADAYS there are many women whose income will not suffice to keep up a comfortable home, and who therefore decide to combine at housekeeping with two or three women friends, or with acquaintances, or even with strangers. The last case is not always the most unsuccessful. As far as friends are concerned the " ills we have " are not more endurable than those " we know not of," and a stranger may prove to have more in common with us than a relative. The money side of these companionships is the chief difficulty. Once the equal sharing of expense is arranged, other things should fall into line, though this by no means follows. More often than not failure is the result of the enterprise.

The fact is that living together, whether in business, friendship, or marriage, is an art so difficult that real harmony and happiness are rarely achieved. Few people are unselfish enough to consider their own faults rather than those of others. Few are patient enough to avoid the hasty word that scatters devastation in its train. If this is a truism, it is time that we looked at it in a new light and lived as if we understood it.

"Live and let live" should be our motto, and in any sort of mutual companionship we should make a point of avoiding undue questioning, interference, or impertinent curiosity. No fuss, no nagging, no endeavour immediately to alter something in our friend's character, probably native to it, and which we never perceived before we lived together. We should try to ignore small habits. Why should a sniff annoy us so intensely? Or talking to oneself, or clearing the throat, or rattling

bead chains? Or the use of strong scents that pervade the whole flat? Yet it is the truth that these things acquire a greater importance to us than the fall of empires.

On setting up house we should try, as far as possible, to find people of similar tastes with our own. We must not be led astray by the fallacy that unlikeness is more interesting. The Sinn Feiner does not assimilate readily with the Ulster woman, or the writing woman with her who practises the violin. If besotted about bridge, we must not consort with the woman who has an objection to cards, nor should we insist on a gramophone when sharing rooms with the composer of oratorios. If punctual, avoid the unpunctual, and if liberal-minded, turn aside from the mean. Between husband and wife, or between relatives, these incompatibilities must be borne with, but between friends, bound by no vow or obligation, they will not be tolerated.

Such matters as the running of the house must be regulated in a business-like way. The most satisfactory method is for one to sign the lease, and make herself responsible for all out-goings, such as gas, light, telephone, etc., also for the housekeeping and the servants. Strict weekly accounts must be kept and both women go over them, the junior partner paying her share of food weekly, servants' wages once a month, and rent, etc., quarterly. Sometimes a trial has been made of one friend taking entire control for three months, then the other having her turn; but this has been found not to answer, as the servants do not like it. With regard to furniture, if one contributes all, a little extra money should be paid into the exchequer by the one sharing the use of this house-

hold gear. In these things the involuntary tyranny of a strong nature over a weaker one sometimes becomes apparent, and leads to the discomfiture of the latter. Here we must again remember the precept "Live and let live." The stronger must encourage her diffident friend to develop her own personality and take her share in the decisions.

The two partners have been known to disagree over one another's choice of friends and acquaintances. This, indeed, is a difficult matter to adjust. For one of the hostesses aggressively to go out or shut herself in her own room every time a certain friend calls on the other soon produces a sense of strain. " Why don't you like her? " " I can't imagine how *you* can. She is—forgive me!—entirely odious." Once that point is reached, forbearance is at an end and this small difference may terminate the arrangement. I have seen many failures in these friendships, but never where a charitable outlook prevailed, or where patience was brought into play and a quality of peace in one's own mind. It is wonderful how this inner peace expands itself on all around and, in the end, brings happiness.

In the words of the great emperor: " Things do not touch the soul, for they are external and remain immovable, but our perturbations come only from the opinion which is within." And he again says: " I affirm that tranquillity is nothing else than the good ordering of the mind."

If we are able to make these considerations a real part of our lives, we shall find that the little irritations of daily life together will seem as nothing, and will fall away from us like withered leaves.

Wireless for the *Home*

Some of the marvellous possibilities of Broadcasting, and its far-reaching effects upon our lives in the near future, are dealt with in this article, which explains how, among other achievements, wireless makes it possible to listen, in your own home, to an opera or concert taking place hundreds of miles away

By John Ellacott Genner

BROADCASTING! The newspapers talk about it daily, politicians and public men make statements upon the subject, but this abundance of information is either too technical to be comprehensible or so vague as to be quite meaningless to mere Man and Woman. There is vague talk about concerts and sound waves, about church sermons and antennæ, yet those who are supposed to benefit most by this innovation are those who know least about the subject. There has been a flood of misinformation, and extravagant claims, which have little or no foundation in fact, have been made.

That broadcasting will undoubtedly be welcomed by all, and in particular by those who value their homes, is not to be doubted, because it offers every encouragement for people to receive their entertainment within the comfort of their homes.

Broadcasting is, in reality, the sending out of messages from a central station through the ether—the name given to the medium through which radio waves travel—so that, with the aid of receiving apparatus in the home, everyone, within a certain area, can pick them up. These messages are not sent out in code, but are actually spoken into one or more special telephone transmitters, the shape of which is somewhat similar to a megaphone. The sound of the voice is carried, by means of very delicate and costly apparatus, into the air so that you may, with the assistance of your receiving apparatus, listen-in (that is the phrase for receiving the messages) and actually hear the voice of the speaker though he may be some hundreds—even thousands—of miles away.

It has been said that this invention is probably the nearest approach to a miracle that the world has known. Think of it: a voice travelling in space, unguided, to be picked up at will by anyone within a huge radius of miles! This is indeed the harnessing of the Air.

The use of the ether is by no means limitless. It will accommodate just so many wireless messages and no more. If this limit is exceeded, then chaos reigns and those who are listening-in with their receiving apparatus hear no more than one incessant conglomeration of noises and discordant sounds.

In order to control the broadcasting of wireless messages, the General Post Office are devising plans whereby Great Britain is to be divided into eight sectors with two transmitting stations in each. Permission to broadcast will therefore be limited to a total of sixteen concerns, and only those capable of giving really first-class transmission and service will receive licences for broadcasting. At the present moment the General Post Office are in negotiation with the various industrial concerns who have applied for permission to broadcast, and nothing in the way of definite information regarding organisation can be given until the end of their deliberations. That which interests most people, however, is the matter to be received and the method of receiving.

At the transmitting stations definite daily programmes will be arranged and information published each morning in the newspapers regarding the times of each performance. If you are interested in any item of the day's programme you listen-in and have all the enjoyment in your own armchair of a concert or lecture.

Many people, particularly women, are scared at the thought of anything electrical, because they do not understand the apparatus. There is the dread fear of "getting shocks." With wireless receiving sets there are no such possibilities of shocks—because they do not exist, and every member of the family, with a little practice, will be able to receive broadcasted messages from broadcasting transmitting stations.

Matter is broadcast from transmitting stations on a definite "wave-length," and before it is possible to pick up the sound on one's apparatus it is necessary to "tune up" to that particular soundwave. This requires a little practice before the best results are obtainable and it is therefore most advisable in the first instance to purchase a Crystal Set with which to experiment and practice. The Crystal Set is not a highly delicate instrument, but sufficiently accurate to obtain satisfactory results.

This set is for use within a radius of twelve to twenty-five miles from the transmitting station, and is supplied complete in a polished mahogany case. Its cost is in the neighbourhood of £5, and certainly no instruments marketed at a price considerably lower are worth consideration.

In the same way that broadcasting is transmitted through an aerial, so must it be received through an aerial; and so this is really the first consideration of those who wish to broadcast at home. The aerial takes various forms, but the Indoor Aerial, as apart from the Outdoor Aerial, will probably be most suitable in this country owing to the comparatively limited garden space of most homes. The aerial for indoor use is merely a few yards of wire coiled round a small frame and can be strung up in an attic or placed conveniently in a living-room. This aerial is connected by a small covered wire to your Crystal Receiving Set, and when you have tuned up your apparatus you place the telephone receivers over your head and on to your ears, and, leaning back in your chair, you listen in comfort to whatever may be in course of broadcasting at that moment.

When the amateur has mastered this Crystal Set his interest will be greatly stimulated and his ambition will be to have a further receiving set of greater range and efficiency, and in purchasing the Valve Detector Set he has an apparatus of an altogether different quality. This set is both delicate and accurate, and will give uniformly better results.

Photo: Yevonde

To every woman who is making a career for herself in science, commerce, the learned professions, or the arts there comes a moment when she must choose between following that career successfully, but alone, or sacrificing it to the ineluctable claims of a husband, children, and a home

Wives, Mothers, *and* Homes

Can a Married Woman Have a Career Outside Her Home?

By

REBECCA WEST

THERE was recently published a book by Mr. A. S. M. Hutchinson called *This Freedom*, which told a lurid tale of the horrid consequences that followed when a married woman went out to work. It was a book that proved nothing, because it was too evident that the author suffered from what lawyers call " invincible ignorance " of the facts of life. One's judgment of the case was prejudiced by the fact that Rosalie, the wicked woman who worked, suffered from a husband who habitually said, " Mice and Mumps ! " when he hit his thumb with a hammer or otherwise felt the need of an expletive. That idiotic trick would, one feels, send any normal woman out of the home not only for the working day, but for good and all.

One was incredulous, too, of the kind

HAVE you ever met a woman who, given a happy comfortable home, a husband and children, insisted on going out to work each morning ? Many earnest anti-feminists apparently believe that such women exist in large numbers. They don't. And the reasons why they don't and never will exist you will find in this article by one of the most brilliant and clear-sighted writers of to-day—Rebecca West

of work Rosalie performed. She was alleged to hold a very high and responsible post in a Bank ; and the directors were alleged to be delighted (and to hold it as a proof of the wisdom of having a woman on the staff) when a foreign client wrote and asked her advice about Christmas presents for his wife and children ; and apparently she found time to give this

advice. Yet would one really be kindly received if one went to one's bank and asked to see the manager, and then began : " You see, it's Aunt Matilda's birthday on Wednesday . . . " ?

Nor was the story of the family's progress convincing. The eldest son was expelled from school, is arrested for drunkenness, is court-martialled out of the Army, makes a disgraceful marriage, becomes a fraudulent company promoter and is sent to prison. This was alleged to be the result of his mother's absence from home during working hours ; but it was almost more likely to be due to her habit of calling him throughout life by the name of Huggo, which she had given him in infancy because his little arms hugged so tight. Few public school boys would really enjoy this. The girl Doda was allowed to *(Continued overleaf)*

Wives, Mothers, and Homes
(Continued)

drift into bad company, though there seems no reason why, because a mother was at the Bank during the day, she should not have prevented her daughter from attending dance clubs all night. She died as a consequence of very gross immorality; and Rosalie's last remaining child, Benji, commits suicide on the Underground Railway after attempting to murder the man who is responsible for her death. Presumably if his mother had stayed at home he would have shaken the man by the hand and thanked him warmly.

The presentation of that particular case need hardly be taken seriously. Nevertheless, though Mr. Hutchinson has put a dunce's cap on the problem, it is a real one. It is not by any means settled in most people's minds whether a married woman ought to have a career outside the home.

That question can be unhesitatingly decided in the affirmative in two cases. The first is the case of the married woman without children. The childless wife who spends all the forces of her being on her home—unless she be so wealthy that looking after her home entails the management of an estate—is putting all her capital into an uncertain investment. Men are apt to take the rosiest possible view of their capacities; and in estimating the extent to which they can provide for the happiness of their wives they are liable to forget that they do sometimes die. When a woman who has wholly absorbed herself in her husband's life intellectually, as well as spiritually, loses him, she endures something worse than widowhood. She becomes a sad cumberer of the earth; and not even means and social position will save her. The childless widow of a famous man, drifting about the world where she figured with him, dressing just as carefully, but not for anybody, is sadly conscious that she is not quite so warmly welcome as she was when her husband was alive. She is also, though more obviously tragic, not really so true to her love as the woman who has an independent career; for that woman can, by the way she works out her career, be loyal to the best things in her dead husband. That career need not, of course, be pursued in the usual wage-earning grooves. There is plenty of work—research in science or in history, service on municipal bodies, work on behalf of public health for which the State, particularly since the war, cannot afford to pay, but which it is desirable in the interests of civilisation should be performed; and here especially is the sphere of the childless wife whose husband can support her.

The other type of wife who ought to work is the antithesis of this woman, the wife with children who is not supported by her husband. She is obviously doing her duty; and a hard row she has to hoe as a rule. A woman who has been married long enough to produce a family has usually lost the habit of working in the way that will be required from her in the factory or shop or office: she goes into the labour market under the disadvantage of having so much depending on her that she cannot bargain fearlessly for good terms; and unless she is exceptionally well-paid and fortunate, all the time she is working her mind must be worrying about the arrangements she has made for her children's well-being during her absence. It is, indeed, a hard lot.

I observe with surprise that of all the anti-feminists who have written to the papers enlarging on the horrors consequent on mothers working outside the home, not one has suggested getting up a subscription

Wives, Mothers, and Homes

list to enable mothers who are forced to do so by lack of means to give up this pernicious habit.

But there remains the problem as to whether a woman with children who is adequately supported by her husband ought to go out to work.

That, however, on consideration, changes into another problem. Can she go out to work ?

There are many reasons which will make it very difficult for her to do so. One of the many things which made women dislike *This Freedom* was its abundance in proofs that though Mr. Hutchinson has written a gasping and palpitating book about children and home life, he knows nothing of children, and little about home life. His ignorance about children was shown particularly badly in the concluding paragraph, when Rosalie's grandchild, whom she adopted to retrieve her errors over her own children, is represented as jumping round her every morning trumpeting in "her tiny voice" ("tiny voice" is a touch that reveals the bachelor) "Lessons! lessons! On Mother's knee! On Mother's knee!" A more experienced person would know that "lessons on mother's knee" would result in frequent pins and needles in the knee, and much damage to the young growing spine.

But even more ignorant was Mr. Hutchinson's assumption that Rosalie's house ran like clockwork, while she, day in day out, kept office hours. It was a large house; her husband was a leading barrister with an income of several thousands a year, and they certainly must have entertained; they must certainly have kept several servants. Yet the reason that brought Rosalie home was that she found that the governess was teaching her children that the flight of the Israelites across the Red Sea was not literally true. The experienced housewife will smile at this. She will know that long, long before the infant ear became corruptible, Rosalie would have been recalled, because she found a rich deposit of dust on the picture-frames; or because the housekeeping books were climbing to the most astonishing dimensions; or because the servants were taking unauthorised days out; or because the housemaid suddenly appeared before her in tears alleging that the cook and the parlourmaid were conspiring against her; or because the housemaid and the parlourmaid were sisters and had to go home because their mother was dying just when Huggo and Doda and Benji were down with measles.

The fact is that there is no task which it is more difficult to hand over to a deputy than household management. A millionaire can find a confidential secretary much more easily (and at a salary not so much more than that of an ordinary secretary for an ordinary post) than a professional woman can find a housekeeper to run her home and family at double the salary given to a housekeeper in ordinary circumstances. There are several reasons for this. The chief is that domestic service, so far from being natural to women, is profoundly unnatural. It is certainly not the perfect destiny for any woman to spend her life looking after another woman's house and children; and the servant's knowledge of this is shown very often in a lack of enthusiasm for her work, and also in a certain discontent of spirit which makes it very difficult to run the household machine smoothly.

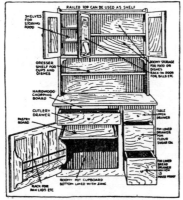

This kitchen has been so planned that when the day's work is finished, it may readily be made comfortable as the servants' sitting-room, the more dirty work, including dish washing, being done in an adjoining scullery

The Ideal Home

Part IV

Things To Be Considered in its Achievement: The Kitchen Quarters

By

Herbert A. Welch, A.R.I.B.A.

LAST month we completed our detailed consideration of the Porch, Hall, Dining- and Drawing-rooms. In passing straight away to consider the Kitchen quarters, we have not forgotten the possible desire for a study or "den," but its provision will rarely, if ever, again come within the range of practicability in a house where our purse is limited to between £1,700 and £2,000, and when four or five bedrooms and other necessities are desired.

The Kitchen Quarters.—Two points of first-class importance will at once occur to us: firstly, that the kitchen quarters are the practical side of the house and therefore need the most exact planning and detailed thought. It is here that we shall, by careful planning, provide a measure of labour-saving far greater than that produced by the many devices we see advertised as such. Secondly, that servants being a necessity in nearly every home, they form part of the members of the household, and good servants being scarce all reasonable consideration must be given to their comfort. Not long since we quite commonly heard the remark that "such and such a detail does not work well, or is not quite

good, but it's only the kitchen—or scullery or maid's bedroom—so it doesn't really matter." It is a sign of progress that such a phase is passing and while we with limited means are unable to give to the servants' quarters that degree of spaciousness and comfort found in the larger homes, we can, nevertheless, see to it that as human beings whose help is necessary to our reasonable enjoyment of life, their comfort at work and leisure receives due consideration.

In houses of the size we are considering the kitchen will be the servants' living-room and as such we must think of it. It should be reasonably cosy during the winter, and bright during the summer. To this end the main features to be considered are lighting, fireplace, table, dresser and doors. We shall do well to give the kitchen sun during some part of the day. A look-out on to the road will also be appreciated. The fireplace should not occupy the wall directly opposite the window or the light will be shut out when the cook is attending to the meals; nor should it be so placed that we have to walk in front of it in passing to the scullery. We shall also be wise to place it reasonably out of the draught.

The above combined kitchen-scullery contains, in addition to the necessary fittings shown, a range and dry store. With this type of kitchen the maids' sitting-room, with a fireplace, is a separate apartment

There should be sufficient room to walk with comfort on all sides of the table, which should be arranged to enable meals to be prepared with comfort during the day and sewing to be done by night. The dresser should be placed close to the range and the scullery door. If all these conditions are to be reasonably met, our kitchen must not be less than 135 to 155 square feet, with 11 ft. 6 in. as a minimum width.

The window should be fairly high off the floor—about 3 ft. or even more—and if a cross light can be arranged for ventilation, so much the better. In any case, we shall make the window—or part of it—open to its full height. Thought too, must be given to artificial lighting. A point over the table is essential and an additional point on or near the chimney breast would be a great advantage. Where electric lighting is available, a hand lamp from a plug near the range is a great help to the cook for inspecting the saucepans at the back of the range.

In mentioning the range we should give the most careful consideration to the method we prefer for cooking our food. The ordinary coal range is still the most generally favoured, as by its adoption the cooking and domestic hot water heating of a small house can be dealt with at the same time. If we decide to use a coal range we shall select one of proved quality with a good thickness of metal, especially for those parts exposed to the fire. We shall pay a fairly good price for it because the comfort of the household depends more upon the range than we sometimes realise. It is more economical in the consumption of fuel to have a "lifting" fire, and if we can afford a double door to the oven—the inner door being of glass—we shall avoid the change in temperature of the oven. By this method the outer door only need be opened to inspect the joint. We shall also select a range the top of which is divided into a fairly large number of sections or it will probably crack as a result of expansion and contraction, with a big fire. A hot-plate—enclosed for preference—at the top of the range in which to keep warm the plates and dishes, will give us all that we can reasonably require. As the draught plays a big part in the success—or otherwise—of our cooking, we must be careful about the formation of the flue from the range. It will tend to added cleanliness if we are able to use glazed tiles to a reasonable extent around the fireplace.

Of late years considerable progress has been made in the development of the anthracite coal range, also in gas and electric cookers. To the anthracite range the above remarks apply to a large extent, its main advantage over the ordinary coal range being that it is less dusty and keeps alight, if needed, throughout the night, thereby assuring a hot bath quite early in the morning. The fuel, however, is more expensive—especially if not used with economy—and it needs a separate compartment for storage. A slow combustion range burning any kind of fuel—including coke—has, however, recently been put on the market, and if it lives up to what is claimed for it, the dirty and dusty range will soon be a thing of the past.

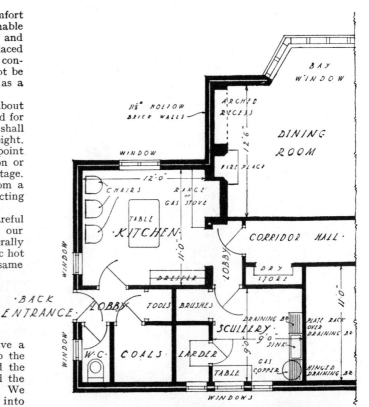

The above plan shows the kitchen quarters with kitchen and scullery separated. The kitchen, whose only fixtures are the range and dresser, may be used in the evening as the servants' sitting-room

Where a good gas supply is available it is frequently considered to be a preferable method of cooking. Its chief advantages are cleanliness, more even temperature, and the oven rises to cooking heat more quickly. It is also claimed to be cheaper, but this depends entirely upon who superintends its use. It will not supplant a fire in the kitchen, and a thermostat or similar arrangement in addition to the gas cooker will be necessary for the domestic hot-water supply. To cooking by electricity much the same remarks apply except that the absence of flame makes it perhaps even cleaner than gas.

Our dresser should be about 5 ft. 6 in. to 6 ft. long and about 7 ft. high, and we shall do well to enclose it at the top, where some of the china will be stored. Glazed doors are preferable, and whether they are hinged to swing or made to slide is a personal matter. Both methods have certain advantages and drawbacks when compared in detail. Similarly, it is a personal matter whether the bottom portion of the dresser should be open with a "pot board" or closed with cupboards and drawers. I think we shall find the latter preferable where the kitchen is to be used as the servants' living-room.

We must not forget to provide one or more cupboards in which to keep close at hand all sorts of dry goods and the like for which there may be no room in the larder or elsewhere. If we can afford it, wood blocks will be best for the floor. The walls and ceiling will more easily be kept clean if painted, and a narrow tile skirting provided. A bright wall-paper, however, of appropriate pattern, and varnished, is generally preferred by the servants. We must not forget to fix to the walls rails for dish covers, nor the possibility of a detachable drying line raised on pulleys and fixed to the ceiling. This, however, is better in the scullery, especially if a fireplace or other means of heating is provided there.

The scullery we shall find in practice to be almost a part of the kitchen. If, therefore, it is arranged to enter directly off the kitchen it will save a great many steps. In some cases the two rooms have been combined—known as a kitchen-scullery.

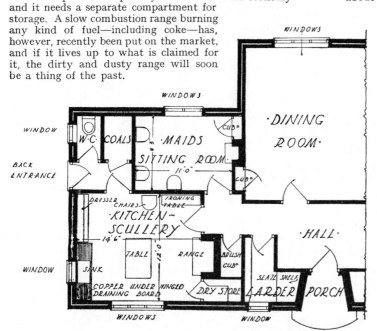

This plan illustrates the kitchen quarters in the form of a kitchen-scullery with a separate maids' sitting-room

THE
20's

Just a Song at Twilight

when the lights are low and Autumn chill is banished by the glowing warmth of the "Valor-Perfection" Oil Heater.

The "Valor-Perfection" is a trouble-free companion, clean and dainty, always ready to accompany you anywhere—radiating healthful warmth—costing little— giving much—dispelling cold and damp—useful in any room in many ways.

Like other sterling articles this famous Heater has imitators. Beware! Buy only the *proved* best — the "Valor-Perfection," now reduced in price but still unequalled in quality.

Look for the Valor Shield, without which none is genuine.

VALOR-PERFECTION
Oil Heaters

SMALL BLACK, 25/-
SMALL BLUE PORCELAIN, 35/-

LARGE BLACK, 30/-
LARGE BLUE PORCELAIN, 40/-

SOLD BY ALL IRONMONGERS AND STORES.

Distributed Wholesale by:
ANGLO-AMERICAN OIL CO., LTD.
Descriptive pamphlet post free.   Address : (108), Stove and Heater Dept.,
Queen Anne's Gate, London, S.W.1.

VALOR
PERFECTION
OIL
CABINET

USE ROYAL DAYLIGHT OIL

VALOR
PERFECTION
OIL DRUM

50 Gall. Capacity, 51/4
30 Gall. Capacity, 46/3

ANGLOCO

10 Gall. Capacity, 12/-
5 Gall. Capacity, 8/6

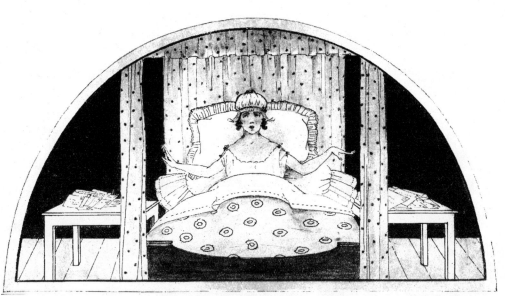

"Breakfast in bed" is not only a tray with a teapot, but a sign of freemasonry which exists between all women. It lengthens the time when we may ignore a swarm of daily cares

Bed As A *Refuge*

By J. E. Buckrose

Author of "The Gossip Shop," "The Tale of Mr. Tubbs," "An Ordinary Couple," etc., etc.

I SUPPOSE there is hardly anyone in the civilised world—particularly of those who do just a little more every day than they really have strength to perform—who has not at some time regarded bed as a refuge.

Even an Eskimo, huddled with his family circle in an airless room and surrounded by the darkness of an Arctic winter, must still feel in the night hours that sense of the agitated and fluttered soul gradually settling down to quiet—like a bird who has reached a safe tree-top after being chased by an enemy—for it is common to us all.

Perhaps, indeed, such a man feels it as fully as he who lies on a house-top under an Eastern sky, with the stars so still in the deep blue above him—though this last does seem as if it ought to be the place in which to experience best that wonderful sense of relaxing the constant, subconscious, bird-like glancing of our minds this way and that, which is our state all day long, our heritage from æons of dangerous living.

For this reason, the most unimaginative can picture David of Israel lying on his bed while the peace of the night settled upon him, until at last he said to himself: "I will both lay myself down in peace, and sleep."

But is it not strange that he is the one poet who has—so far as I am aware—given bed its right place in the spiritual history of human beings? We all know from experience that most of the important conflicts of the soul are carried on there; that early all the decisions affecting our whole existence are really taken during those hours, though we may not be quite aware of it at the time; and yet we are apt to miss that part of existence out of our calculations, as if it did not matter. You even hear talk of time wasted in bed, from persons who would consider they had

IT is strange that bed, as a place of refuge in all moments of spiritual doubt, of sorrow, or of joy, has been left entirely unsung by the poets. But this oversight has been repaired by J. E. Buckrose, who writes, with the simple, good-humoured philosophy that makes all her work delightful, in praise of bed as a sanctuary in which we may—for a time—evade the need of living dangerously

done something definitely useful if they sat up and read an Encyclopædia.

It is in bed that we learn to bear the inevitable. We are learning this all the time while we lie with our face turned to the wall thinking we are doing nothing. And we wait until those silent hours to realise some great happiness, because we know there will be nobody watching to see how we take it.

An aspect of the question more entirely feminine is conjured up by the words, "Breakfast in bed!" which implies at once that the breakfaster is in the habit of rising early and is simply lengthening by two or three hours her time of refuge before she must get up to face the usual swarm of little, gnat-like cares. For "breakfast in bed" is not only a tray with a teapot, but a sign of a freemasonry which exists between all women, high and low.

If a wife loses her husband, or a mother her child, or a girl is jilted by her lover, some other female—if there be one in the house, should it be only the youngest "tweeny" with a kind heart —will feel this is the most delicate consolation that can be offered.

Men do not seem to share this point of view, excepting one of whom I heard years ago, who lost his lady-love in some fashion unknown and retired to bed for life. This seemed to me, even at that early, romantic period, to be carrying the thing too far; and I can

still see the picture formed in my mind at that time, of a poor gentleman sitting up in bed wearing an unbleached calico night-shirt, and eating bread and milk with a metal spoon. I do not know why I imagined him thus, but I suppose that bread and milk and unbleached calico must have been, in those days, my idea of the fitting accompaniments to such a situation.

All the same there are a great many grown-up people who at present experience the same feelings as that man did when he retired for good, doubtless saying to himself: "I have had enough of this!" For every time we take up the newspaper the headlines about murder, misery, anarchy, and starvation fall on the sensitive soul like drops of hot iron, until we feel we could run and hide anywhere to escape them.

Only we cannot do that—because there comes an hour in the middle of the night when bed is changed from a refuge to a place of torment. Some people may not have experienced this horrid transformation, for it is a thing seldom talked of, but I cannot help thinking that most of my neighbours know all about it.

At any rate those who have awakened in the middle of the night to a feeling of heavy depression, without any actual, present cause, will understand why the following lines—which do not pretend to be poetry—once floated at such an hour into my mind:

> "There's a dull end of things
> Where no words come,
> Where every moment brings
> Some old grief home;
> With every thought that's born,
> How memory aches—
> Oh, come to-morrow morn,
> When hope awakes!"

HOUSING

Conducted by Herbert A. Welch, A.R.I.B.A.

THE
20's

Entrance front of the £1,000 house : A quiet, restrained effect, avoiding " fuss " in all forms, has been aimed at in this house. The external walls are intended to be brick roughcasted, with a plain band of brickwork immediately beneath the first-floor windows, and the roof is to be tiled. All the windows a e casements, with glazed doors or " French windows " giving access to the garden from the dining-room

The One Thousand Pound *House*

By F. J. Watson Hart

IN the years before the war the architectural profession, or quite a large part of it, was hard at work trying to devise a cottage which could be built for £100. This problem, which even then was not satisfactorily solved, of providing more than money will buy, is perennial, and, in these days of high prices and house shortage, is with us in a greatly intensified form.

In the good old days the struggle was chiefly confined to the provision of cottages. To-day it has spread to all types of houses except those for the very rich. Clerical workers and smaller professional people whose incomes have, generally speaking, not risen in proportion to the advance in prices, find it very difficult to get any place in which to live. They must buy or build. In buying they may go either to some decaying suburb and content themselves with a roomy but dilapidated and entirely unworkable house, built in the eighties of the last century, or they may get "an artistic home" in a new district from a speculative builder. In following either of

SO many have been the enquiries on building called forth by the architectural articles we have published in "Good Housekeeping" that we have arranged to give our readers the benefit of expert advice on this subject. Mr. Herbert A. Welch, A.R.I.B.A., will direct the Housing Section of "Good Housekeeping" in future, and all queries regarding suitable sites, building costs, etc., should be sent, accompanied by a stamped addressed envelope for his reply, to The Director, " Housing," "Good Housekeeping," 1 Amen Corner, London, E.C.4

these alternatives the purchaser, even if his property proves structurally satisfactory, has to sacrifice his individuality and content himself in surroundings adapted merely to meet general requirements. Only by building a house can one hope to escape from the slough of unimaginative mediocrity which is offered by the average speculator. And the building of a house is, to the man of limited means, a momentous undertaking involving the sinking of the bulk of his capital in something which he can only

see on paper in the shape of plans which he and his wife seldom really understand.

There is a general feeling that if one buys a ready-made house one at least knows the worst, but that the alternative of building one is somewhat of a gamble, which, if it fails, may end in years of inconvenience and dissatisfaction. But building one's own house is worth doing all the same. There is real joy to be had in helping to design it, for architects *are* helped by their clients, not technically, but by finding the limitations of the client's requirements and seeking to carry out in the plans his individual desires. Then there is the joy of watching the house grow stage by stage, through early chaos until it assumes understandable shape. It is doubtful if any other spending of money can give so much genuine interest and joy as this. What a feeling of satisfaction is gained on entering the house to feel that one has contributed some real thing towards its accomplishment !

As suggested at the beginning of this article, the greatest difficulty in building is to realise how much your money will buy. Builders offer no equivalent for "clearance lines" and "bargain sales." Merchants will not supply materials below the market rates, however charming a client may be, and the architect can do no more than plan economically; he cannot produce "something for nothing." The general ignorance about the cost of building is remarkable. Almost all those who embark on the undertaking have a very real hope that Providence will be specially kind in their case and cause the builder to provide them with more than their money's worth.

The cost of building is generally roughly arrived at by calculating the number of cubic feet enclosed within the walls and roof. The approximate price per cubic foot being a known quantity, it is not difficult for an architect to form a fairly reliable conclusion on the matter.

As a basis of argument, the house here illustrated has been designed to show how much may be expected for £1,000. Under ordinary circumstances it could be erected for that money outside the London building area; within it, it might cost a little more, and in certain highly favoured spots, where bricks and sand and other materials are locally available, it might cost less.

The design, within limitations, could and should be varied to meet individual requirements and the exigencies of site, but on the basis previously indicated it gives a representation of value for money at the present time.

An effort having been made to establish this question of value on some kind of understandable basis, it is possible to pass on to more interesting and intimate matters. The most important factor in building a house is the site. It is not unusual for people to buy their plot of land before thinking of an architect, and a good many avoidable mistakes are made in this way. If possible, the architect should be decided on and consulted first. To the man who wants an economical house a level site is essential; sloping land necessitates much additional digging and extra brickwork which adds nothing to

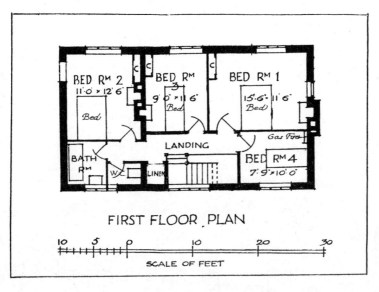

FIRST FLOOR PLAN

SCALE OF FEET

the accommodation of the building. In the choice of a site the aspect needs most careful consideration, otherwise it may be almost impossible to keep the living-rooms in the right place and still get the sunlight into them. Before buying cheap land in outlying districts, roads, drainage, and the provision of water must be thought of. Unless a water company's main is accessible, endless difficulty and expense may be met with. Therefore if it is only to be a small house, one must not be led away by a romantic site, lots of trees, sudden falls in the land, and other picnic attractions; romance of this kind is expensive.

Land and architect having been decided upon, the design for the building should not be hurried.

If a satisfactory home is to result, the architect must have time to consider thoroughly even his clients' impracticable dreams, so that he may try to translate them into something tangible. Even if this proves impossible, knowing them will help him to form definite ideas of his clients' requirements and turn of mind, so that a scheme may be prepared that will fit itself to their individuality and which will become not just *a* house but *their* house.

There are so many fascinating possibilities about the modern house, even a small one. So many are the different ways in which available space may be subdivided, so many little points have to be decided, that it is well to take time over the preliminaries. The first ideas may be good, but it is quite possible that they may be improved upon with further thought.

First of all, the vital question of aspect has to be considered—that is, the position of the rooms with relation to sunlight and outlook. In the builder's house this must of necessity be largely left to chance, for in speculative building one plan has to do duty for many sites, and though it may have had a larder facing north in the first design, when repeated on land for which the plan was not intended this important point will probably have been entirely lost sight of. But in a specially designed house such matters can and must have due consideration.

The most debatable question in this class of building is the space to be allotted to the kitchens. There is very little doubt that in these days there is a general tendency to cramp this all-important section of the home, and it is indeed true that, with the necessity of providing a good-size living-room and a room for meals on the ground-floor, restriction of the working quarters, though undesirable, is difficult to avoid. It is therefore necessary that the space allocated should be used to the utmost advantage—that every item of equipment should be planned to come in the best possible position. For example, assuming that the kitchen and dining-room are adjacent, as they should be, it is desirable that the sink should not be at the farthest possible point from the dinner-table. The larder, also, may with advantage be placed between the kitchen and dining-room, so that cold food need not have an unnecessarily long journey in either direction.

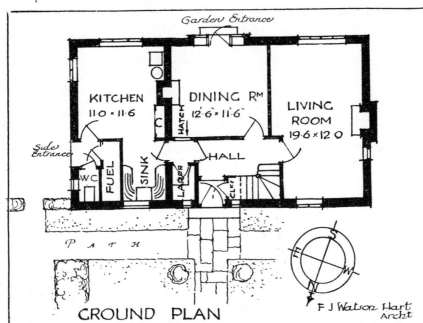

GROUND PLAN

F J Watson Hart
Archt

These plans indicate the accommodation obtainable to-day in many districts for an outlay of about £1,000. The planning is very direct and simple, no space being available for other than necessary uses. The plans, rectangular in form, are designed without breaks to reduce the cost of building

THE
20's

Built amidst the Hampshire pines on the spur of a hill, the ten-roomed house illustrated
above faces south, and is constructed of hard local bricks roughcasted in cream colour

The Fifteen Hundred Pounds House

By H. V. M. Emerson, A.R.I.B.A.

THE house illustrated in this article was built amidst the pines of Hampshire, the site being on the spur of a hill commanding magnificent views over the country to the south and west. The accommodation consists of two reception-rooms, convertible into three if required, a kitchen, and the usual offices on the ground floor; and on the first floor, four bedrooms, dressing-room, and bath-room.

The cost of this house at the present time would be about £1,500. On the ground floor an open, oak-framed entrance-porch with tiled or small paving-brick floor, leads to a good-sized entrance-hall. The drawing-room is provided with a wood-panelled, folding partition, which, when in use, converts this room into a smaller drawing-room and a morning room, with a fireplace in each room. The partition is so arranged that it can be folded back into a cupboard recess, and does not in any way form an unsightly object in the room. The size of the large drawing-room is 22 feet long by 11 feet wide, extending to 18 feet 6 inches in the wider part. The size of the small drawing-room (with the partition in position) is 18 feet 6 inches by 11 feet 6 inches, and the morning room is 11 feet by 10 feet 6 inches.

External doors from either room give access to a covered loggia, with a tiled floor, oak timber framing, and a tiled roof forming a protection from inclement weather. From the loggia charm-

ing views of the surrounding country are obtained, and being placed on the sunny side of the house it really constitutes an extra room in the summer, not unlike the "sun" rooms so usual in American houses.

The dining-room is pleasantly situated and well lighted with a large bow-window, in addition to smaller windows on either side of the fireplace. These small windows facing east, the benefit of the early-morning sun is obtained. A recess is provided to take the dining-room sideboard, which might, if desired, be a built-in fixture, an arrangement that adds considerable space to the room.

The kitchen faces east, and is provided with an up-to-date kitchener, which also operates the hot-water service. The dresser is entirely enclosed with glazed doors to the upper part and cupboards in the lower portion, thereby eliminating dust and reducing labour. Scullery and stores are in close proximity to the kitchen, whilst the larder and pantry are conveniently placed alike to the kitchen and dining-room. Service to the dining-room from the kitchen is given by means of a hatch-way, which is placed just outside the kitchen, thus obviating the objections to direct communication between kitchen and dining-room. The hatch-way is within easy reach of larder, pantry, and kitchen, and is fitted with shelf and cupboards on the passage side, for the placing of dishes, etc.

The staircase has a lavatory under it for washing purposes only. A large

window gives ample light both to the entrance-hall and the first-floor landing.

On the upper floor four bedrooms are provided, also a dressing-room, lavatory, and bath-room, with a heated linen-cupboard. Cupboards are provided in the bedrooms, that in the servant's bedroom (over the kitchen) being large enough to form a box cupboard.

The walls of the house are constructed in hard local bricks, with a 2-inch cavity, roughcasted outside and tinted a light cream colour. The porches and gables are framed in oak and the roof covered with hand-made, sand-faced tiles. The ground floor has a surface layer of cement concrete with sleeper walls, joists, and tongued and grooved boarding. The walls of the scullery, pantry, lavatories, and bath-room are tiled, and the remaining walls are plastered and distempered. The internal woodwork is finished in white enamel, and the external woodwork in dark green with white sashes to windows.

The particular site chosen for this house was upon a spur of rising ground, which necessitated cutting an angle into the side of the hill in order to obtain a level surface to build upon. The south and west sides were free from any obstructions in outlook over the surrounding country, but the windows on the north and east sides were partly obstructed by the earth-banks which, beginning at ground-level at the north-west and south-east corners of the building, reached a height of about 8 feet at the north-east corner.

In designing this house, it was very necessary that the principal rooms should be so placed that they should face south or west, and that the windows to less important rooms of the house should face the earth obstructions. A glance at the plans will show that this was successfully accomplished.

For those intending to build, it is very important, when choosing a site, to bear in mind that the levels of the ground form a very important factor in the aspect and cost of the building. The cheapest site to build upon is a level site, as rise or fall in the ground means extra cost incurred either by excavating the earth or by the unproductive use of materials in the foundations.

The nature of the soil should also be taken into account. Clay is unsatisfactory in many ways. It is cold, liable to expansion and contraction, which, in the absence of deep foundations to the structure, often cause serious cracks and settlements in the walls, affecting the construction and stability of the building and entailing considerable expense in repairs. It is not considered healthy, and as water cannot readily percolate through the soil, it does not form an ideal subsoil during the winter months. Gravel is one of the best formations to build upon: it is very healthy, water readily drains away, and it is not liable to the disturbances that a clay soil experiences during variations in the weather. One precaution should be taken in erecting a building upon gravel: the foundations of the walls should be carried down to the ordinary water-level. Water is an incompressible body, and whilst water is in the gravel your building is safe, but any drainage of this water from the gravel allows the settlement of small particles to fill up the voids, and in course of time a settlement takes place. Rock and chalk make excellent foundations, but the latter soil is not considered good for persons suffering from gout and similar complaints.

Drainage is another problem with country houses. Where you can discharge the drainage into a sewer, your troubles are practically at an end; but where sewers do not exist, care must be taken in the disposal of sewage. The most common method in use for small country houses is to discharge the drainage into a cesspool, i.e. a brick underground chamber, but this requires periodical emptying. A method I have

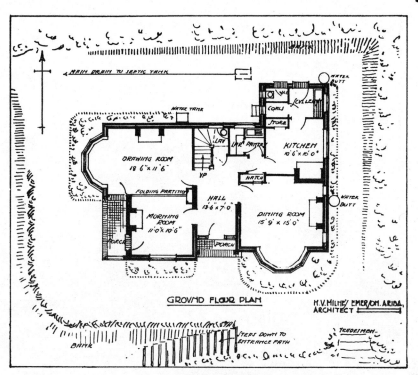

GROUND FLOOR PLAN   H. V. MILNE/ EMERSON ARIBA, ARCHITECT

Plan showing the ground-floor rooms and porches of the £1,500 house described in this article

employed with success for this class of house is to carry an overflow pipe from the cesspool, and discharge the same by means of branch pipes over a soakaway situated some 5 or 6 feet away. The soakaway is formed by digging a hole some 10 feet below the level of the overflow pipe, and about 6 to 8 feet square, and filling the same with broken bricks, breeze, gravel, or other hard loose material, which allow the water discharged from the cesspool to be partly filtered and to percolate freely into the surrounding ground. The tops of the cesspool and soakaway are 2 feet or more underground, thus eliminating any unsightly arrangement and also preventing any nuisance arising. This arrangement really forms a septic tank upon a small scale, and the water being allowed to escape, the receiving chamber does not require cleaning out for a number of years. The soakaway should have the filtering material changed when required, a matter of every five years or more being sufficient. For larger houses it would be advisable to have a more complete system installed, consisting of the septic tank and open filtering beds, etc. In this case the plant would be situate some distance from the house, adjoining an open stream or brook, in order that the water from the filter beds may find a ready outlet. As the water after passing from

the filter beds is perfectly pure, no harm will arise from this water being turned into a stream.

The water-supply to a house is an important item. Town houses are usually supplied with water direct from the street main, but the country house is more often unable to obtain its water-supply from this source and other means have to be adopted. Drinking-water is the first consideration, and it must be clean and pure. The usual sources of supply are from well and spring. If a well is used, care must be taken that no source of contamination shall be within 100 feet of the water. Although it is recognised that impure water is a great danger to health, it is no uncommon thing to find in country houses and farms that the well is often within a few feet of a stable-yard or cow-sheds, and the drainage from the same will in time contaminate the water surrounding the well. The well can be fitted with the usual winch and bucket, but a more convenient method is to provide a large storage tank in the roof of the house and to connect it to the well with a pipe fitted with a small rotary pump. The latter can be fixed to the wall of the scullery, is easily worked, and will pump up to 60 gallons per minute. An indicator can be fitted showing the amount of water in the tank. From the tank the usual service pipes can be taken to various parts of the house.

Rain water should be conserved as much as possible, and for this purpose an underground tank should be constructed of brick and cement, water-proofed, and holding 1,000 gallons or more. The tank should be connected to the rain-water pipes from the eaves. Water can be pumped to a storage tank in the roof with service pipes to points required. The taps should be labelled "rain water." A small quantity of lime thrown into the rain-water tank will clear away any impurities.

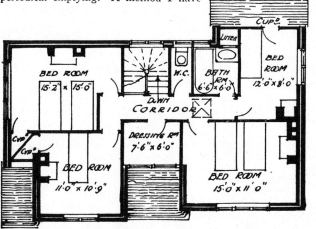

First-floor plan of the house illustrated on opposite page

THE 20's

Occupying, with a well-planned garden, half **an acre** of ground, the servantless house is as ornamental as it is practical

The *Servantless* House

Solving the Problem of Costly Living

By DORA J. MOORE

CONVENTION dictates a certain standard of living for the professional and upper middle-class, be the individual family rich or poor; and since the days when dividends dwindled and prices soared, retrenchment has become a necessity in many a post-war household.

My own particular ménage was no exception to the rule. Life soon resolved itself into a sordid struggle to make two ends meet. It was during a caravan holiday that first the idea of defying convention and revolutionising our whole mode of living occurred to us. After a few peaceful days of the simple life, one begins to realise how unnecessarily encumbered is domestic life for the average housewife.

Admitted that caravan life might not be practicable for family life, I conceived the feasibility of enlarging on the idea and building a home that would have all the advantages of a caravan—except mobility!—and none of the disadvantages of an ordinary house. A compact little place, with one big room over the ground floor wherein children might play, out of sight and out of sound. A home built and equipped to reduce housework to a minimum—so that servants might be entirely dispensed with.

It did not take us long to put the scheme into action. An

A CARAVAN holiday was the inspiration of the enviable house described in this article, which many women will recognise as the cottage of their dreams come true. Planned very cleverly it fully lives up to its name, and few people, given the opportunity, would refuse to undertake its management unaided. The cost of its construction at the present time is about £1,500

architect friend was commissioned to professionalise our own rough plans and sketches, and soon the cottage of our dreams was materialising on half an acre of ground on the river-side.

The venture held for us all the thrill of pre-married days, with this difference: after ten years of housekeeping, we now knew exactly what we required of our roof-tree—and the practical way to set out to get it.

Nearly all our old, cumbersome furniture was disposed of at a sale. The proceeds more than paid the expense of installing, throughout the entire cottage, fitments to our own design, to suit our personal requirements. Thus we utilised every inch of space to advantage and reduced housework, by abolishing the dust-traps that lurk below and above ordinary articles of furniture.

My long-suffering architect friend must have found us exacting clients; for we determined the cottage should be as picturesque as practical—combining all modern conveniences with the minimum of housework. Luckily, he is a man of resource as well as an artist, and rose to the occasion.

The living-room of the cottage is 16 feet by 16 feet 6 inches, and is literally panelled with oak bookcases. These, with their leaded lights, provide a comfortable home for our treasures, pleasing to the eye, *and dustproof.*

The window-seat recess is long enough to be used as a lounge couch, and under it are fitted handy cupboards. Beams and other woodwork in this room are stained brown. A floor of polished oak is partly covered with Indian rugs. The restful, dominant colour throughout the room is soft-toned green. It was a debatable point whether the sitting-room should or should not have a fireplace, for though ample provision had been made for heating it adequately by radiators, there is cheeriness about an open fire that most English folk find indispensable on dull days.

My architect produced such a fascinating sketch for a log-burning hearth that I succumbed to the idea; the more easily as he suggested that the space under-stairs should be utilised to store firewood, this being loaded in from a door opening into the garden, while another door opening *into the sitting-room* enables the logs to be thrown straight into the hearth. Though we are not dependent on the wood fire for heat, we find it an additional winter comfort entailing, however, some extra work.

All the fitment furniture and panelling of the downstairs bedroom is enamelled pale grey; and an artist friend has decorated the panels with medallions of old-world ladies gowned in soft lilac and rose. The Axminster carpeting is rose and midnight blue, the same colours appearing in the curtains. The wardrobe recess is furnished with patent fittings, which treble the hanging capacity of a wardrobe.

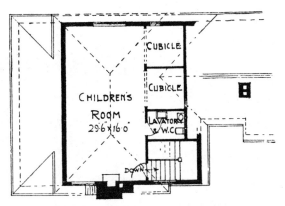

FIRST FLOOR PLAN

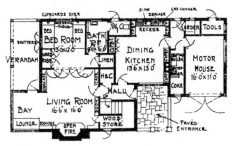

GROUND FLOOR PLAN

The covering curtain is secured *top and bottom* with rings, and the space below is utilised for drawers. The bed adjoining the wardrobe is panelled to the ceiling.

Both beds are fixtures, and fitted underneath with nests of drawers. The cupboard fitments at the head of each bed open well above the pillow line; these projecting cupboards act as draught-screens for the beds.

The larger window in the bedroom is fitted with outside shutters for use in rigorous weather: though the verandah roof prevents rain from driving in at any time. The large linen cupboard also has additional shelves and hooks for clothes.

The bathroom leads off the bedroom, and is tiled in

white and turquoise blue; a gutter (with outlet) runs round the black-and-blue mosaic floor, and the corners of the room are rounded (as elsewhere throughout the house) to avoid dust-traps. The room is heated with radiators. It has a hot towel-rail, and there is a cupboard under the washing basin, and glass shelves above. The taps are of special white enamel, so that there is no nickel or brass to clean.

In the curtained, white-tiled recess of the dining-room-kitchen is the sink (with a draining-board at each end), also an electric cooking-stove. A slate-topped table, which takes no hurt from hot pans, provides a cool surface for pastry-making. Above the sink are patent racks, into which cups, saucers, plates, and dishes can be placed after rinsing in clean water.

The shelves above the stove and table are of iron, with a specially prepared *white-enamelled surface.* These shelves, for cooking utensils, etc., were a " brain-wave " on the part of the architect, and made to his special order. They are excellent in every way. Two minutes' work a day means spotlessly clean shelves with a glossy white surface, which does not chip or crack. We use these shelves in the larder, too, where the tiny north window and the door panels are of perforated zinc, and a commodious ice-box proves a boon in summer.

The most fastidious need find nothing distasteful in partaking of meals in this combination room, discreetly curtained. The sink and stove are spotless. No bits of any description are ever allowed to escape down the outlet. Over the sink is a window, and outside, within easy reach, hangs a bucket into which all bits from the plates can be emptied. Where coal and oil are abolished for cooking, pots and pans can be kept spick and span without any undue labour.

The curtain across the recess is secured with rings top and bottom (the lower rail being inset in the floor); this arrangement does away with the flapping nuisance on windy days.

When a table serves several purposes, a white cloth, before even a meal begins, too often shows the stains and rims

Though heated with radiators the servantless house succumbed to tradition in having a fine open grate for the cheerful blaze of logs on cold days

We could all of us tell tales of houses and their temperaments, remembering the bad tempered and the good tempered, the unhappy and radiant houses we have known—but it takes an artist like Annie S. Swan, whose books have delighted so many thousands, to write, as she does here, a story in which houses are the main characters and full of personality

Photo: Rita Martin

Houses I Have Lived In

By Annie S. Swan

Author of "Aldersyde," "A Victory Won," "The Curse of Cowden," "Sir Roderick's Will," etc. etc.

DURING my considerable experience of this mundane sphere I have lived in all sorts of houses: big houses, little houses, old houses, new houses, period houses and houses of no period at all, but merely blots on the landscape, so I know nearly all there is to know about houses, their vagaries and moods, their faults and their good qualities, their maddening inconveniences and subtle methods of torment, their exasperating habit of letting you down at the most critical and inopportune moment.

Also I have proven, in full measure, pressed down and running over, their comforting qualities, their queer intimate comradeship and understanding. I have even sampled a haunted house. Houses interest me as much as anything in the world; quite as much as the people who live in them, because you cannot separate them. It is a dual life. Houses influence us far more than we imagine, and play a stupendous part in our lives, helping to mould our outlook in every direction.

When memory begins to get busy with houses there is a momentary sense of confusion. One has seen so many, that

to sift out the types seems a hopeless task. As one can never totally eliminate the personal element from anything, I will content myself with describing briefly some of the houses I have lived in.

My early recollections are of an old ivy-covered farm house on a bleak upland in the south of Scotland. It was a roomy family house containing the lowest percentage of comfort and convenience of any house I have lived in since, save one. Picturesque without, it was draughty within, minus water, sanitary convenience, and coal-cellar. Everything had to be brought in from outside, and the winters of those days were the real thing. Weeks and weeks of snow and desolating frosts which necessitated the thawing out of pump-handles with kettles of boiling water. I can remember watching my mother winding ropes of straw round and round the pump, until it looked like the inflated car tyres with which advertisement has made us familiar. That was to prevent it freezing—but it never did. It might delay the process, but that was the utmost limit of achievement. In the long run everything got frozen up, and a well

at some distance had to be broken into every morning, the ice inches thick smashed with a hammer, and buckets let down to bring up the precious fluid.

Yet I believe there was then less grumbling over household affairs than there is now. People were not so much afraid of work, they put their backs into it because circumstances demanded it. Anyway that was a very happy house, full of children, and it had delectable gardens, and woods spreading away behind it where grew every known species of wildflower, and all the fruits: raspberries, brambles, the wild strawberry, cherries and crab-apples; always there was something for us to seek and to find.

I migrated from that old, but never-forgotten family house to a very small cottage on the edge of a desolate moor.

These were the far-back days when love was very venturesome and material considerations mattered little, if at all. No capital was needed in such case, save love and hope, and hard work and determination to succeed. Those for whom the going is made easy, miss the best in life.

This cottage *(Continued overleaf)*

Houses I Have Lived In
(Continued)

I can only describe as a Presence. Also occasionally there was a hint of soft inexplicable footsteps! I also remember distinctly a man who came as *locum tenens* for my husband telling me after we came back from our holiday that the house was haunted. He was a very solid, level-headed person, and we did not pursue the subject. There was never any sense of fear or dread accompanying our rumoured ghost. She had no grievance against the family! Her distress was peculiar to herself. One who knew the history of the house assured me that a good few years back the apparition had been "laid" by the rector of the parish coming to exhort her, afterwards visiting her grave and admonishing her to lie still. I never asked any questions about the lady, however, nor sought to probe her story. In a house where vivid imaginations are rampant it is better not.

And now we have achieved the last word in a house of modest dimensions "replete (*vide* catalogue) with every modern convenience." It is a long, low, comfortable-looking house of the Queen Anne type, built of soft-toned red brick and having numerous high, rather narrow windows.

The sitting-rooms, built to catch every ray of sun, are on the ground-floor, also the domestic offices. There is neither pantry nor scullery, and the kitchen is the workshop of the house. It has a floor of smooth red brick with rounded corners so that there is no dust-trap, also a skirting of the same brick, so that the wash cloth makes no sad line of discoloration on the walls.

The sink, a large, deep, roomy one is across the window, and has enclosed cupboards underneath with broad shelves for the reception of the pots and pans. There is a large cupboard with enclosed doors, and ample shelving space.

No crockery, or tin, or silver ware is permitted to stand outside to receive the attentions of the housefly and other household enemies.

The window is large and opens on the garden, so that there is plenty of light and air. Close by is the larder with a slate shelf and a good window for ventilation. The power-house which provides the central heating opens off the back passage and is entered through a door and down two steps. It has a red-tiled floor, a large wash table with a surround of white tiles, an ironing table, and a copper, so that part or all of the family washing could be done at home. The cellar for the coke opens off, so that everything required lies to hand, and innumerable steps are saved. The furnace heats the house from top to bottom and provides unlimited hot water.

There is no kitchen-range. Cooking is done entirely by gas or can be done if preferred by electricity. In the meantime, however, gas is cheaper and entirely satisfactory. There are no flues to clean, no stoves to polish, no coal to carry, the only fire in use being one in the living-room for appearance sake. It is not really necessary for comfort.

The maids have a comfortable and pretty sitting-room, heated by a radiator, and there is also a small fireplace. It has basket-chairs, rugs, and pictures on the walls. They can, by the mere closing of a door, shut themselves off completely from their workshop, and enjoy their leisure or their needlework in equal comfort with the other members of the house.

As there are wash-basins in all the principal bedrooms, hot-water cans for inmates or guests have become a thing of the past. The taps are porcelain so that there is little to polish. A dull house, you say! Not at all, but right from top to bottom flooded with sunshine and air and great

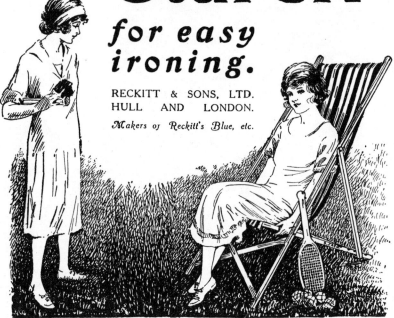

comfort with the least expenditure of labour. It is coal-fires that create most of the dust which torments the housewife, and with a stout vacuum cleaner in regular use the nightmare of the spring clean becomes a thing of the past.

In the old days, and in the old houses it would appear as if a conspiracy had been entered into to complicate the housewife's life and give her the minimum of comfort for the maximum of work. Labour-saving devices were not known. Even yet they are coldly welcomed in some quarters, for women are the most conservative creatures on earth.

In the process of removal we eliminated most of the heavy curtains, harbourers of dust, and all articles of unnecessary furniture. The result is surprisingly beautiful and satisfying to the eye. There is space for really worth-while things to be seen. Most of us have lived too long in bondage to our stuff. We endeavour to bring to our new house the spirit of hope and contentment of loving-kindness and good-will, to establish it all there, so that it shall be a happy house for all time.

Houses are not so inanimate as people imagine, they are extraordinarily sensitive and responsive to the atmosphere. They cannot create it, living beings have to do that, but they can receive and retain impressions and give them forth. Thus we are conscious of the spell of some

Our Guarantee

houses, of their restfulness, their gaiety or charm, or, in quite marked degree, of their dulness and sadness.

I have a friend whose house breathes quiet, both for the body and the soul. It is only a little house, but that is its atmosphere. It is impossible to hurry or have nerve-strain or be impatient under its roof.

I go to another sometimes where one is immediately made conscious of sadness and gloom. I have never inquired into its history, but am certain that it would reveal the fact that there had been much sorrow, even tragedy, under its roof. Then there are disagreeable, bad-tempered houses which wreak vengeance on those who live in them. They have creaking doors and smoking chimneys and draughty corners; nothing ever goes right in them, and comfort, true comfort, is unknown. My theory is that it was a curmudgeon who planned and built that kind of house, a man whose hand was against his fellows, and who found enemies at every corner. But never friends!

It is a fascinating study, this business of house-planning. If you have a little imagination it is more fascinating than writing novels. Because you deal with real things, and real people, and all the romance and witchery of life. Longfellow was aware of all this when he said:

"The houses wherein men have lived and died are haunted houses."

THE 20's

THE 20's

34

A plan that has been found to work excellently is to give the " daily " maid a list of the silver, valuable china, and fine linen in daily use, making her responsible for their care, with instructions to report mishaps at once

Daily Maids in the *Small Town House*

By Margaret Benn

HOW much valuable space, obtained at a premium, is given up, more especially in the small town house or flat, to provide bedrooms for a resident staff! So long as this can be spared, so good. But a time may come when the needs of an expanding household will necessitate the redecorating and adapting of this accommodation to some such uses as a dressing-room, night nursery, or bedroom for an older child.

The reluctant decision once made, a vista of inconvenience opens up, and to the mind's eye the daily maid appears as slovenly, unpunctual, perhaps actually dishonest, introducing burglars, and herself vanishing from sight or, it might be, not appearing at all on some critical occasion. Chosen with care, the " daily " will fulfil none of these fearful expectations. Frequently she is a woman of a competent and superior type, the wife, perhaps, of a disabled soldier, obliged to return to service in this form, and highly recommended by the better-class registry which supplies her.

Whether cook or house-parlourmaid, it is a first essential that she should have a sense of responsibility, a quality to be fostered and tacitly acknowledged by the giving of responsible work. Special pains must be taken to attach her to the household so that she will not feel herself to be a mere casual worker. A plan which has been found to work excellently in this connection is to give the house-parlourmaid a list of the silver, valuable china, and fine linen in daily use, making her responsible for their care—and with instructions to report mishaps at once. And to the cook, if she is that pearl of great price (and experience) who will do all her own marketing, give on a certain day the sum of money allowed for food, cleaning materials, and ordinary expenses. Provide her with a book to be

kept up to date, balanced, and, above all, inspected at a regular time every week. If selection has been made of a cook whom catering interests, or of a house-parlourmaid proud of her pantry, that second essential, the sense of co-operation, is thus secured, and she feels that her part in maintaining the general health and well-being of the household meets with the appreciation and respect due to the good performance of skilled work.

That there are inconveniences cannot be denied. Bells must perforce remain unanswered after " kitchen hours," and adjustment may be called for in order to ensure that during these hours—perhaps between 7.30 a.m. and 9 p.m.—someone shall be on duty. For the small house a workable scheme consists in engaging a cook for the earlier " shift " who will, if necessary, leave dinner so far advanced that it can be easily served by the house-parlourmaid who comes and goes proportionately later. Another drawback is the somewhat higher rate of wages asked by the woman who has to find her own rent and laundry. That this is met on the balance will be shown presently. In any event it should be a matter for thought to a daily employer,

whether commercial, industrial, or domestic, to pay an employee less than a living wage—particularly if that employee is a woman entirely on her own resources.

It is not an inconsiderable piece of social work to-day to make of domestic service a more pleasant profession. Of late years it has broken down, except in the case of very large establishments where the society of other servants, and some good degree of comfort, and off-time were not wanting. It has broken down mainly because it asked too much and gave too little. It gave, for one thing, an insufficiency of fresh air. It demanded the whole time, and gave back, as a concession, an afternoon now and an evening then. Thus even the concentrated strain of the factory and the office have come to seem preferable, for some part of the day at least brings back the outside world.

The mistress of daily servants will find first and foremost that the morning and evening journey infuse a new tone and vigour into the daily round. Not only is it healthy, but it gives variety and makes for cheerfulness. She will find, too, that where everything has to be done within hours, the day's work will tend to be better arranged and generally better done. Meals are ready to the instant, and dinner is served with perfection and dispatch. But best of all compensations (if any are needed), as the door closes finally the chancellor of the domestic exchequer may sigh with contentment, for she knows that below stairs everything invites inspection. The kitchen table has the whiteness of a dreadnought's deck. The larder is fresh and clean. And she knows, too, that the kettle will not boil again until to-morrow, that the kitchen teapot will remain on its shelf, and the tea undisturbed in its tin. The lights are out and the fire is low. Nothing but the rent runs on.

THE
20's

These old-fashioned homes persist, but they grow fewer as time goes by, because they are too difficult to maintain.   Woman has not been so much a home-maker as a home-endurer.   The war set her free

WHAT IS A HOME?

W. L. George *predicts a world that will not know the answer*

IT is a platitude to remark that the word "home" exists only in the Anglo-Saxon and Teutonic languages, but a platitude is merely a truth that has grown accepted; thus, when we talk of the home and strive to make our view world-wide, we must extend our rather narrow idea of what it represents.   In the broad sense the home is more than the house one lives in, one's ways of entertainment, one's cat, one's dog.   The idea of home must cover also the relations between the parents, and those which exist between parents and children.   In the main, how-

ever, the home means the conditions under which woman performs her domestic tasks.

If we confine it for a moment to that meaning, the home is the organisation which changes slowest.   Kings rise and fall, religions wax and wane, but boiled bacon is always the same.   For boiled bacon is not a matter of faith but of fact, and one cannot doubt that when the prehistoric tribes along the Rhine boiled portions of pig, they had to boil them for exactly the same time as does the most modern chef in the most Ritzian of modern Carltons.   That is why the

home has become so detestable to many women.   Loving variety and excitement, as is the way of their sex, they find that here is an invariable thing, the only invariable thing, at least in appearance.

It is only by force that changes were brought about in the white man's conception of home.   Force of circumstance is, of course, the most effective.   It is not so much that civilisation offers more and more labour-saving devices, carpet-sweepers and oven-thermometers; it is that the vast resistance against novelty takes its natural form.

Though this article began by a plati-

What is a Home?

tude that was true, I must contradict myself and acknowledge that all platitudes are not true; one of those platitudes is that woman is a home-maker. She is nothing of the kind. She has made homes for hundreds of centuries because she was compelled to make homes. All that time she has been dumped, first in a cave, and now in a block of flats, provided with none too many resources, with still less toleration of error, and told: " You are a home-maker. Get on with the job. Make a home."

Woman has made the best home she could, swept without conviction, cooked with fortitude, and nursed in weariness. Until recently there was nothing else for her to do, and even now the best way she knows to keep alive the little god of love is to make him " turn the spit, spit, spit." But woman has never enjoyed it. Even in the days of Queen Victoria woman seems to have felt that she had so many children she didn't know what to do. If she grew interested in her home, it was as many a galley-slave has become proud of the smartness with which he pulled his oar; it is typical of mankind that it should take some interest in its work . . . but that does not mean that it does the work it would have chosen if it had had the chance.

To my mind, woman has been not so much a home-maker as a home-endurer, and she has done well, given the conditions, economic, social, and political, with which she was confronted. In other words, she has compromised with the conditions that were forced upon her by man. She made homes during the Great Plague, and in the middle of the Hundred Years' War; she made homes on the trail while her men fought the Red Indians. But all this, pestilence, migration, war, amounted to impediments; the making of homes is the curse of Eve.

What is happening to-day, what has been encouraged by the Great War, is therefore not at all a development in the mind of woman, who not more than man cares for the home, but yet another feminine reaction to the circumstances of the day. Her rebellion against the heavy weight of the home is not new, but it has become vocal. If the home has changed, it is not so much because woman is changing as because men are altering the atmosphere; it is men who are home-makers, but they do it by deputy, which saves them a lot of trouble. If to-day there is among women a rising against kitchen ranges and brass, it is because mankind has produced conditions that make these

things intolerable. To-day we still find a fairly large number of old-fashioned homes, houses with rather too many rooms, containing too much furniture that needs dusting, where meals for several people are regularly served, where children are sent to school, where the slippers of the lord are placed (as the case may be) before a coal fire or on the top of the radiator. These homes persist, but they grow less as time goes by, because they are too difficult to maintain.

During the last few years a new type of home has been prepared for the coming of the new world. It was prepared very slowly, in virtue of something that looks like a series of accidents, for there is no obvious connection, for instance, between the decay of the home idea and the spread of wage work for women. When women first entered factories, the public vaguely told itself that one of the daughters would look after the house, this being what one of the daughters was created for. For a long time all went well: some of the daughters took up wage-work; another one offered up her youth and her hopes on a pyre of black-lead and metal polish. But the war, the rush of women into patriotic service, their stay in service no longer patriotic but remunerative, all this has deprived the old home of its kitchen-fodder. The modern daughters are of step-cleaning

take on a home as well as a husband. The result is that in England large houses are being converted into small apartments, while in America dwellings of two rooms are being built, sometimes with a concealed kitchen, sometimes attached to a communal restaurant. It is difficult to say what creates what, just as one never knows whether one has a cold because one has a cough or a cough because one has a cold. Thus we do not quite know whether it is the revolt of woman that alters the home, or the new kind of home which " corrupts women." The " serious " section of the public says that new conditions are corrupting women, but then they say that about everything.

My own suspicion is that these things play on each other; what the eye sees the heart hungers for; example has its influence. It is impossible for a woman to witness the operations of the vacuum cleaner, and then to go home contentedly to a broom in an advanced state of mange. The vacuum cleaner exists because one woman, who hated the mangy broom, happened to be married or sistered to a poet who thought nature might be controlled and mangy brooms done away with. Also, this is part of the tendency (which many people deplore) to make life easier than it was before. Europe put its foot on that slippery slope when in 1786 Jonas Hanway appeared in the streets of London carrying an umbrella; this, of course, was very bad for mankind, likely to lower its physical fibre, its resistance to the weather. With the spread of education mankind has become maniacal in its desire to have things easy: life in itself being a difficult affair, I shall not join those who complain. If women are blamed for their desire to draw light from an electric bulb instead of from a tinder box, it is because women have only recently begun to express such desires.

Now what is notable is that in this new world the home has become a problem that men recognise. Until the war, even, they took it as it was and cursed it for not being what it wasn't. Now they have realised that there is money in home reform, and that has made reform more agreeable. Hence the vacuum cleaner, the radiator, the mechanical potato-peeler, the plate-washer, all the beautiful things, the clear, lovely things that take the weight off the back of life. Many old-fashioned people hate these devices because they reduce effort, but I confess that if ever it is given to me to see a machine receiving pigs at one end and discharging at the other pork-pies, hair-brushes, and pocket-books, I shall *(Continued overleaf)*

Little Ships of YESTERDAY

By Martha Haskell Clark

LITTLE ships of Yesterday, laden deep with dream,
Sailing through the sunset with your silken sails agleam,
Light-heart Youth and dancing Hope laughed upon the quay,
When across the harbour-gold you breasted to the sea.
Oft and oft shall almond bloom scent the springtime rain,
Ere the ships of Yesterday homeward turn again.

Gull that skims the distant waves where the dawn-star pales,
Can you catch a glimmer of the rainbow-tinted sails?
Winds that toss the silver spray past the dipping prow,
Can you say if sunny skies smile upon them now?
God of little, speeding ships, guard them on their way,
Guide them safely back to us, our ships of Yesterday!

Little ships of Yesterday, wind and tempest-borne,
Beating through a winter sea, scarred and soiled and torn,
Homing slow on weary wings under leaden skies,
Still within each clasping hold the precious dream-gold lies.
God of little, gallant sails beating to the grey,
Send my ships of Yesterday safely back, I pray!

---

age and their retort is : " Do away with the steps." A revolution! Now there are less daughters in the home, while their mothers are still desperately making jam and mending table-cloths, are doing so without optimism, by force of habit, because they never had anything else to do.

The daughters, as they become wives, proclaim that they are not going to

What is a Home ?

(Continued)

experience an emotion that I cannot draw from the poems of Walt Whitman.

We are on the way to that golden age. The savage " home " is being muzzled. Even the children, for which it is supposed to be kept up, are being taken over by the new world. Instead of expecting a mother of eighteen to be born a doctor, a food expert, and a dress designer, we now see spread all over the civilised world an organisation of welfare centres, baby clinics, nursing organisations. In the beginning these bodies were looked upon with suspicion. I once read in an American magazine the story of a young man who formed a day-nursery for busy mothers, and put it in charge of a trained nurse. No mother would send her children there. So he put in Old Mother Johnson, who'd " had fourteen," and it was a great success. How decayed all that is! The new woman knows that if Old Mother Johnson had had fourteen she also buried ten. We are not so afraid of the trained nurse and the clinic as we used to be. Little by little, mothers are accepting the fact that babies should not be fed on pickled herrings. Even the Chinese women have unbound their feet. This does not mean that the new world will not extend its work. For instance, in the great city of Pittsburg we still in 1920 had an infant death-rate of 110 per 1,000, say, one life in nine, before the baby attained twelve months. This was being coped with only by a centre of 35 physicians, 18 nurses, and 14 assistants, most of whom were employed in the medical inspection of schools. This gives one an idea of what remains to be done. The new world must give us four physicians and twenty nurses for every 1,000 babies. Ours may be a new world, but it is going to be much newer before it has done.

A little earlier in this article I pointed out that there were less daughters in the home; those who are there tend to play the part of the catfish in an aquarium. More and more, we find the daughters chafing against the home and trying to get out of it; a little while ago, in an English police-court, a girl was offered the option between a month's imprisonment and returning to her parents. She chose gaol. That is an extreme case, but it reflects the new attitude: that the daughters' demand for a home is waning. Very seldom does the new woman use as a threat to her husband "that she will return to her mother": he wouldn't believe her. So, at the same time, we find the home deprived of those who were deemed to be its natural vassals, and ceasing to be an object of affection. It is a sleeping-place, an eating-place, an entertainment centre, but not a holy. To many people it is already an unholy.

Among the special features of the present time we find another factor which has its effects even in America, where money is more abundant and enterprise is more reckless than it is in Europe. I mean the house shortage. Owing to the great increase in the cost, building has either stopped, or dwindled to small proportions, or been confined to the division of large old houses into small new apartments. The tendency of the home is to become smaller and smaller; there is no more money for the maintenance of the parlour, that sacred room, kept chilly all the week and not much warmer on Sundays. The tendency is towards the living-room, where all may take their ease. This has accentuated family disunion, for families quarrel when

kept too close together. Father cannot sleep while Jack plays the flute and Mabel rehearses her part in the amateur dramatic company. The old home stood because its members could get away from one another; by bringing them together we encourage the effect of bringing together flint and steel. Besides, now that the home is small, it is uncomfortable; it drives its members to find pleasure elsewhere; it no longer offers the old domestic joys. The new woman acquires an outside habit, finds this attractive, and turns more and more away from the focus of domesticity.

Other causes also intervene. One of them has been operative in the United States much longer than in England, and that is the servant shortage. The American servant problem is not an old story; it has been partly coped with, but in these years after the war we find coloured domestic labour scarce and dear. The problem and its effects are therefore renewed. In England we have always been dependent upon what might almost be called slave labour. Badly paid, badly fed, badly housed, given never more than twelve hours' freedom a week, our domestics at last revolted, and either went into other trades or refused to sleep in. In America this had happened long ago, and the present state is merely one of scarcity. That does not matter: whether the servant cannot be obtained, or whether when obtained she refuses to work more than eight hours, she over-sets the old idea of home. To-day, all over the world, the old home is being kept together only because the old housewives have accepted slavery. The young housewife refuses, and thus the shortage of domestic help also helps to reduce the size of the home, because the large home cannot be kept up. It is almost impossible to-day to find a tenant for the fourteen-roomed house of our grandfathers. One such house, known to me, a good house, was leased twenty-one years ago for £200 a year; it was recently offered at £150 a year; to-day the landlord would gladly take £100. We are not short of money so much as of domestic servants, and it is that, rather than high prices, which keeps down the size of the home, and is creating a new civilisation, based upon minimum space, helped out not only by labour-saving appliances, but by restaurant feeding. That is the last brick heaved at the old home: thirty years ago, to dine at a restaurant was a rather fast thing to do. A sort of virtue attached to the boiled mutton and capers, the slabs of cabbage, the suet pudding of the home, a home which in many ways was much like the pudding. Privacy was the sauce poured upon the meal. To-day, all that is vanishing because there is nobody to cook the meals, except the mother who can't and the daughter who won't.

Lastly, there is a fall in the birth-rate, which in the home-keeping middle class has supervened from California to Poland. Less children are born, and so the need for multiple nurseries is going, together with the power to staff those nurseries. Everything contributed to reduce the importance of the home, and at the same time to liberate the housewife. She no longer expends all her energy and hopefulness in domestic labour. She is gaining a little freedom, a little time for culture, and even for pleasure. The older woman maintains the tradition, but of the younger woman it may almost be said that her attitude to the home is that there is no such thing.

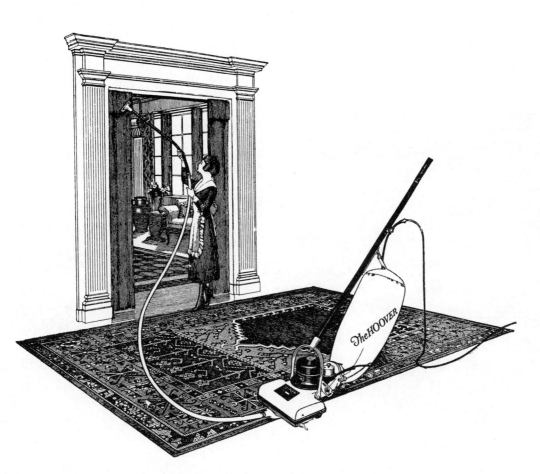

Dust in this easy, dustless way

Ordinary dusting simply perpetuates house-work.

Most of the dust is not removed from the room. Much of it is stirred up into the air and shortly settles again.

To dust efficiently needs the electric Hoover Suction Sweeper.

The long-armed Hoover air accessories suck every particle of dust into a detachable dust-proof bag which can be emptied out of doors and its contents burnt.

The Hoover makes dusting dustless and makes it easier, too.

These Hoover accessories dust from floor to ceiling, reach every nook and cranny, easily and surely. There is no stooping or balancing precariously on step-ladders.

And the most difficult of all household tasks needs the Hoover most of all. Only the three-fold cleaning process of the Hoover can ensure the constant cleanliness and beauty of your carpets. In one easy opera-tion it beats out all the pile-wearing, gritty dirt from their depths; electrically it sweeps, and erects crushed pile; powerfully it cleans by air suction, and brightens colours.

The Hoover is no longer a luxury. It is to-day a necessity. It frees you and your servants for ever from the tyranny of the broom; ends that wasteful, unavailing ex-penditure of human energy; and to you it means a home that is always scrupulously clean—because it can be thoroughly cleaned so easily and so rapidly.

Only £3. 19s. down and 31s. a month for a short time pays for the Hoover while you use it. There is also a larger model for hotels, clubs and large residences. Write for illustrated booklet and names of nearest Hoover dealers.

Hoover, Ltd., 288, Regent Street, London, W. 1, and
at Birmingham, Manchester, Leeds and Glasgow

The HOOVER

It BEATS.... as it Sweeps   as it Cleans   REG. TRADE MARK

This bungalow has been planned to give its inmates all the
advantages and none of the inconvenience of life at sea

A   HOME   BESIDE   THE   SEA

Planned on nautical lines, there is a holiday atmosphere about this
bungalow though it is built for a permanent home.   Its cost is £1,500

By H. V. M. EMERSON, A.R.I.B.A.

UPON the bracing east coast, the
sunny south coast, or the picturesque west coast of England
are to be found sites with
charming views over land and sea,
sheltered from the cold winds of the
north, ideal in every way for the
bungalow we illustrate and describe in
this article.   It is called a seaside
bungalow, and is planned and designed
to be used during holidays and week-
ends, or all the year round, the aim
being to create a nautical atmosphere
for the occupants, which will enable
them to enjoy all the benefits and beauty
that the sea affords, without the inconveniences that are occasionally experienced by those whose home is afloat.

The living- and sleeping-quarters are
arranged so that the full benefit of the
sea breezes and sunshine is obtained.
The saloon and billiard-room is large
enough to hold a full-sized billiard table,
and at the same time allows ample room
for social intercourse without causing
any inconvenience to those playing at
the table.   Such a room is a necessary
feature in a bungalow of this description, for the weather is not always
favourable for outdoor pursuits, and indoor recreation has to be provided.   The
interior decoration of this room is half-
timber work for the upper walls and
ceiling, and panel filling for the lower
part of the walls.   The large fireplace,

with its brick hearth and dog-grate, sur-
mounted with a stone mantel of the
Tudor period, is the central feature of
the room.   The floor could be made of
polished oak boards or blocks, and
covered with rugs.

Leading from the saloon is a winter
garden, fitted with glazed doors that
can be easily removed during the
summer months, and replaced for the
autumn and winter, providing a delightful lounge.   The interior walls are
plastered and covered with patterned
lattice-work, upon which are trained
creepers and flowers, whilst the floor
is of the jointless variety, being practically noiseless and impervious to water.

Through a curtained opening in the
saloon is a small dining-saloon.   Provision is made for service from the
galley by means of a hatch of the cupboard type, which is more effective than
a hatch with a single door in preventing
noise and the smell of cooking from
reaching the dining-saloon from the
galley.   A well fire is provided, and the
decoration of the walls is carried out
with a dark dado, a white frieze, and the
space between the dado and the picture-
rail painted apricot colour.   Upon the
ceiling, which is white like the frieze,
there is a light plaster band ornament,
in the position shown by a single line
on the plan.

Behind the dining-saloon is the galley,

fitted with a full range, or, if gas is
installed, a smaller type of range can
be substituted, consisting of an open
fire, boiler, oven, and hot-plate.   Around
the walls and within easy reach are
placed the necessary stores and appliances for the work that has to be done
here.   Near the galley is the tradesmen's entrance, bunker, and lavatory.
Facing the sea is the maid's cabin fitted
up in a similar manner to those described
later, and of sufficient size to accommodate two maids.

The sleeping-quarters in this bungalow
are similar to those found in an ocean
liner.   Cabins are provided with one or
two berths.   Under each berth drawers
are fitted for the reception of clothes,
and at the end of each berth is a narrow
wardrobe fitted with sliding hangers,
which can be pulled out, and any article
of clothing removed or added without
disturbing the remainder.   Each berth
is provided with a wire spring mattress
and side curtains.   Sliding seats are also
provided, which can be pulled out for
use and pushed back when not required
—an advantage in limited spaces.   At
the end of the cabin a lavatory basin is
fitted with hot- and cold-water supply
and waste, an arrangement which very
materially reduces the work of running
the bungalow.   Racks and fitments are
provided for the reception of water-
bottle, glasses, and toilet requisites, while

Cabins, in place of bedrooms, have built-in fitments that are space-saving and labour-saving

a small cabinet let in the wall holds a shaving outfit. The door is fitted with a mirror, which can be opened to any angle for use when shaving. In the women's cabins full-length mirrors are fixed to the entrance doors and adequately protected against accidental breakage.

The doors, which open outwards, are hung on rising butts, and are self-closing. The floors are formed with the jointless material before mentioned, which has rounded angles and is covered with rugs.

The state-room is a more important apartment, with oak floor and decorated ceiling. It is fitted with a lavatory basin, and upon either side there are a wardrobe and drawers complete with all fittings. An angle cupboard is provided with a full-length dress-mirror, and the opposite angle is fitted with an electric or gas stove.

A separate entrance to the sleeping-quarters enables bathers to undress and dress in their cabins and to pass in and out of the bungalow without traversing the main apartments.

The building is constructed in brickwork upon concrete foundations, the walls being covered externally with cement roughcast, treated with a waterproof solution, or, if a brickwork finish is preferred, hollow walls should be used in order to withstand the penetrating rains experienced upon the coast. The thickness of the walls will depend upon the position of the site: the more exposed the position, the thicker they will have to be constructed. The roof is covered with plain tiles or small thick slates of varied colour laid in courses. The position of the site should allow the building to be erected with the main front facing practically due south and allowing the rooms on the sides to obtain the benefit of the rising and setting sun.

The drainage from the house can be carried into a septic tank such as that described in a previous article in GOOD HOUSEKEEPING, or, if the position is favourable, the drain can discharge into the sea; but careful consideration should be given to this point, so as not to cause any offence upon the shore or interfere with the bathing.

The lighting and heating of this bungalow call for consideration if the public gas or electric-light supplies are not available. The lighting of the bungalow can be effected with oil, petrol, gas, acetylene, or electricity. Lamps burning petroleum are too well known to call for any special comment. An improvement upon the oil lamp is the petrol-gas lamp. This is a portable lamp fitted with a reservoir, mantle, and glass. In the reservoir is an absorbent block. Sufficient petrol is poured in to saturate the block, the surplus being returned to the can. With an ordinary

incandescent mantle, a light of about 50 candle-power is obtained from this gas. The lamp is perfectly safe, will not explode, and if accidentally knocked over, automatically goes out. A petrol-gas installation is very economical in working, gives a splendid light, and can be used for cooking. The plant is automatic in working, and consists of a container for petrol and another for the gas, which is simply a mixture of petrol-vapour with a given quantity of air. This mixture is obtained by the action of a small machine worked by a suspended weight. When the gas container is full, the machine automatically stops, but comes into play again as soon as gas is withdrawn from the container. The only attention the apparatus requires is the winding up of the weight and filling the petrol container. The gas is conducted to the various points by means of pipes somewhat larger than ordinary gas pipes. As the air is already mixed with the petrol-gas, the air in the room is not consumed. Unlike coal-gas, petrol-gas is practically odourless, and should the tap be accidentally turned on, no harm will arise, as the gas is non-asphyxiating, and an explosion from the introduction of a naked light is practically impossible, as the mixture of petrol-vapour and air have to be in the right proportions before an explosion will take place, and the air in a room being in a constant state of movement prevents the right proportions being obtained.

Suitable fittings for this form of lighting are on the market. Small mantles are generally used, giving a light of about 50 candle-power each. Gas-stoves and boiling-rings can be obtained for petrol-gas as for use with ordinary gas, the burners being slightly different. The gas is turned on and off in the usual way, the machine producing sufficient gas to meet the demands made upon it. The cost of petrol-gas is much less than coal-gas, as a gallon of petrol will produce between 1,000 to 1,500 cubic feet of gas, according to the grade of the spirit used.

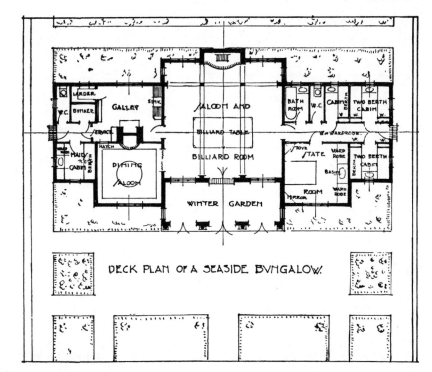

DECK PLAN OF A SEASIDE BUNGALOW.

THE
20's

Repose and dignity are given to a simple rectangular brick house by the arrangement of its entrance porch and windows

The Well-Mannered House

By C. H. JAMES, A.R.I.B.A.

Individuality in treatment need not mean the sacrifice of all conventional standards

WHEN the idea of the Capital Levy was first mooted, it was estimated that there were no fewer than three hundred and sixty thousand people whose capital exceeded £5,000, and who would, therefore, come within its scope. This being so, it is fair to assume that there are at least that number of people who can afford to choose, within limits, in what neighbourhood and in what manner of house they will live. In addition to these, there is undoubtedly a large body of people who, although not possessed of that amount of capital, have incomes sufficient to pay the interest on a considerable loan such as would enable them to build a house for themselves.

Of these two classes, a few thousands are very rich, and no doubt own both country and town houses; but it is certain that the great majority live in fair-sized residences in the suburbs of London and the larger provincial towns.

FEW people can doubt the need for improvement in house design in this country and, dealing with the subject constructively, the author of this article gives many excellent suggestions. Readers needing information on any phase of house building should send their enquiry with a stamped addressed envelope for his reply, to the Director of Housing, "Good Housekeeping," 153 Queen Victoria Street, E.C.4.

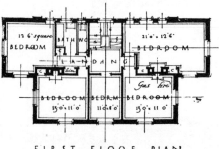

FIRST FLOOR PLAN
of the house shown on the opposite page

It is the purpose of this article to examine to some extent the kind of houses they inhabit, and to make a few suggestions which would, if carried out, improve the standard of house-design in and near our large towns which, since the last great Exhibition of 1851, has reached a deplorably low standard.

People who wish to build a week-end cottage in the country have been amply catered for by articles in this and other magazines, and in many volumes dealing with small houses. But with very few exceptions the problem of the urban house has been left untouched.

Much as people may desire to live in the country, it is impossible to effect this end by putting up a large number of country cottages on small building plots near our towns. It will be obvious to all who think intelligently about the matter that houses which in the nature of things have to be erected at a short distance one from another cannot, if a sense of fitness is to be preserved, have too much individuality, in other words, too many worrying little features and excrescences. Just as many persons of different habits and temperaments will not be able to live happily together without, to a certain extent at any rate, sinking their own points of view, so houses, to be well-mannered, must not vaunt themselves at the expense of others in their neighbourhood.

The external clothing of a house, no less than of an individual, must conform in some degree to conventional standards. A man who goes to his business in the City in " plus fours " and a " pull-over " is little more out of place than a country cottage dressed in rough-cast and half-timber work in an urban area.

It should be understood that no plea is being made for absolute uniformity of design, although that to many people would be preferable to the utter discord which at present prevails; but it should be realised that the exteriors of houses, while retaining good design and proportion, can be varied greatly in detail without becoming inharmonious. The doorways, the shape and correct placing of the windows, the colour and texture of the brickwork, and the design and materials composing the roof can be made to give all the relief necessary to prevent monotony, and in any case the different requirements of the inhabitants themselves, having their effect on the plan of the house, will inevit-

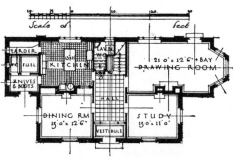

GROUND FLOOR PLAN
of the house shown below

ably change its external appearance.

The great town houses of London, Edinburgh, and Dublin, of which we ought to be really proud, will be found when analysed to be singularly quiet and restful in appearance. Their external effect is almost entirely due to the careful placing of the windows, to well-designed doorways, and, in the case of many of the London squares, to nature in the form of trees and grass lawns.

The owners of these houses are free to express their individuality and talent for decoration and furnishing within the rooms themselves.

The house in its own grounds, by which term is meant two acres or more, becomes an entity, a work of art or otherwise in itself, and can by means of trees be cut off from its surround-

ings and so judged. On the other hand, a house in a street is part of a larger whole, and must be treated as such. To ignore one's neighbours of brick and mortar will soon be looked upon as a serious breach of etiquette.

It should be clearly understood that the repetition of features, such as bay windows and gables, merely defeats its own ends, and is far more monotonous when carried to extremes, as in our suburbs, and far more difficult to bear than the monotony of absolute simplicity.

The bulk of the large number of people mentioned at the beginning of this article live in houses which, striving each to shout its importance more vigorously than its neighbours, have become mere units in a confused din. People are no longer judged by the mere size of the house in which they live; they are more likely in the future to be judged by its design, and the manner in which it is built. No person of taste could ever be deceived by mere expensiveness or extravagance. The lay-out and appearance of the front garden, the curtains, and the colour of the paint on the front door will tell the keen observer much about the character, tastes, and habits of the occupants of a house.

It may be said with a certain amount of justice that the average person lives in the kind of house provided for him by the builder, but it should be remembered that the *(Continued overleaf)*

THE
20's

This house shows the restfulness produced by good proportion and the direct expression of various parts

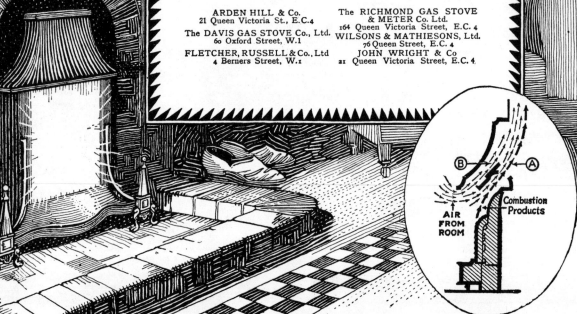

The Well-Mannered House

(Continued)

latter builds for a livelihood and not for recreation. He must needs erect the type of house which experience has proved to him to be most likely to attract purchasers with the least possible amount of delay. He cannot afford to cater for the one person of taste, but must set his bait for the other nine, who, having eyes, apparently see not.

It is evident, however, that the number of persons having educated taste is greatly on the increase, with the consequence that the best architects are being increasingly employed for the design of even very small houses. Many enlightened builders have also realised the wisdom of erecting well-designed houses, even as a speculation, and no doubt effect considerable savings by going to the so-called expense of a trained architect's assistance.

The house designer of the past seventy years appears to have gone about his work in quite a different manner from that adopted to-day. He apparently added rooms one to another until the required number was reached, and afterwards attempted to make these into a shape capable of being roofed over and of producing an elevation of the "rambling" type. Nowadays, however, economy is much to the fore, and it has had one very good result, it has forced house designers to avoid as far as possible unnecessary walling and unnecessary labour in cutting roof timbers and tiles.

The requirements of a householder are now taken as a whole, and forced into a shape approaching the rectangular. This has resulted in considerable economy in cost, and no loss, often indeed great gain, to the convenience of the house.

The desire for detached houses is in many ways a misfortune, for great savings could be effected by the agreeing of two or more prospective house owners to build their houses together. The objection to the party wall and the trouble with noise from the next-door neighbour could be overcome by thickening that wall, at less expense than would be entailed in building two or more separate houses. Great gains in appearance would also be effected owing to the drawing out of the horizontal lines, which would help to compose the street frontage.

There is, however, no reason why individual houses, bearing in mind the points mentioned above, should not have dignity and repose, for they can always be linked together by out-buildings, garages, etc., while it is more than likely that within a few years the American method of eliminating the front division hedges and fences and having open front gardens will be adopted.

It should be the aim of everyone intending to build a house to build it of the best materials that he can afford. This will ensure a minimum repair bill and weather and time will but improve the appearance of the property.

It is foolish to ignore the influence of nature and its ultimate effect on the design. A house of the utmost simplicity will answer to good garden treatment far better than one of a more elaborate kind, and will ultimately yield far greater satisfaction.

The enduring things in art are always the most simple. Many people who have discovered this to be true of music and of furniture will need little convincing to prove to them that it is true also of houses and of gardens.

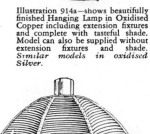

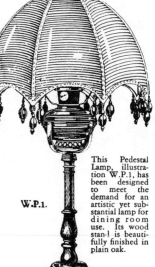
THE 20's

The home is very much more Eve's castle than it is Adam's. Of course he has " his chair "
in the living-room, but his personal belongings seem to be always in the wrong place

THE
20's

ADAM *at* HOME

By Clara Savage Littledale

Illustrated by Henry Raleigh

THIS is an article for women only. It would never in the world do to let Adam get hold of it. Even as I write, I realise the peril of that possibility. Because men do read GOOD HOUSEKEEPING. Just when you are most anxious to finish the next instalment of a particularly interesting serial, you find Adam deep in your latest copy. He reads straight through—fiction, articles. He lingers, wide-eyed, over the fashions, and then becomes absorbed in an article on electrical appliances. He smacks his lips over recipes. However, it is to be hoped that if any man begins this article he will stop at the first paragraph. Because it is a piece of frankness between women only. And every woman knows that there are things she will admit to another woman or in a group of women that she would carefully avoid mentioning if Adam were present. It wouldn't be safe to mention them. There is no use in encouraging Adam to be any more unmanageable than he naturally is.

Now that men readers have been discouraged, it is urged, at this point, that every woman reader borrow a pair of Adam's shoes and put them on. (He probably has a cupboard full of them. You know how strangely attached he is to his shabby, outworn, useless old pairs.) Only when Eve has put herself in Adam's shoes will she be in the proper mood to read this article.

Have you ever found yourself wondering why men marry? Or does that question seem ridiculous to you? It's easy enough to see why women marry. Most women want just what marriage has to offer—a home of their own to decorate and arrange and enjoy, a chance to keep house, time for their friends and social engagements, the wonder of children, the companionship of Adam. Marriage, when it is happy, is so exactly calculated to give a woman what she wants of life that it seems as though she must have invented it.

But Adam! Is domesticity what Adam most wants? Does marriage have as much to offer him as it has to offer Eve? Perhaps some marriages would run more smoothly if Eve asked herself that question. So many women seem

to take it for granted that once Adam is married he should be the happiest man on the face of the earth. And some women, working on that theory, are willing to take so much and give so little!

A great deal is being written nowadays about women by women. Times have changed since woman was a docile little thing who kept house and kept still. She has now become startlingly articulate. Glance over any list of new books, and you will be struck by the number written by women bent on self-revelation —telling what they think, how they feel, and why they do what they do. We hear a good deal about woman's need for self-expression. Can she express herself if she has to do housework? This is a much-discussed question. Women have won the title of "the restless sex" and seem rather proud of it. And all the time, poor, dear Adam stands by patiently, rather puzzled by these strange upheavals among the ladies, but trying to be kind and sympathetic.

It never seems to occur to Adam to make a point of being restless, too. He doesn't go about declaring that his office routine gives *(Continued overleaf)*

Adam at Home
(Continued)

him no time for self-expression. No, Adam goes quietly off to his office in the morning, works from nine till five, comes home at night carrying bundles, and is very patient and good about it indeed. While his wife is struggling with the servant problem—and telling him all her difficulties every evening—Adam is hiring and firing office help and not making much fuss about it.

But it isn't Adam in his office as much as it is Adam at home who should give us pause. After all, he is more or less supreme in his office. But though he may be listed in the census as Head of the House, what is actually Adam's position in his own home?

Sometimes one can't help wondering what early feminine ancestor of ours first had the temerity and the power to get Man into a home and keep him there. Was it a palæolithic maid, brawny and strong as her mate, or was it her sister of the polished stone or neolithic age? Was it one of these who succeeded in luring him within the four walls of a cave? True, Man shows signs of being interested in a home. He likes to build it or buy it. But often one detects in present-day Man traces of that balkiness which must have been his when he was first told to wipe his prehistoric feet on the door-mat and come into the house. By that entering, Man brought upon himself far-reaching and unimaginable consequences. So did Eve bring unforeseen complications upon herself.

We have now come to believe that a man's place is in the home. From the time he is born, his liberty is plotted against. If a boy baby only knew what infinite capacity for harnessing, for confining, for attacking him, lurked within the tousled golden head of every little girl baby! Why, as soon as she can talk, what does she play? "House." Yes, "House" is from the first her favourite game. Her brother prefers "Injuns" and "Policemans," and he wants to be the whole fire-company, but his small playmate is perfectly contented with an endless, all-satisfying game of "House." And if he isn't very careful, he is included in the game in spite of himself. Perhaps it is fortunate that men do not see any more clearly than they do the vast feminine intrigue in which Woman is engaged from her babyhood up—that of making a home and finding a man to put in it. Women used to be more outspoken about it than they now are. Maidens used to admit that their desire was to "make a home for some good man." It sounds altruistic, doesn't it? Girls don't come out quite so openly on this point now. And yet, in nine cases out of ten it is the fundamental desire on the part of women.

And Adam? Once he is safely married, have you ever stopped to consider what an odd figure he often cuts in his own home? Not your particular Adam! Oh, dear me, *no*! But consider your neighbour Adam, or your brother, Adam, and practically all other Adams.

"Every man's home is his castle," is an English saying. It is seldom if ever used in the United States. Perhaps that is why Mr. Gilbert Chesterton, on a recent tour of the States, was so overwhelmingly surprised at American husbands who helped their wives with the dinner dishes. Mr. Chesterton pointed out that this was never the custom of English husbands living in England. He said it would not have occurred to them to do such a thing, and it would not have occurred to their wives to ask them to do such a thing. The originality of the idea must be credited to American women. When Mr. Chesterton asked the American woman about it, she said it was "sociable." And she said it made Adam feel "at home." There is no record of what Adam said.

If Eve is at all fair-minded, I believe she will admit that the home is very much more her castle than it is Adam's. Perhaps she will even maintain that that is as it should be. But wait a minute. Remember you have put on Adam's shoes and can look at things from his point of view. Just consider Adam and his home.

In the first place, it is very hard for him to enter it satisfactorily. He seldom wipes his feet as thoroughly as Eve would have him. Ten to one, if Eve is not looking, he will walk over the clean floor without even seeing the door-mat.

Once safely within, in just what part of the house can Adam feel most at home? Well, Eve points out, he has "his chair" in the sitting-room. But he must be very careful not to change the position of that chair by pulling it over the rug. That will wrinkle the rug. It is a priceless rug, a wedding-gift, and on no account are ashes to be dropped upon it. It seems to Eve that Adam is always on the point of dropping ashes. To circumvent their fall she places a neat, small ash-tray by his chair. Now Adam's ideal ash-tray would be about the size of a salad-bowl, but the one Eve has given him for Christmas is about the diameter of a button. Somehow, even in his chair, and with his ash-tray, Adam does not feel that he is any great addition to what Eve's friends describe as her "perfectly lovely living-room—so homelike."

Then the dining-room! The dining-room wouldn't be so bad if white table-cloths didn't seem to attract drops of gravy. And Adam never can get over crumpling his napkin in his best restaurant manner. Then there are centrepieces to wrinkle and spatter. Eve is very touchy about centre-pieces and those mats she calls "d'oyleys" —silly name, Adam thinks. The dining-room makes him nervous.

But surely Adam finds the bedroom a restful place? Well, it might be if women weren't, by necessity, the putters-away. Of course, as Eve points out, someone must "pick up the house." And so it is naturally Eve who puts Adam's clothes away, who decides that his collars and socks and handkerchiefs shall go in the top tray of his wardrobe, his shirts in the second, his pyjamas, et cetera, in the third. All very neat! But can you, Eve, imagine yourself letting some other person arrange your dressing-table drawers without consulting you? Eve even arranges Adam's cupboard—if she lets him have a whole one for himself.

THERE are some sad households where Eve has never learned that two main requirements for a happy marriage are a separate wardrobe for Adam and a separate cupboard for him—each separate and sacred to him. No, much as she is tempted to put her stuffed figure for dressmaking in Adam's cupboard, she should restrain that impulse. The bride who thinks it will be sweet to share half her dressing-table drawers with Adam and to go halves on one cupboard is making the first big mistake of her married life. It is true that the minister has said that "these twain shall be of one flesh," but she must not take that to mean that they shall also be of one cupboard and one chest of drawers.

"If I only had a chest of drawers all to myself!" I heard one Adam lament.

"Well, you have—all but one drawer," said his wife.

"That's just it—all but one drawer. I wish I had that drawer."

(Continued overleaf)

THE 20's

THE
20's

Adam at Home
(Continued)

" But you don't need it," Eve came back. " What have you to put in it ? "

" I don't know," admitted this exponent of the reasonable sex, " but I want the feeling of having that whole thing to myself. It's the same way with my cupboard. I wish you'd take your summer hat out of it ! "

But it is not only so far as the house is concerned that Adam frequently gives the impression of living on the fringes of his wife's domestic arrangements. It goes farther than that. When there are children, often he misses his share in them.

Adam is off to his office before the children are up in the morning. He comes home after they have gone to bed. Saturday afternoons and Sundays are practically his only chance to get acquainted with his own youngsters. But there is dancing school on Saturday, or mother wants to take the children shopping, or any one of a dozen things interferes with their being with their father. On Sunday comes Sunday-school and a large dinner, after which Adam is too sleepy and too overfed to be an interesting parent. There is something all wrong with such a state of affairs. A small boy or a small girl ought to have their fair share of picnicking, tramping, fishing with father, romping with him, or listening to the stories he can tell. Father ought to have a chance to show them what an altogether fascinating, delightful, ingenious, and lovable person he is. That is only fair.

THERE is something dangerous about the maternal instinct. There is a fierceness about it, a sense of superiority, and an assumption of power that often accompany it. If a woman is not very careful, she finds herself assuming omnipotence in regard to the children. " My children," she says instead of " our children." Deep in many a woman's consciousness lurks the sublime conviction that no man on the face of the earth—not even their father —can possibly know anything at all about *her* children. The best kind of mother will admit this tendency of hers and will struggle against it. She will be very careful to see that fatherhood gets its rights and that there shall be no motherhood monopoly in her family.

There are households that are divided against themselves in the matter of fun. This is a very serious division. If two people can't have fun together, they are apt to develop a case of incompatibility which may lead to divorce. The trouble is that Adam likes out-of-door amusements —golf, tennis, long walks, camping. Eve's favourite diversions are the theatre and dancing. When Adam declares he dances " like a house afire " and hates it, Eve comes back at him by maintaining that

tennis tires her out and that golf is stupid. In some cases Eve is more successful at dragging Adam to dances and the theatre than he is at getting her to put on her hat and coat and come out into the fresh air, or perhaps they agree to disagree and enjoy themselves separately.

This last solution of the difficulty is a poor one. Both Adam and Eve are losers, and neither of them is being a good sport. Besides, they are missing something that every single one of us really wants—an opportunity to be someone else for awhile. Everyone gets tired of being just the same old self. That is one reason why women like new and different clothes, because they hope that when they wear them they will feel like new and different persons. That is why we often enjoy an entirely new group of people, because they don't know us as our old friends do, and we hope through their eyes to see ourselves from a fresh point of view. Eve has a splendid chance actually to discover a new Eve by entering into Adam's kind of fun. Perhaps she will find there is an out-of-door Eve who is most fetching in jaunty sports clothes set off by rosy cheeks. This is an Eve with whom Adam will fall in love all over again.

As for Adam—Adam stands a very fair chance of discovering a self who likes the theatre, if he chooses nights when he isn't tired out after a hard day's work, and if Eve doesn't select all the plays. As for dancing! Do you know the real honest truth about Adam and dancing? The more he says he hates it, the more capacity he has for immensely enjoying it! Deep in Adam's heart is the unadmitted desire to glide over a ballroom floor, arms encircling Eve, with such grace, precision, and masculine charm that everyone will stop to look, admire, and envy. It is his conviction, based on fact, that he falls far short of this vision, that hurts. It hurts so much that he can't bear the thought of dancing.

But if Eve goes half-way in joining in Adam's favourite amusements, she can appeal to his sense of fair play and get him to join in hers. Before she insists upon his dancing, however, she should persuade him to take a few lessons. For the whole trouble with Adam's dancing is that he doesn't know how; he isn't up-to-date; he isn't sure of himself. But let his teacher be someone other than Eve! It is trying for Adam to be put in the position of pupil to his own wife.

An accusation frequently brought against Eve is that she robs Adam of the friends of his bachelor days. Out of this belief in the ruthlessness of Eve has grown up the custom of the bachelor dinner which the prospective bridegroom gives to men friends on the eve of his marriage. It is

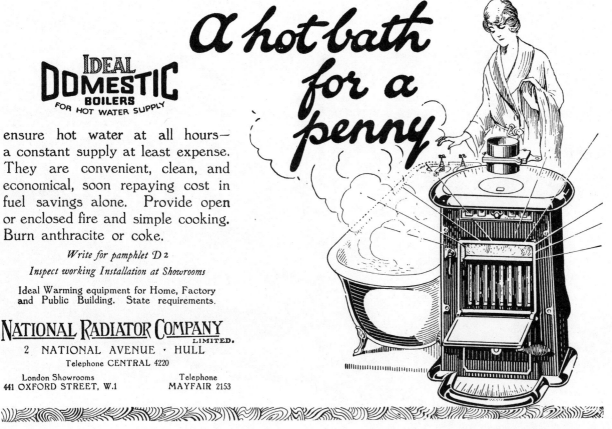

THE
20's

A Home *in*
London *or*

By Lady Violet

*The choice is not so much that of one's
lives in the country : in*

FIRST, let it be either in one or the other. Let me, at all costs, live either in the very heart, at the humming hub of London itself, or else in real wilds. Not at any price in one of those unsatisfactory compromises, those half-way houses called suburbs and garden-cities, which cheat one both ways; nor even on the accessible fringes of Surrey, Essex, and Hertfordshire, where villas grow like weeds and one sees gleaming between the boughs of every Scotch fir the red roof of a "bungalow."

There may be hygiene, comfort, cleanliness, convenience to be found in the suburbs, but there surely can never be atmosphere of romance? They have no soil, no key or colour of their own. They can never hold solitude. One can lose oneself as effectually in a crowd as in a desert, but among villas and "semi-detached residences" privacy is almost unattainable. Villadom is argus-eyed. A terribly vigilant neighbourliness pre-

vails in garden suburbs. (I know one in which the building of a wall and even the growing of a hedge round houses is forbidden, in order that the inmates may be encouraged to have "nothing to conceal" and to display the apple-pie order of their lives to all around!)

Half-way houses then are dismissed—and the choice remains between the country, the real country, and London. I say London, because, if one *is* going to live in a town, it obviously must be London. London is the town of towns. In it can be found the merits and demerits of a town, all at their zenith. For smoke, dirt, noise, fog, density of houses, traffic and people, what town can beat it? For personality, variety, atmosphere, tradition, freedom, what town in the whole world can come near it?

But though far more than ninety-nine people out of a hundred, given the choice, would ask for a home in London *now*, most of them would choose to have grown up, to have spent their

childhood at least, in a home in the country. And surely they would be right?

A home in London has narrow limits. At its best it must be bounded by the four walls of a house with, perhaps, one peep out of a window that one loves thrown in. A home in the country may mean, besides a house, a river, a mountain, a garden, a moor, a beech wood, or the bare shoulder of a down, even the whole sea or the whole sky, as intimately known and as surely possessed as one's own front door. To those who have grown up in a home in the country, sunsets and wild-flowers and birds and trees will be a part of the familiar furniture of daily life—held and remembered like the pattern of the chintz in the night-nursery, the shiny floor of the drawing-room, our favourite rocking-chair, or the clock in the hall.

We may not have thought of any of these things as "beautiful." Children rarely pass conscious æsthetic judg-

THE
20's

in the Country

Bonham-Carter

Decoration by C. A. Wilkinson

ments, and it is particularly difficult to appraise at all critically anything that we can never remember being without. Those of us who have grown up in the country can never guess at the startling ecstasy, the sudden dramatic revelation of beauty it gives to the London child. We are apt to take it quite calmly for granted, as a matter of course. But its beauty does reach us somehow, nevertheless, almost without our being aware of it. It strikes a root in us long before we consciously register our impressions or experiences. We draw it in with our breath, through our pores, and make it ours. Whatever chances await us, we shall feel safer all our lives for having a bit of the earth that surely belongs to us, to which we can always return as to a friend, with the certainty of finding even in the soil itself peace, welcome, and renewal. Of this sure possession, this birthright, country children can never be disinherited.

There are so many different kinds of wonderful homes one might have grown up in in the country. I (who have never, alas! owned more than a window-box or a square of red flannel to sow my mustard and cress in) shut my eyes and see a procession of perfect alternatives.

Red-brick Queen Anne, a perfect House-that-Jack-built, straight from the pages of a Caldecott, standing in four-square serenity among shaven lawns. There is a rose-garden, walled in with black yew hedges on which vast birds in topiary are perched precariously; a cedar-tree with branches sensitively out-spread, like the hands of a pianist poised above the keys; a herbaceous border, rolling towards us, a river of colour. A wide lime avenue stretches downhill away from the house into blue distance. Behind it lies a kitchen garden with octagonal walls, rose-red, cut like a jewel.

The next is in the Cotswolds. A manor built of golden stone, silvered with lichen here and there. One great Eliza-bethan window of old latticed glass lets the sunlight filter greenly through into the long hall. A big magnolia grows on the south wall. Under the tulip-tree on the lawn we sit for happy hours, lotus-eating. Sometimes we walk away a little, but always we are constrained. as though by a spell, to look back and back again over our shoulders at the house, lying in golden peace in its green cup. It has the beauty of a face.

A tiny home, hardly more than a keeper's cottage, on Northumbrian moors. Great sweeps of heather, moss, and orange grasses stretch away from it to wide horizons. Their colours change with every mood of the sky. Brown streams, full of tiny trout, tumble down into the valleys over grey stones. One can tramp for miles over the moors without meeting any living thing except a curlew or a flock of black-faced sheep. But in this solitude there is no desolation. . . . *(Continued overleaf)*

Like a Film of Flexible Glass

It Protects and Beautifies

THE
20's

For Motor Cars

Johnson's Liquid Wax is recommended by leading motor-car manufacturers for polishing and preserving lacquer-finished cars against wear and weather

For Woodwork

Johnson's Liquid Wax never becomes soft and sticky. Consequently, it does not gather dust and lint or show finger-prints

For Furniture

On fine furniture Johnson's Liquid Wax, the greaseless furniture polish, gives a glass-like protection

Johnson's Polishing Wax will fill a real need in your home—cleaning, preserving and beautifying all finished surfaces. It is so hard, dry and greaseless that a thin coat spread on floors, furniture and woodwork is like encasing them in flexible glass armour.

Johnson's Wax instantly cleans off all soil and grime, polishes easily and is very economical. Very little Wax is necessary and the finish it gives is most lasting.

Use it on *all* your floors—wood, linoleum, tile or composition. Johnson's Waxed-floors are wear-resisting and add beauty and charm to your home.

JOHNSON'S WAX
Electric Floor Polisher

Hire a JOHNSON'S WAX ELECTRIC Floor Polisher from your dealer for a few hours at the rate of 5/- a day or 3/- a half day, and polish your floors electrically. Ten times faster than other methods. Works from any lamp socket for less than 1d. per hour. You can purchase a JOHNSON'S WAX ELECTRIC Floor Polisher for only £6 . 6 . 0, and with each is given FREE a 14/- tin of JOHNSON'S Liquid Wax and a Lamb's-wool Mop, value 7/-. Deferred payments arranged.

Tested and Approved
Good Housekeeping Institute

1/- size Reduced to 9d.

From Grocers & Ironmongers at 9d., 2/6, 4/-, etc.

S. C. JOHNSON & SON, Ltd., West Drayton, Middlesex
" The Floor Finishing Authorities."

JOHNSON'S
POLISHING WAX

A Home in London or in the Country

(Continued)

A small flint farmhouse lying in a fold of the downs. They roll away in great bare curves on all sides, scarred here and there by a chalk quarry and dappled by the cloud shadows that scud across them on a windy day. No garden is wanted here. Wild orchises and giant cowslips leap out of the close-growing turf that smells of thyme. Along these high uplands one can walk for hours with the sky above one and the world spread out like a coloured carpet at one's feet. . . .

What alternatives can London offer which will compare with these? To begin with (says the rustic) all London houses are alike. A London house is just a box—a big box or a small one, a dark box or a light one. No matter who lives in it, the outside looks almost exactly the same as that of seventy or eighty other boxes standing by its side. The colour of the front door and the number on it are often the only things to show that it belongs to me. And even the insides of an enormous proportion of London houses are depressingly alike. One enters the "front hall" (a passage somewhat dimly lit from the coloured glass of the half-landing window on the stairs) and one knows blindfold that on one side lies the dining-room, and behind it a quite uninhabitable man's sitting-room (the "study" the caretaker calls it), fit only to keep the perambulator in. One knows again, with gloomy certainty, that the inevitable L-shaped drawing-room will lie overhead divided by double-doors, and that the dado on the stairs will probably be made of lincrusta. . . .

But, it may be objected by the loyal, lifelong Cockney, these reach-me-down houses exist everywhere, not only in London, but in the country too. As for variety and contrasts, if *that* is what you are after, London can more than hold its own. It would be much easier to mistake Hampshire for Berkshire, or Sussex for Kent, than for one moment to confuse Belgravia with Bloomsbury or Chelsea with Mayfair. The difference between downs and moorland pales, shrinks and dwindles beside that which distinguishes—say, Soho from Marylebone. The component parts which go to make up London have as distinct and definite a character as anything in nature. Each has its own atmosphere, its own inhabitants, its own language, almost its own smell. . . .

Where would one choose to live in London? I do not hesitate to put Belgravia *last* of anywhere. I would rather live in Whitechapel, Shoreditch, or Chinatown than in Belgravia. Belgrave Square itself may be redeemed for some by dying echoes of Thackeray, but for dingy, dreary gentility I give the Eatons and the Sloanes (whether Streets, Squares, Gardens, Places, or Crescents) first prize. Those vistas of complicated high-church houses (pseudo-Gothic? pseudo-*what*? I'm not sure, only certainly pseudo) made of dark red brick, thickly veiled in smuts—who *can* the people be who voluntarily live inside them? The fact that they *are* inhabited has shaken my faith in Free Will. There is a good deal to be said for Bloomsbury, with its old bookshops, cheap polyglot restaurants, wig, mask, and false beard-makers, niggers, *fairs* (there is usually a merry-go-round to be found in a waste space off Tottenham Court Road), and splendid squares falling into dignified decay. Mayfair is grossly overrated—the Mecca of house-agents and Americans. Curzon Street, Hill Street, and Charles Street have always struck me as dull, dark, narrow, and noisy. No one

(Continued overleaf)

ARE YOU A GOOD COOK?

Thousands of the women who read "Good Housekeeping" would tell you that *they* are good cooks. Far better cooks now—after using the excellent recipes that Florence B. Jack has prepared for the magazine for the past three years—than ever before.

In the book whose cover is illustrated above—"Good Housekeeping's" First Cookery Book—you have in handy, inexpensive form all the delicious and wholesome dishes needed to give your meals interest and value. These recipes are economical and practical. They do not demand the use of extravagant quantities of expensive food. Explicit directions are given with the recipes, all of which have appeared in "Good Housekeeping" after being carefully tested in the Model Kitchen at the "Good Housekeeping" Institute. The book costs 2/9½ post free. Address your order, with P.O. enclosed, to "Good Housekeeping" Book Dept., 153 Queen Victoria Street, E.C.4

THE 20's

A Home in London or in the Country
(Continued)

could be happy there except the very rich. Chelsea is of course a Paradise—for the owner of several motors. (Without these getting to and fro just halves the day.) Living in Chelsea one may own a panelled room, a staircase, a sundial, even a garden, and best of all one may look out through the branches of a lime-tree on the river. If distance is "no object," there is a good deal to be said for Church Row, Hampstead. The real Hampstead is essentially *not* a suburb. Church Row is like the close of an old cathedral town in the country, and the Heath with its donkeys standing patiently saddled round the White Stone Pond, and its infinite views past London roofs and spires over rolling Constable landscapes, is like nothing anywhere except itself.

On balance, I am sure that the home in London I should choose if I could afford it would be in Westminster. Trafalgar Square, its lions and its fountains, the curve of Whitehall, the old Admiralty with its guardian dolphins, the Houses of Parliament, the Thames ("liquid history," as it was described by Mr. John Burns to some transatlantic visitors), the Whistlerish twilight on the Embankment—these are to me the essence and the soul of London. I love the labyrinth of streets and slums behind Dean's Yard; North Street, Barton Street, the College Streets, Great and Little. I love above all Smith Square, that silent square so difficult to find, built round its curious church—the only square in London in which no wheel is ever heard, only the chime of clocks and clang of bells.

If one is obliged to live in London, I am sure that it is imperative to avoid what is called a "residential neighbourhood." In my present home in Paddington I feel crushed and stifled by the prosperous uniformity of the vast impersonal stucco houses which hem us in on all sides. In my old home, a tiny Georgian manor-house on the edge of the slums in Marylebone, the realest home in London I have ever known, we had a baker's shop at the corner and a palmist over the way. Small ragged children played hop-scotch on the pavement in front of our door and twirled round the lamp-posts on ingenious swings twisted out of knotted rope. Our children knew and were known by all our neighbours. The porter of a block of rather gloomy flats would run out and stop me in the street to ask me how much they weighed and whether their colds were better. . . . It was like living in a village.

And when we talk of the difference between a home in London and a home in the country, what we are thinking of is not so much the home itself as the life of which that home is the basis and the frame. The difference between life in London and life in the country for a child is, of course, quite incalculable. It is not merely a question of red-letter treats like picnics, bonfires, and bathing. It is only in the country that children can be really free and that they can ever be alone. In the country "going out" does not involve the tedious treadmill of walks in the park, gloved and gaitered (oh, the slavery of gaiters!), with a tight elastic under one's chin. It means, instead, happy hatless hours spent poking about in shrubberies and potting-sheds, climbing trees, eating warm fruit in kitchen-gardens, swaying, deeply ensconced, in a giddy nest on the top of a hay-cart. It may mean (joy of joys!) a pony of one's own. It must mean at least a guinea-pig. Above all, it means long tracts of leisure free from the irrelevant interruptions of grown-ups, tracts of time in which one can spin one's

own web of fancy and settle in it.

Do what we will in London, we cannot provide substitutes for these things. The Zoo, the Serpentine, even the Squirrel Walk in Regent's Park do not begin to make up for them. One is taken to these places as to a peep-show, given half an hour to enjoy them in, often reminded to hurry up about it, as it will soon be time to go home again. . . . And so it is.

And the experience of childhood in this respect is an accurate presage and foreshadowing of that of our grown-up-hood. "*J'aime la campagne, cela repose les cheveux,*" said a Frenchwoman ("I like the country, it rests the hair"). Those to whom the country is merely a rest-cure for the hair are town-dwellers no matter where they happen to be. We all know the Saturday to Monday country-house which appears to be let down like a drop-slip on Saturday afternoon and rolled up again and packed away with the tennis net on Monday morning. This again as "country life" does not count. It is just an extension of London. There is all the difference in the world between a visit to the country and having a home there.

The great difference (and it is the same one) between the home in London and the home in the country is not so much that of one's outer as of one's inner life. One *lives* in the country; in London one passes the time.

I remember being told by a friend who knew Turkish that in that language the adjectives "happy" and "unhappy" do not exist in the masculine gender, because (the Turks say) only women are capable of being "happy" or "unhappy." Men take their emotions on a shorter lease. They are either bored or interested, irritated or amused, pleased or annoyed, but they cannot be said to be definitely or lastingly happy or unhappy as women can. The same distinction applies, to my mind, to life in town and country.

In London one lives in staccato half-hours. No single day even can ever be a homogeneous entity. Its colour and its temperature are constantly changing. It is a tight mosaic of plans neatly dovetailed into one another. It is, or it may be, a chequered succession of work and play, including a committee meeting, a shopping expedition, a debate in the House of Commons, a picture gallery, a hospital, or a play. In this broken rhythm of experience one has no time to reach or rest upon the real background of one's thoughts or feelings. A hundred false bottoms are interposed between one and the foundations of one's life. One knows exactly what one is going to do, whom one is going to see, where and at what time, but as to why one is doing any of these things, what goal, if any, one has in view, one hardly has time to wonder. Life is a journey with a perfect time-table, but without a starting-point or a destination.

In the country, on the other hand, there is no time-table, one measures life not in half-hours but in terms of weeks and months, almost of seasons. Two factors only determine their shape and colour—the weather and one's own state of mind. One may be able to avoid reading in the country (it is difficult), but one cannot help thinking and feeling. It is impossible to keep realities, inconvenient or otherwise, at arm's length through the long winter evenings and the endless days of summer. Therefore it is only the very happiest, or the very bravest people, those who do not fear to be left alone face to face with themselves, who can afford to choose without misgiving "a home in the country."

THE
20's

IN
SIXTEEN
ARTISTIC
COLOURS

There is room for this beautiful furniture in your home

How *invitingly* a Lloyd Loom coloured chair or settee would fit into your hall, how *comfortably* it would fill a vacant corner in your sitting-room. Or for your garden—imagine the joyful colour-contrast of vivid scarlet on a summer lawn. There are 16 Lloyd Loom colours, from Geranium red and clear green to misty blue frosted with gold and silver. This brightly-hued, gracefully-fashioned furniture is produced by weaving improved fibre on to sturdy hardwood frames. It is resiliently comfortable, and long enduring. It does not creak like wicker and has no split ends to tear the clothing. For extra comfort, many of the settees and easy chairs are sprung in both seat and cushion. There are also glass-topped tables, artistically designed Linen Baskets, Work Boxes, Lamp Shades, etc., all very moderately priced. You can see a Lloyd Loom display in the furniture section of most good stores. Write now for free illustrated booklet.

SEND FOR FREE BOOKLET OF THIRTY PHOTOGRAPHS
Write your name and address on a postcard and send it to W. Lusty & Sons, Bromley-by-Bow, London, E.3, for the Lloyd Loom Booklet which shows photographs of 30 useful designs and the name of your nearest Lloyd Loom dealer.

Lloyd Loom
Woven Furniture

W. LUSTY & SON, MACAULAY WORKS, BROMLEY-BY-BOW, E.

ANNE ORR'S NEEDLEWORK

Anne Orr will furnish patterns and instructions for the boy's blue room, above, as follows: Hot iron pattern No. 6701, price 1s. 2d. post free, with designs and directions for sampler bedspread and pillow. Pamphlet No. 6703, 1s. 2d. post free, working pattern and directions for making both choo-choo rag rug, above, and sunbonnet-girl rug opposite. Hot iron pattern No. 6704, 1s. 2d. post free, carries 3 each of the two designs of boys on window shade, with directions for painting in silhouette on shades and embroidering on runner and chair back. Double pattern of No. 6704, 2s. post free

The little girl's room in rose, above, has also been designed by Anne Orr, and patterns and instructions are as follows: Hot iron pattern No. 6702, 1s. 2d. post free, designs and directions for the Bo-Peep sampler bedspread and pillow. No. 6703, 1s. 2d. post free, working pattern and directions for sunbonnet-girl rag rug, above, and choo-choo rug, opposite. Hot iron pattern No. 6705, 1s. 2d. post free (double, 2s. post free), 3 each of the figures to be embroidered on runner or painted on shades. Hot iron transfer No. 67-1001, 1s. 2d. post free, quilting design and directions for chair seat

HOW TO ORDER

To obtain any of the designs shown on this page send stamps or postal order, stating exactly what you require, to Anne Orr, Good Housekeeping, 153 Queen Victoria Street, London, E.C.4

Paper patterns and directions for making baby's first clothes may be ordered as follows from Good Housekeeping Pattern Service: plain dress or slip, petticoat, and long coat are 7d. post free; dress with trimming and set-in sleeves, 9d. post free; all 4 patterns, 2s. post free

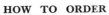

Among the delightful furnishings designed by Anne Orr for the little people's pleasure comes the play rug and pillow on the left. Hot-iron pattern No. 4704 carries designs, with full directions. Price 1s. 2d. post free. Double pattern for complete nursery set, 2s. post free

So This Is

*A little guide to the hills of mat-
being lost these days because they*

By Clara Savage Littledale

*The way of a man with a clean,
probably embroidered towel will
never cease to be a constant source
of despair and irritation to his wife*

JUST here, my husband looked over
my shoulder.

"Good heavens!" from him.
"What *are* you writing now?"

"Something for the *women* readers
of a *woman's* magazine," I said by way
of a hint.

"Don't you believe it," he returned.
"Women are not the only ones who are
going to read what comes after that title.
Men are going to, too. I for one."

In spite of this terrifying threat,
here is the article.

There are some things one doesn't
know a thing about until one has tried
them. Marriage is one of these. You
can read about it, think about it, see
pictures and plays about it, live almost
entirely surrounded by it, and yet, when
a girl marries, she finds that marriage
is no cut-and-dried affair that can be
studied in advance by diagram and rule.
It is endlessly surprising and ever-
changing. From one day to the next
it is different. It keeps her guessing.
That is one reason why marriage is so
fascinating an institution. It is also one
reason why it is a hazardous one. It is
a thoroughly sporting proposition—is
matrimony.

*Needles and pins,
Needles and pins,
When a man marries
His trouble begins.*

What crabbed old cynic
wrote that horrid little
rhyme?

The author was no femin-
ist, that's certain, or he
would have been fair enough
to admit that what there is
of truth in it is as true for
wives as for husbands. Just
between ourselves, we might
as well be frank. We all
do have our troubles in
matrimony. We all do have
our ups and downs, even our
quarrels and our makings-
up, times that are decidedly

bumpy and hard to bear, and
times that are as happy and
serene as we could possibly
wish them to be.

"These married people who
tell you they have never dis-
agreed on any subject in their
lives!" that doughty exponent
of woman's rights, Dr. Anna
Howard Shaw, of fighting
Scottish ancestry, used to exclaim. "In the first place, I
can't believe 'em. In the
next, I don't want to! Such
a marriage would be about
as stimulating as the stagna-
tion of a frog-pond! No normal man
and woman can possibly agree on every
single everlasting thing always. But
let them agree to disagree and then
live happily ever after, and you have a
marriage that is worth while."

But not every one of us can be as
philosophical as that when it comes to
our own particular disagreements. The
other day I had a letter from a woman
who is very unhappy.

"My husband is fascinating, clever,
talented, capable of earning big sums of
money, but absolutely unpractical," she
wrote. "Money slips through his
fingers as fast as he gets it. I am just
the opposite type. I like to save and
look ahead. I hate his spendthrift
ways."

That woman has been hating her husband's "spendthrift ways" for ten

years—as long as they have been married. And, apparently, she has every
intention of going on hating them till
death do them part. Her letter stressed
the fascination of her husband, his lovable qualities, his generosity, his cleverness. Evidently she is proud of him,
proud of his love for her. One would
say, after reading her letter, that here
are two people who are very much in
love with each other. And yet the wife
insists that they are unhappy.

Now, this woman is a perfect example
of what is the trouble with ever and ever
so many of us, to a greater or less extent.
We are spending our lives, wearing ourselves out, making ourselves and other
people miserable by hating, scolding, rebelling at something which we cannot
change.

Hating and scolding are poor weapons
at best, but rebellion is a mighty good
one, at times, provided it is intelligent
rebellion with some constructive plan
ahead of it. There's no use rebelling
just for the sake of rebelling. Before
you begin, decide what definite programme you have to put into operation
once your rebellion is successful. Then
go ahead and rebel for all you're worth.
But rebelling for the sake of rebelling
—there's something a little foolish about
that.

"Phil is never going to be different,"
wails this wife.

What that woman should do, and
what a lot of us should do, is to sit

MARRIAGE!

*rimony, where so many couples are
think they are among mountains*

Illustrations by Stuart Hay

There is one never-ending source of argument: Who works harder, Adam or Eve? Every woman would like to put her husband through her regular routine

down and sort out the things at which we are rebelling, or feeling hurt or angry or irritated about. In one column list all those that are capable of being changed—perhaps by herculean effort, but capable of betterment. In another column put down those that are plainly immutable, that will always be as they are till the heavens fall. Sort them out and list them carefully. Then consider those things that must remain as they are. Take them up one by one. Think them over. Realise all their disadvantages, all the difficulties they entail, all their unpleasant aspects. Then be capable of the next step. Accept them. They are as they are. Nothing will change them. No use to grieve or worry or rebel against them. It will do no good. Stop all that and accept them. Bitter as that acceptance may be, have courage enough and character enough to face facts.

"Phil has always been unpractical, improvident, a spendthrift, and he always will be," complains this wife.

She seems to admit the facts. But she doesn't. If she had actually accepted them—deep down in her consciousness, not just by word-of-mouth —she would stop rebelling against them, she would stop making herself and "Phil" miserable because he is as he is and she is as she is. She would stop storming and fuming and fretting over something that will, by her own statement, never change.

Custom invariably dulls appreciation. How can you expect a daily expression of their joy in you that your men folks reveal after you have left them to shift for themselves for a while?

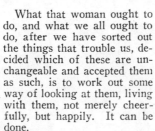

What that woman ought to do, and what we all ought to do, after we have sorted out the things that trouble us, decided which of these are unchangeable and accepted them as such, is to work out some way of looking at them, living with them, not merely cheerfully, but happily. It can be done.

"My husband never enjoyed big social affairs," said a certain woman.

For years his wife had dragged him to formal dinners, to dances, to receptions, to teas. He went, out of a sense of duty, but hated it. Then, quite suddenly, they dropped out of society columns. This is the inside story of what happened as his wife told it:

"Tom just said he was through," she explained. "He said life was too short for any human being to waste time doing needless things he didn't enjoy. I was in despair. But Tom was absolutely in earnest. I couldn't do a thing with him.

"Finally I sat down and thought the thing over. I had to admit that my husband had been perfectly fair. For years he had been doing the social stunt just to please me. If he wanted to stop, I couldn't blame him. But, of course, it meant that I must stop too, and the thought of it made me miserable. Relief came when I realised that while Tom didn't care for big formal gatherings, he did enjoy small groups of people. He is thoroughly hospitable, not to crowds, but to two or three good friends at a time. We reorganised our social life on a small, informal scale. And the result is that we have more real friends, more real sociability and fun, than we ever had before in our lives."

That woman is on the right track, sure-bound for happiness. She accepted facts, and then she set about finding a way to live happily with those facts. She did not make the mistake of utter renunciation. Suppose she had said in a sudden burst of generosity and self-sacrifice:

"I'll give it all up. I won't try to have any kind of social life. I'll give it up for Tom's sake."

Now, for a while, this might have worked. She might even have got a good deal of satisfaction out of thinking how self-sacrificing she was. But, ten to one, this fine fever of self-sacrifice would have worn off. She would have come to think of herself as a martyr, and martyrs are trying people to live with. Instead, she showed sound common sense in her solution. She analysed the situation carefully, she took into consideration her disposition and her husband's disposition, and she came to a practical solution—a compromise that suited them both. That's the ideal solution in many a matrimonial difficulty. And it's almost always a possible one.

"But," someone objects, "you talk about things that can't be changed. Why can't they be changed? Why can't the woman with the unpractical husband help him to be practical? Isn't it weakness to give up trying to improve a bad situation?"

THE
20's

Dad put it this way

THE boy sat with his father. His best pal in the world was "the guv'nor." The older man turned to his son and wagged his pipe—like he always did when he was going to say something more important than usual. "Dick, my boy: when I married your mother I was getting very much less money than you are getting. It wasn't until we'd settled down in our little home and you had arrived that I realised that the greatest moral obligation of my life was to make the future safe for her—in case anything happened to me. It troubled me for a while because I'd saved very little. Then I wrote to my Dad. He gave me some advice which I took. I paid my first premium for a Friends' Provident Life and Endowment "with-profits" Policy. Since then my life has been adequately insured. Next month, when my endowment is due, they'll be sending me a sum of money amounting to a good deal more than I've paid in premiums. Your mother and I have always felt safe because of that—and the other policies I took out as I got more money. Better do as I did, Dick; it's safer! And if I wasn't certain of that money coming along soon," he added, with a grin, "I'm not so sure I'd be able to give you and Betty that two-seater for a wedding present!"

You should insure this easy way. Write to-day stating your age and full particulars will be sent.

The *MENDING BASKET*

Remodelling with New Printed or Knitted Fabrics

By Caroline Gray

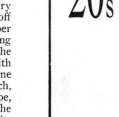

WHEREAS the smart woman of to-day eliminates every superfluous item of clothing, she admits the almost invariable necessity of an under-slip, particularly with frocks of the transparent fabrics of spring and summer. These slips should be dainty, well-made, and shadow-proof. Of all fabrics, radium silk is perhaps the nicest, if you are choosing something new. However, new material is not essential, and as silk of one sort or another is desirable, you will find that your evening or afternoon gowns, whose first freshness is gone, will cut over to excellent advantage as under-slips, or as a slip worn with a tunic blouse.

For the spring and early-summer wardrobe, a light under-slip and a dark under-slip are almost a necessity. Perhaps a black satin evening gown will furnish the dark one and a beige, white, or pastel shade pussy-willow satin afternoon gown the lighter one. Crêpe de Chine night-gowns, which are worn round the neck and arm-holes, may also be converted into charming slips of a lighter variety. Three gowns will make two slips. That is, the twenty-inch shadow-proof hem of each slip may be supplied by the third gown. The upper part of the slip is cut in a straight line from just under the arms to the hip-line, where it fits rather snugly, while the extra fulness for the skirt of the slip is gathered into slashes on the hips.

For the younger generation, what could be more practical and spring-like than a straight-line flannel frock, such as the one illustrated? So straight and simple this one is, and so little material is needed, that should you not have anything in the house to convert into this charming little frock, a bit from the remnant counter will supply new material at little cost, while the odds-and-ends bag may produce some piece for collar, cuffs, and vest. Pongée vest and cuffs, vividly outlined with heavy embroidery silk,

completed this frock.

Discarded capes lend themselves surprisingly well to remodelling of various kinds. A three-piece knitted suit, composed of cape, skirt, and sweater, was an interesting problem, which turned out well as the one-piece frock shown below, which was for a taller person than the original wearer. The sweater was left untouched, to wear with separate skirts, while the skirt was ripped off the belt and allowed to set low on the hips, giving the additional and necessary length. The scarf collar was ripped off the cape, and the pattern for the upper part of the frock, including the long sleeves, was pinned to the cape. The pattern was then faithfully outlined with tacking cotton, and the entire outline stitched by machine with a fine stitch, and silk matching the wool of the cape, as the stitching was to remain after the tacking was removed, to hold each knitted stitch and prevent ravelling. After sewing the seams in the new upper part, and joining the skirt to it in a flat seam, the neck and wrists were bound with a braid of self-colour to correspond with the finish at the bottom of the skirt.

Again, a full-length, tweed cape became a tailored, wrap-over skirt, overlapping eight to ten inches in the front, with the original buttons and button-holes and facings again in use down the opening of the skirt.

The ensemble costume pictured at the extreme left was the happy outcome of an unfashionable two-piece twill suit. Of printed silk, harmonising in colour with that of the suit, a simple, one-piece frock was made. The bottom of the old skirt made a fourteen-inch band at the bottom of the dress. This was cut in points at the top, following the pattern in the silk, thus making an effective finish. The revers and front of the coat were faced with the same fabric to a depth of about eight inches. If the coat lining is at all worn, it is advisable to reline the entire coat with the material used for the body of the dress.

The child's frock at the top of the page was made from a surprisingly small amount of material. An unfashionable two-piece suit was the inspiration for the smart ensemble costume seen at the immediate right

At the left is pictured a frock which was the successful result of making over an old cape and skirt of last season. Fresh linen collar and cuffs gave the finishing touch for a smart and practical sports frock

FOR HALF-A-CROWN A WEEK!

Perhaps you've always regarded the telephone as an expensive luxury—beyond your means?

Perhaps you'll be astonished to know how little it costs?

NOTHING—to instal.
NOTHING—for the calls you receive.
ONE PENNY—for each local call you make.
RENTAL—2/1 to 2/6 a week.

Is that too much to pay for the luxury of being within a few seconds' talking distance of everyone else who is on the 'phone? After all, nearly *everyone* is on the 'phone—your friends, your shops, your doctor, your theatre, your office . . . . A luxury, did we say? Isn't the telephone a practical need of modern life?

Why aren't YOU on the 'Phone?

Write your name and address in the space below, post the coupon (½d. stamp only if envelope is left unsealed) and you will receive a free booklet which will tell you everything you want to know about getting the telephone into your own house, **also particulars of £100 Prize Competition.**

Please write clearly.

NAME

(Mr., Mrs., Miss, etc.)

ADDRESS

("F." April 1926)

Post to The Telephone Development Association, 10, Bedford Street, London, W.C.2

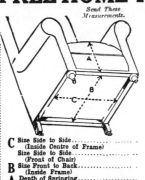

THE
20's

Cheap Living

In —

The Third Article in "An

Illustrations by

Stella Steyn

BOULANGERIE

I HAVE often been asked by English friends if the fall of the French franc has not produced a corresponding rise in prices; whether, in fact, the low exchange is really as profitable to the English as it appears to be. The only satisfactory answer to that question is to give actual facts; but I may begin by noting that where the prices involved are those of goods imported from abroad, any serious further fall of the franc will be followed in nearly every case by a corresponding rise in the price of the article—as a rule within a week or two. Even here, however, there are some puzzling exceptions of which I will quote one.

A certain brand of English-made cigarettes that I often smoke were priced at 2.75 francs for a packet of ten when the franc was below 100 to the English pound. Later on they rose a little, but to no more than 3.00 francs. This means that whereas two years before I was paying 7½*d.* a packet I am now paying only 4½*d.*; an anomaly I cannot explain. There are a few others of the same kind. Now, in order to save my readers the trouble of trying mentally to convert French francs into English money, in what follows, I will take the rate of exchange at 160 francs to the £ and give all my figures in the familiar British coinage. The actual rate at the time of writing is 170, so that the prices I shall give will all be a shade more than they really are. (But see my postscript!) Thus at 160, eight francs is worth exactly a shilling; at 170, a shade below 11½*d.* But in what follows I shall rarely have to touch such a high figure as a shilling!

I will begin by describing for the benefit of the London housewife a four-course dinner I took in the Boulevard St. Michel a few nights ago. It was a decent-looking place, a little above the Luxembourg Gardens, calling itself the Restaurant du Luxembourg, a few doors from the short turning that leads to the Panthéon. There were not more than half a dozen tables on the pavement, but inside there was accommodation on two floors, for from two hundred to two hundred and fifty people.

I have said that it looked decent—there were white cloths on the tables for instance—but it must not be imagined that it was in any sense "smart." If I wanted to find a place in London with which to compare it, I should cite "Flemings." There are differences, but they are not important, and the only one I shall mention is one that struck me as representing an interesting contrast between the English and the French attitude. On the wall facing me in the Restaurant du Luxembourg was a notice to this effect (I translate), "To waste the bread is to contribute towards a rise in the price of the meals." Bread, I may add, was *à discrétion*, which means that you may eat as much as you like. And the French eat a lot of bread.

Let me now give you some idea of the menu. The fixed price for the meal included the following: Soup or Hors-d'œuvre; Fish or Entrée; Vegetable or Pudding; Cheese or Dessert; a quarter bottle of red wine or a pint bottle of beer or a bottle of table water; and, as I have mentioned, bread *ad lib.*

There were two kinds of soup, sustaining in quality and liberal in quantity, served very hot in ornamental metal bowls which you immediately empty into your soup plate. The hors-d'œuvre included sardines, anchovies, fillet of dried herring with potatoes, smoked sausage and *pâté de foie*—the last-named served in small china pots covered with paper

By J. D. Beresford

PARIS

Author in France" Series

Stella Steyn

and tied down. Only one of these dishes can be taken, but the portions of each are reasonably generous. I noticed two young women near me making an excellent beginning with *pâté de foie* and unlimited bread.

The fish that night was fried whiting *au gratin,* and cold boiled cod with mayonnaise sauce. The entrées included, among fifteen items, braised beef and peas, ham and potato salad, roast shoulder of veal and haricots.

The vegetables—a separate dish in the French fashion, independent of the vegetable served as a matter of course with the entrée—were red haricot beans *à l'étuvée* (the stock of stewed meat), spinach *à la crème,* new carrots *à la paysanne* and rice boiled in milk, among a choice of nine dishes. The puddings included cream caramel, apple tartlet,

vanilla or chocolate cream.

There were six different kinds of cheese, and for fruit, bananas, peaches and strawberries.

And the price of this meal, including as I have said wine or beer and unlimited bread, was precisely sixpence-three-farthings (4.50 francs). I defy

anyone to make such a satisfying and wholesome dinner for the same price in London. Consider, also, the wide range of your choice.

The diners included many students from the neighbouring Sorbonne and the Art Schools, young men and women from many countries of Europe, though I did not that night hear either an English or an American voice. And it was not difficult to guess that most of them were regular customers. They had their own napkins with numbered rings which were kept in a special chest of small drawers—somewhat resembling a big nest of card index drawers—at the end of the room. The charge for

this luxury is rather less than a half-penny a week and the napkins are changed every Sunday.

But there was another class in evidence, which is worth a moment's thought and consideration: the *rentiers,* those people who before the War were living on fixed incomes derived from

French investments (*rentes*) and whose money is now worth, at most, one-fifth of what it was then. Some of them, no doubt, have found employment, as *concierges* or what-not, to eke out their resources. But others, those who were perhaps too proud to take menial service, come with a touch of furtiveness to such restaurants as these I am describing.

Before the War they had an income worth perhaps £600 of English money, and could keep up appearances, pass as being comfortably off. Now, they are reduced to living on the equivalent of £120 a year; and would not like their friends to know that they dined every night among the students in the Boulevard St. Michel. And to them this absurd price of four and a half francs still means what three shillings and ninepence means to us. They count not by the falling value of the franc but by the enormous increase in the cost of living.

I must admit to being exceedingly sorry for these poor gentlefolk, and so far as one can see worse is still to come. It is not long since the price of the Restaurant du Luxembourg was raised from four francs to four francs, fifty centimes. I picture them denying themselves small extras in order to feed decently with a napkin. For there are possible extras to the bill of fare I have given. By paying another three-farthings, for instance, you can have a grilled steak and fried potatoes for your entrée. I saw one and it looked excellent. The accepted amount for the waitress's tip is also three-farthings.

DESIR

On the happy day on which Miss Mapp got back to her own spaciousness, several hampers of apples were smuggled in through the back-door

Illustrations by L. G. Illingworth

HOUSES in Tillingham are in much request during the months of August and September by holiday-makers of the quieter sort, who do not want to stay in large hotels on esplanades in places where there are piers, to flock to the shore in brilliant bathing-costumes, to pose for photographers in the certainty of winning prizes as plump sea-nymphs, to dress for dinner and dance afterwards. But families in search of tranquillity combined with agreeable pastimes, find Tillingham much to their mind: there is a golf-links, there are illimitable sands and safe bathing: no treacherous currents swirl the swimmer out to sea when the tide is ebbing (indeed the shore is so flat that the ebb merely leaves him stranded like a star-fish miles away from his clothes): there are stretches of charming country inland for exploratory picnics, and Tillingham itself is so full of picturesque corners and crooked chimneys and timbered houses that easels in August render the streets almost impassable.

The higher social circles in this little town are mainly composed of well-to-do maiden ladies and widows, most of whom, owing to the remunerative demand for holiday-residences, live in rather larger houses than they otherwise would and recoup themselves by advantageous letting. Thus towards the middle of July a very lively general post takes place. Those who own the largest houses with gardens, like Miss Elizabeth Mapp, can let them for as much as fifteen guineas a week, and themselves take houses for that period at eight to ten guineas a week, thus collaring the difference and enjoying a change of habitation, which often gives them rich peeps into the private habits of their neighbours. Those who have smaller houses, like Mrs. Plaistow, similarly let them for perhaps eight guineas a week and take something at five: the owners of the latter take cottages, and the cottagers go hop-picking. Many householders, of course, go away for these months, but those who remain always let their own houses and are content with something smaller. The system seems to resemble that of those thrifty villagers who earned their living by taking in each other's washing, and answers excellently.

Miss Mapp on this morning of early July had received an inquiry from her last year's tenants, as to whether she would let her house to them again on the same terms. They were admirable tenants who brought their own servants, a father who played golf, a mother who wrote letters in the garden and two daughters with spectacles who steadily sketched their way along the streets of the town. Miss Mapp instantly made up her mind to do so, and had to settle whether she should take a smaller house herself or go away. If she could get Diva Plaistow's house, she thought she would remain here and take her holiday in the winter. Diva was asking eight guineas a week, including garden-produce. The crop on her apple-trees this year was prodigious, and since garden-produce was included, Miss Mapp supposed she would have the right to fill hampers with what she couldn't eat and take them away at the end of her tenancy.

"I shouldn't have to buy an apple all winter," thought Miss Mapp. "And then fifteen guineas a week for eight weeks makes a hundred and twenty guineas, and substract eight times eight which is sixty-four (I shall try to get it a little cheaper) which leaves—let me see . . ."

She arrived at the sumptuous remainder by tracing figures with the handle of her tea-spoon on the table-cloth, and having written to the admirable tenants to say that she would be happy to let her house again at the same price, hurried to the house-agents to make inquiries. She could, of course, have gone to Diva direct, but it would not be pretty to haggle in person with so old a friend. She put on her most genial smile, and was artful.

"Good morning, Mr. Hassall," she said. "A cousin has asked me to inquire about houses in Tillingham for the summer. I think Mrs. Plaistow's little house might suit her, but I fancy she wouldn't pay as much as eight guineas a week."

"Very nice house, ma'am. Very good value," said Mr. Hassall. "Garden-produce included."

"Yes, but eight guineas is rather high. But perhaps you would tell Mrs.

ABLE RESIDENCES

A Delightful Comedy of Robbing Peter— and Barely Paying Paul

By E. F. Benson

Plaistow that you've had an inquiry offering seven. And what about servants?"

"Mrs. Plaistow is thinking of getting another house for the summer, and taking her servants with her."

Miss Mapp considered this, still smiling.

"I see. Then would you make inquiries, and let me know as soon as possible? I am going home at once. Good morning. What a lovely day!"

This question about servants was, like all Miss Mapp's manœuvres, much to the point. If Diva was leaving servants, her plan was to pick a quarrel with her cook without delay, and give her a month's warning, which would bring her to the beginning of August. But there was no need for that now.

Miss Mapp stepped out of the office into the hot sunshine, and failed to observe Diva, round and red, trundling up the street behind her. But Diva, whose eyes were gimlets, saw Miss Mapp and where she came from, and popping in to see whether there were any inquiries for her house, heard from Mr. Hassall that he had just received one, offering seven guineas a week. Such evidence was naturally conclusive, and she had not the smallest doubt that this nameless tenant was Miss Mapp herself. Mr. Hassall allowed that the inquiry had been made by Miss Mapp on behalf of a cousin, and Diva laughed in a shrill and scornful manner. She no more believed in the cousin than she believed in the man in the moon, and it was like Elizabeth—too sadly like her, in fact—to attempt to haggle behind her back. She also drew the inference that Elizabeth had received an offer for her house, and already rolling in prospective riches, wanted to roll a little more.

"Kindly ring Miss Mapp up at once," she said, "for I saw her going up the street towards her house, and say that I am asking eight guineas a week, and will not take less. I should like a definite answer at once, and I'll wait."

The telephone bell saluted

Miss Mapp's ears as she entered her own door, and the ultimatum was delivered. It was tiresome to have used the cousinly subterfuge and have got nothing by it, but the difference between even eight guineas a week and fifteen was quite pleasant. So she accepted these terms, and since it would soon be obvious that she was her own cousin, she admitted the fact at once. Diva was so pleased to have seen through the transparent and abject trick so instantaneously, that, full of self-satisfaction at her own acuteness, she bore poor Elizabeth no grudge whatever. She only sighed to think how

like Elizabeth that was, and having thus secured a very decent let, inspected a smaller house belonging to Mrs. Tropp which would suit her very well, and obtained it, for the period during which she had let her own, at four guineas a week.

Some fortnight later, Miss Mapp was returning from an afternoon bridge-party at Diva's. She had won every rubber, which was satisfactory, and had caught Diva revoking beyond all chance of wriggling out of it, which made a sort of riches in the mind of much vaster value than that of the actual penalty. But it was annoying only to have been playing those new *(Continued overleaf)*

But Diva had had a similar inspiration, and scorning concealment, took away with her a hand-cart piled with cooking-pears

Desirable Residences

(Continued)

stakes of fourpence halfpenny a hundred. This singular sum was the result of compromise: the wilder and wealthier ladies of Tillingham liked playing for sixpence a hundred, but those of more moderate means stuck out for threepence. Diva who hardly ever won a rubber at all was one of these. She said she played bridge to amuse herself and not to make money. Miss Mapp had acidly replied, "That's lucky, darling." But that was smoothed over, and this compromise had been arrived at. It worked quite well, and was a convenient way of getting rid of coppers if you lost, and the only difficulty was when there happened to be a difference of fifty or a hundred and fifty between the scores.

"If a hundred is fourpence halfpenny," said Miss Mapp, "and fifty is half a hundred, which I think you'll grant, fifty is twopence farthing." . . . So after that, they all brought one or two farthings with them.

Still, even at these new and paltry stakes, Miss Mapp's bag this evening jingled pleasantly as she stepped homewards. But one thing rather troubled her: it was like a thunder-cloud muttering on the horizon of an otherwise sunny sky. For she had heard no more from the admirable tenants: there had just been the inquiry whether she was thinking of letting, and then a silence which by degrees grew ominous. She wondered whether she had acted with more precipitation than prudence in committing herself to take Diva's house, before she actually let her own, and no sooner had she reached home than she became unpleasantly convinced that she had. The evening post had come in, and there was a letter from That Woman who had written so many in the garden, to say that a more bracing climate had been recommended for her husband, and that therefore with many regrets . . .

It was a staggering moment. Instead of raking in a balance of seven guineas a week, she would possibly be paying out eight. July was slipping away, so the pessimistic Mr. Hassall reminded her when she saw him next morning, and he was afraid that most holiday-makers had already made their arrangements. It would be wise perhaps to abate the price she was asking. By the twentieth of July, anybody could have had Miss Mapp's house for twelve guineas a week: by the twenty-fourth, which ironically enough happened to be her birthday, for ten. But still there was no one who had the sense to secure so wonderful a bargain. It looked, in fact, as if the Nemesis which has an eye to the violation of economic problems, had awakened to the fact that the ladies of Tillingham took in each other's washing (or rather took each other's houses) and scored all round. And Nemesis, by way of being funny, did something further.

On July the thirtieth, Miss Mapp's most desirable residence, with garden and the enjoyment of garden-produce, could be had, throughout August and September, for the derisory sum of eight guineas a week. On that very day two children in the cottage which Mrs. Tropp (Diva's lessor) had taken for herself developed mumps. A phobia about microbes was Mrs. Tropp's most powerful characteristic, and with the prospect of being house-

less for two months (for she would sooner have had mumps straight away than be afraid of catching them) she came in great distress to Diva, with the offer to take her own house back again at the increased rental of five guineas a week. Besides, she added, to turn two swollen children out into the hop-fields was tantamount to manslaughter. Upon which, to Mrs. Tropp's pained surprise, Diva burst out into a fit of giggles. When she recovered, she accepted Mrs. Tropp's proposal.

"So right," she said, "we couldn't bear to have manslaughter on our consciences. Oh, dear me, how it hurts to laugh. Poor Elizabeth!"

Diva, still hurting very much, whirled away to Mr. Hassall's.

"A cousin of mine," she said, "is looking out for a house at Tillingham for August and September. Miss Mapp's, I think, would suit her, but seven guineas a week, I feel sure, is the utmost she would pay. I should like a definite answer at once, and I'll wait. Why, if I didn't use exactly those words to you, Mr. Hassall, when last you telephoned to Miss Mapp for me! I won't give my name at present—— Just an offer."

Miss Mapp was in the depths of depression that afternoon when the telephone bell summoned her. She had practically determined to stay in her own spacious and comfortable house for the next two months, since it was of quite a different class to Diva's, but the thought of paying out eight guineas a week for a miserable little habitation (in spite of the apple-trees) in which she would never set foot gnawed at her very vitals. Of course with the produce of her own garden and Diva's, she would have any amount of vegetables, and with the entire crop of Diva's apples added to her own cooking-pears (never had there been such a yield) she would do well in the way of fruit for the winter, but at a staggering price. . . . Then the telephone bell rang and with a sob of relief she accepted the offer it brought her. She hurried to Mr. Hassall's to confirm it and sign the lease. When she knew that the applicant was Diva, and divined beyond doubt that Diva's cousin was Diva too, she moistened her lips once or twice, but otherwise showed no loss of self-control.

So for two months these ladies stayed in each other's houses. Mrs. Plaistow's letters were addressed to "Care of Miss Mapp," and Miss Mapp's letters to "Care of Mrs. Plaistow." Every week Diva received a cheque for one guinea from her tenant (which was the balance due) and another from Mrs. Tropp, and immensely enjoyed living in quite the best house in Tillingham. She gave several parties there, to all of which she invited Elizabeth who with equal regularity regretfully declined them on the grounds that in the poky little house in which she found herself it was impossible to return hospitalities. . . . It may be added that on the happy day on which Miss Mapp got back to her own spaciousness, several large hampers of apples were smuggled in through the back-door. But Diva had had a similar inspiration, and, scorning concealment, took away with her a hand-cart piled high with cooking-pears.

THE
20's

Your health—Your home— and Frigidaire

THE primary consideration of every home should be Health—and nothing so vitally influences the health as the food you eat. But the health of the home to-day is assailed by a greater danger than ever before, because since chemical preservatives in food are now prohibited, food will not keep.

This new housekeeping problem can fortunately be overcome because the safety of the food you eat can be assured by proper provision being

made for its preservation in the home. Frigidaire Automatic Electrical Refrigeration is the solution to this problem, for in the automatically maintained, dry, crisp cold of Frigidaire food stays fresh. There can be no risk to your *Health* if *Frigidaire* is installed in your *Home*.

Frigidaire is air-cooled, self-starting, self-stopping, self-oiling and needs no water.

Send coupon for full particulars and details of deferred payments.

London Showrooms :
Frigidaire House, Chapter Street, Vauxhall Bridge Road, S.W.1, and Imperial House, Kingsway, W.C.2.

Frigidaire
Automatic Electrical *Refrigeration*

Branches at :
Birmingham, Manchester, Leeds, Brighton, Glasgow and Edinburgh.

FRIGIDAIRE LIMITED (*Incorporated in Canada*).
Dept. A-602, Frigidaire House, Chapter Street, Vauxhall Bridge Road, S.W.1.
Please send me, without obligation, complete information about Frigidaire.

Name..

Address ....

No. in Family ....

Linoleum and oilcloth have no better cleanser than Zog

With Zog no harsh scouring, that destroys the surface or pattern, is necessary. To make them look like new and to keep them so, simply sprinkle a little Zog on a damp rag or mop, rub gently, then rinse with a damp cloth — that is all.

Zog is just as valuable elsewhere in the house. It removes dirt and grease. It *polishes* glass, windows and metals. It enables you to finish your housework in half the time, and gives you more leisure.

Zog is agreeable to use and safe. When used on the most delicate surface nothing but good results.

Zog does not scratch

It does not redden or chap the hands; it is good for them. You want Zog everywhere in the house. Buy it now. Sold in two convenient sizes —giant container 6¾ in. deep—7½d., and handy size 4d. From all grocers and oilmen.

*From all grocers
and oilmen*

WINDOWS & GLASS

POTS & PANS

POLISHES ALUMINIUM

WHITE PAINTWORK

THE HANDS

In the giant container
7½d

Handy size 4d. Zog comes back with 100 new uses. There is nothing else like it. Nothing else can do what Zog does — cleans glass and white paint-work *without scratching*; *polishes* aluminium as well as cleans it.

CLEANS PAINT

For cleaning paint and enamel work, windows and mirrors use a damp ZOG cloth shake on a little ZOG and rub gently and firmly to and fro. Wash off with clean water and sponge, finishing with a dry cloth. ZOG cleans and polishes without scratching.

ZOG

There is nothing like Zog for cleaning and polishing

PAINT-WORK
ALUMINIUM & TIN
LINOLEUM & OILCLOTH
WINDOWS
GLASS & MIRRORS
CHINA   PORCELAIN
ENAMEL
BRASS & COPPER
SILVER & PLATE
TURNERY   CUTLERY
BATHS, WASH-BASINS
TILES & SINKS

LEVER BROTHERS
LIMITED
PORT SUNLIGHT

ZOG 24-5

By *Lady Violet Bonham Carter*

Are YOU a GOOD Housekeeper?

The mechanism of a house well kept should be silent and absolutely invisible. Really good housekeeping is neither seen nor heard. It is only deeply and gratefully felt

THE
20's

IT seems an act of almost mad temerity to choose this theme to write upon between these covers, and I want in my first sentence to ward off (if at all possible) the inevitable misunderstanding which such a choice must bring crashing down upon my head. If I venture to write about housekeeping at all, it is not vaingloriously, dogmatically, helpfully —as one who knows her job, and wants to let others know it. It is in a humble, a groping, almost a broken spirit.

I am not going to say, " But it's all *so* easy! Don't you know how to make new pitch pine look like old walnut? Why, just take two old banana skins, dip them in the tea-pot (after you've finished tea, of course) pass them lightly two or three times over the surface of the wood—and there you are "; or give an equally painless, economical and impossible receipt for wringing out flannels with button-hooks, making omelettes out of egg-shells or persuading last winter's cabbage-stalks to taste like next spring's asparagus. . . .

No, that, alas! is not my line of business. (Would that it were!) I want on my own behalf to explore, I want, if I can, to discover by what mysterious method, trick, knack, science or inspiration that miracle, good house-keeping, is achieved.

Though we may not know how it is brought about, yet how unmistakably we recognise it, how joyfully we hail it directly we come up against it. On crossing the threshold of a well-" kept " house we are immediately enfolded by an atmosphere of comfort and well-being which it seems almost irreverent to dissect and analyse.

What are the ingredients that go to make up this perfection? How are they put together? Coldly summed up, they will be as useless to us as a friend's receipt of her own ambrosial dish is to our own fumbling cook. We find that the prescribed proportions do not really vitally matter. It is the spell one mutters over them. Some people come into the world knowing the spell, others die without having learnt it. A little greed, and much kindness, an inventive appetite, an imaginative sense of comfort, linked with a Permanent Under-Secretary's power of running a machine, these all play their part, but in the main good housekeepers are born and not made. But I hope (sometimes against hope) that bad ones may be improved.

Let us, starting at the wrong end, first consider " effects," coming to causes later. What are a few of the symptoms of a really well-kept house?

First and foremost it is important that the door should be opened to us by a familiar figure, one whom we have learnt to regard as an integral part of the human structure of the household, and who welcomes us as a host and a friend. A sense of personal responsibility on the part of the servants towards the guests of the house is the lynch-pin of the comfort and well-being of both, mental as well as physical.

One of the next things one notices on entering the house is that it *smells* good, though one can't quite say of what. Wood fires? Pot-pourri? Lavender in linen cupboards? No—it is more subtle—mixed—pervasive and inexplicable. It is simply the smell of a nice house.

Upstairs in the bedroom there is a fire burning—a *real* fire of coal or wood. Not gas peering luridly through skulls or licking the lichen off a sham log, not even (to my mind) electricity glowing through large blocks of amber and coffee-sugar (though both these devices are great time- and labour-savers). There are dark blinds to pull down over the windows and wedges to stick in the sashes in case they rattle, for a bedroom *must* be " a chamber deaf to noise and blind to light." A reading-lamp, a bell and a pencil and paper are within reach of the bed, perhaps even a good novel as well.

The bed itself and particularly the pillow should be exquisitely comfortable. When one considers that we spend nearly half our lives in beds, the mattresses which the majority of human beings, quite gratuitously and of their own free will, elect to sleep on, are amazing. I have a fairly wide experience of " taken " houses in various parts of England and it is the rarest thing in the world to find an even tolerably comfortable bed. There are infinite varieties of discomfort, ranging from mild malaise to torture.

There is the soft lumpy and spring-less kind in which one sinks deeper and deeper into a suffocating grave, dug by one's first unwary wriggle. There is the hard ditto, in which one tosses, bruised and aching, making not the smallest dint by one's most convulsive effort at adjustment.

There is the bare, lean, springy mattress of wafer thinness, sagging in the middle almost to floor level.

Good mattresses are expensive no doubt, but there are few things I would not forgo by day in order that my nights might be spent on the exquisite surface of a best hair or (still better) best white hair mattress.

In the well-kept house nothing is tepid. The bath-water is always boiling, and the drinking water icy. The bath-towels are enormous. (The luxury of a hot bath is more than half undone if, on getting out, one is received by a meagre pocket-handkerchief which barely covers one to the waist, instead of in the all-enfolding embrace of a bath-sheet.) The bath-soap also is large and smells delicious, with no suggestion of disinfectant properties to produce the illusion of being treated like a dog.

But let us leave washing and sleep on one side for a moment and turn to food. And here I long not for the tongues of men and of angels but for the pen of one woman—Lady Jekyll— who has shown us in her masterly book, *Kitchen Essays*, how food can be treated lyrically. Only a poet who was (incidentally) also a millionaire could aspire to her great efforts, the joints rinsed in the best burgundy, the birds studded with truffles and bathed in cream, the jellies like " an emerald green pool set in a flat glass bowl, reminiscent of Sabrina fair in her home below translucent waves, or of Capri caverns, cool and deep." . . . But what we all ought to be able to achieve (and it really is the thing most worth achieving) is to make the ordinary, everyday food of life not a banal, wearisome treadmill of the jaws, but a constant surprise and delight.

That bacon should be crisp, brittle and curly instead of pink and limp; that toast (most difficult and testing of all feats) should not be a flabby sandwich stuffed *(Continued overleaf)*

Are You a Good Housekeeper ?

(Continued)

with cotton-wool; that hot milk should have foam and bubbles instead of skin on the top of it; that bread should be new; jam a delicious *compote* in which real fruit floats as units, instead of an anonymous and undiagnosable amalgam of dull red slush; that beef should be red and mutton brown, not *vice versa*; that vegetables should be cooked in butter and cream rather than tepid water; that the soup should not have floating in it the alphabet carved out of custard; that elaborate arrangements of parsley, cherries and lemon peel should be rigidly eschewed (it matters so much more what food looks like even than how it tastes)—these are things that really cost little but count infinitely much.

Nice food need not be any more expensive than nasty food.

Oysters, caviare and *foie gras* are treats, of course, once in a way, but they are not things it occurs to us to miss from the menu of our daily lives. It is humiliating to reflect that it is not to want of money but to want of skill, taste, intelligence and resource that we owe our nasty or our dreary fare. We are food-bores, food-Philistines, where we might be food-wits, food-artists, food-poets. We try to avoid platitudes—we do our best not to sing flat, but do we ever reflect how many old threadbare tags and *clichés* we utter, how many false notes we sing in terms of food?

Men are as a rule far better hands at ordering a meal than women. In fact it is quite arguable (if one rules out extravagance as a disqualification) that they are better housekeepers. They are either superlatively good at planning comfort or else quite helpless. In a bachelor's household one touches top or bottom. One suffers the extreme of hardship or enjoys the highest degree of luxury. Both are to be explained by the fact that in household matters men rule by abdication. They make one crucial decision when they choose their servants. Then they hand over completely, delegating all detail. There is a great deal to be said for this system. People naturally work better when they are given responsibility and opportunities for initiative, and every servant must feel a floodtide of energy released by serving a man who is busy and absent all day, rather than a woman who is always about the house telephoning, ringing bells and generally giving trouble.

For the same reason good housekeeping, even for a woman, is child's play in a house in which no nursery exists. No one who has not experienced it can guess at the strain imposed by constant diplomatic missions between nursery and kitchen, the difficulties of conveying tactfully to the cook that "grease" was again detected on the top of the children's chicken-tea and had to be removed with tissue-paper, that the "twice-cooked meat" which is gratefully received by the dining-room is regarded in the nursery as a con-

fection planned by the Borgias, that the Yorkshire pudding was fried in fat, that there was pepper *and* onions in the Irish stew, and that they had again sent up (or failed to send up) tomatoes for Nannie's supper.

Then the perambulator scratches off the paint in the hall, the children fall down and hurt themselves on linoleum that the housemaids have overpolished. . . . Above all the nursery is seldom away and never "out." A nursery is in the words of Sherlock Holmes (applied by him to love) "sand in the clockwork, a fly in the amber, iron near the magnet."

I have said nothing about economy because that is a dragon which every one of us must wrestle with single handed and in our own way. We each have a separate scale of values as to what are and what are not essential extravagances. With some of us it is the fruit-bill, with others the laundry; to others again warmth comes before dessert or washing, and they would sacrifice all for the sake of a fire (even in the dining-room) or hot pipes at full blast throughout the winter. Sometimes one puts a thing so high in the scale that one dare not indulge in it at all for fear of going too far. I have a passion for flowers, and realising that if I bought them at all I should go to dangerous lengths I made it a rule when I married to give them up altogether and this I found easier and less painful than having too few.

I regretfully admit that I think one ought to "do" weekly books if one wants to learn anything at all about one's household expenditure. None of them present any difficulties at all except the grocer's; and that after ten years' baffled perusal floors me completely to this very day. The grocer's book is a nightmare. To begin with it is always enormous. And why? There's the rub. One knows so well as one glances through the butcher's (for instance) whether one has or has not had several more legs of mutton or shins of beef this week than usual, and if so why one has had them. But when one sees mixed up with macaroni and currants, and Demerara, Demerara (a recurring rhythmic wail that seems to have come straight from Synge), quite arbitrary quantities of cleaning materials and incredible numbers of bundles of sticks, one's power to check and still more to criticise dwindles to vanishing point.

My advice to would-be economists is: "Conquer the grocer's book." Once you have laid that many-headed hydra low the game is yours with the reluctant respect of your cook thrown in.

One last warning. The mechanism of a house well kept should be silent and absolutely invisible. There should be no sense of strain or hustle anywhere and nothing should be or appear difficult or inconvenient. Really good housekeeping is neither seen nor heard. It is only deeply and gratefully felt.

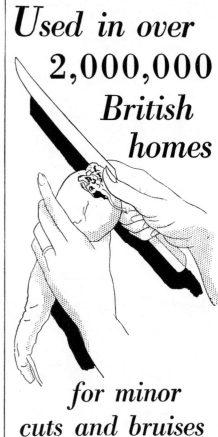

THE 20's

THE
20's

Anglo-Saxon Silver Bowl belonging to the Eleventh Century. By courtesy of the Trustees of the British Museum.

When Alfred went to Rome

When Alfred the Great (the one who burnt the cakes) was a boy, his father Ethelwulf took him to Rome to be blessed by the Pope. They took with them as presents crowns and dishes and images of silver and gold — in those days the work of Saxon silver-smiths and gold-smiths was admired all over Europe. The Pope himself had invited Saxon smiths to live permanently at the Vatican.

The eleventh-century Anglo-Saxon bowl shown here is particularly interesting, because it is one of the very few purely domestic Saxon vessels ever found. It would seem that silver had its place in the every-day equipment of Saxon households, just as it has in ours, but cleaning it must have been something of a task then! Now-a-days, of course, Silvo is available for giving a deep, mirror - like polish to all kinds of silverware. And as Silvo contains neither acid nor mercury, it is equally safe for electro - plate as well.

SILVO

"*Good Housekeeping*"

By Herbert A. Welch, F.R.I.B.A.

Director of Good Housekeeping Housing Department

and by

D. D. Cottington Taylor

Director of Good Housekeeping Institute

SINCE its first number GOOD HOUSEKEEPING has always been the medium for the expression and illustration of our own views, as well as the views of many eminent architects and domestic economists upon a subject which, by the very nature of things, must be an absorbing one.

All readers of the magazine who study the Housing and Household Engineering Sections will know that the former has hitherto dealt mainly with the architectural side of house planning, and the latter with general household equipment and management, and that in spite of their natural tendency to overlap in many respects, the two sections have not up to the present actually co-operated either in theory or practice.

The Household Section gave birth, in 1924, to the Institute, an organisation which has enabled precept to become practice in regard to the reliability of domestic equipment and many other points in connection with the successful running of a house, and it is perhaps the logical sequence of events that the Directors of the two sections should pool their knowledge and experience in the actual building of a house. In doing this it is hoped that some of our cherished theories, as well as our proven practical experiments, may be dovetailed together in demonstrative form within the walls of one home.

This article is not intended to treat in detail, nor even to touch upon many of these theories, but only to give an outline of what it is planned to accomplish. We shall therefore reserve much to be said when we are quite sure we have carried out our ambitious desires and accomplished them successfully.

The search for a site was at once a pleasant but difficult task. We felt it must satisfy three main essentials; it must be not too far from London, the train service must be good and the site must be

At Oakfield Park, Weybridge, this announcement marks the site of the "Good Housekeeping" House

such a one that we would ourselves be happy to live in the house.

The site selected at Weybridge in Surrey, which has an excellent train service, we consider meets all these requirements, and will be easy of access, not only for its permanent occupiers but for readers desirous of inspecting it when completed. Many people know the natural beauties of the district, but even to them the illustration of the site (taken in late March before the leaves had broken) will not be superfluous. The trees are delightful oaks and beeches, and the situation—at the junction of an old road (along which a bus service runs to the station) with a newly formed one—makes for convenience of approach and at the same time assures a measure of seclusion behind the deep belt of trees.

With regard to the accommodation of the house, we decided it must not be too large, but well suited to the requirements of an average family.

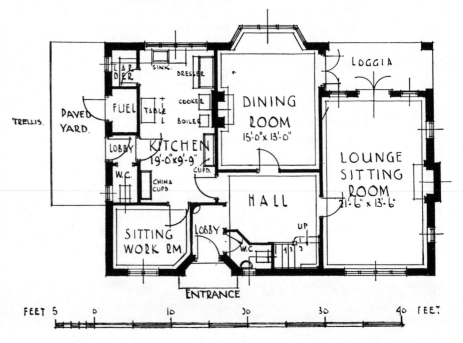

Builds A HOUSE

"Good Housekeeping" hopes that its cherished theories, as well as proven practical experiments, will dovetail together in demonstrative form within the four walls of this house. Two bathrooms are considered essential and a special feature is the sitting-work-room leading from the kitchen, the dimensions of which are 19 ft. by 9 ft. 9 in.

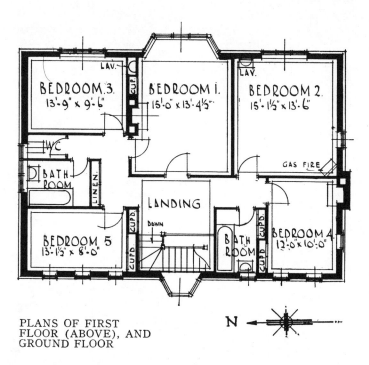

PLANS OF FIRST
FLOOR (ABOVE), AND
GROUND FLOOR

To commence upon the first floor, it was thought that four bedrooms would not be sufficient for the reason that these would all be put into constant use by parents, son and daughter, and a maid. To make provision for visitors, five would probably be required. Of bathrooms there must be two, and in addition washbasins—placed as unostentatiously as possible—in two at least of the bedrooms. Cupboards, as many as practicable, are considered essential provided they do not "eat up" too much room. Cupboards have therefore been provided "in recess," so avoiding the unseemly appearance produced by projections from the walls, which in addition make cleaning more difficult.

On the ground floor are a sitting-room and dining-room of moderate size. It is pleasant particularly during spring and summer months to have somewhere in the open in which to sit, but where the sun does not worry, and a loggia has therefore been provided on the south-east side. A fair-sized hall not too occupied by the stair-case and lavatory, with the entrance lobby separate from but in close contact to it, is also included.

Close at hand are the working quarters, the pivot of the home's comfort. We have decided upon a large kitchen, rather than one of smaller dimensions and a separate scullery, and a small sitting-work-room entering off it, the reason for which decision will be touched upon later.

(Continued overleaf)

THE
20's

(Continued)

To deal with the planning in greater detail:—the house is approached by way of a recessed porch on the west side giving access to a lobby, off which is entered the w.c. and lavatory (placed under the stairs) and the hall. The hall provides a reasonable amount of wall space and a sufficient means of access to the sitting- and dining-rooms, the kitchen, and to the stairs. The sitting-room (21 ft. 6 in. by 13 ft. 6 in.) is placed on the south-east corner with external walls on the east, south and west, thereby securing the maximum of sunshine. At the east end of the room a pair of glazed doors open on to the loggia and thence to the garden. The fireplace is recessed in order to secure the maximum of available room.

The dining-room is a comfortable size (15 ft. by 13 ft.) for its purpose, and has in addition a bay window facing east-south-east which ensures the enjoyment of sunshine in the early morning and retains it until after lunch. In addition, it commands a full view of the garden. It is placed in close touch with the kitchen and —like the sitting-room—has been provided with a pair of glazed doors giving access to the loggia.

The kitchen is entered directly off the hall but the door is not apparent upon entry. The planning of the kitchen, or workshop of the house, has naturally received the specialised attention of the Institute, for it is here that great scope is offered for putting into practice the lessons we have learnt during our five years' experience. Bearing in mind that cramped conditions are not conducive to comfort and efficient work, it was decided to devote a space of 19 ft. by 9 ft. 9 in. to a combined kitchen-scullery. We make no claim to be infallible but we confidently assert that no detail has been included or excluded without very careful thought.

Although often misapplied and somewhat hackneyed, the words "labour saving" can, we think, be rightly given to the arrangement not only of the service quarters, but of the whole house.

Among the points which have not been forgotten are:

(a) The elimination of dust-traps in angles, mouldings, etc.

(b) The placing of equipment in the service quarters with a view to step-saving and the gaining of necessary light when working at the sink, gas stove, etc.

(c) The provision of power points for use with electric cleaners, etc.

This photograph, taken before the leaves were out, shows the natural beauty

(d) Hardwood floors.

(e) Window glass to permit the penetration of ultra-violet rays.

The various conditions under which the house is likely to be run were carefully considered, and it was decided that whether an ordinary domestic or trained worker were employed, a sitting-work-room, entirely separate from the kitchen but closely adjacent, was to be an essential feature of the house. The advantages of this arrangement are many, and should the house be run by the mistress with the assistance of a resident or day worker, this room will be available for the use of the mistress in the morning for such purposes as

ironing, sewing, or dressmaking, and as a sitting-room for the domestic worker during the afternoon and evening.

The first floor is provided with a landing of good size, the main features

I F   Y O U   A R E

Any reader who desires free a house is asked to write to Housekeeping, 153 Queen Vic stamped, addressed

THE
20's

of the site, which is at the junction of Oakfield Glade and Oatlands Drive

south. It will accommodate a double bed or twin beds and will be provided with a lavatory basin. The small one (12 ft. by 10 ft.), for a single bed, faces south and west and has a cupboard in recess. The two last mentioned bedrooms immediately adjoin the second bathroom, all three rooms being approached within a separate lobby off the main landing. The fifth bedroom (13 ft. 1 in. by 8 ft.) faces west and has been provided with a double cupboard in recess.

Although the actual fabric of the house will receive very careful thought, our interest will extend to other considerations, such as the treatment of the woodwork, whether it is to be left in its natural state, stained, or painted. To some people the width of the floor boards would hardly seem to call for much attention, but we consider that it is on small points such as these that the charm of the house largely depends, and distinguishes it from the house of the mass production type.

The provision of adequate lighting and power points is considered no less important than their disposition.

The elevations, illustrated by a perspective sketch viewed from the south-west angle as indicated, will be treated with multicoloured facing bricks, grey, red and purple-grey, up to the head of the ground-floor windows. From this level up to the roof elm weather boarding (which will tone to a silver grey tint) will be fixed to brick external walls. The windows will be steel casements with leaded glazing having easy opening lights and special hinges to facilitate cleaning from the interior of the house. The roof will be covered with green glazed interlocking pantiles having a wide projection at the eaves oversailing the walls.

The garden of the house is of good size, having some well-grown trees and shrubs, mainly on the north side. It is hoped that the front portion of the garden may be laid out—if the season is not too far advanced—on a simple formal plan in keeping with the house and its natural and beautiful surroundings. A frontage of 90 ft. and a depth of about 200 ft. provides an ample area for the average householder to cultivate.

A garage is an essential addition to any house in the eyes of the majority of people to-day, and a house allowing no facilities for its erection is likely to have but a limited appeal.

It has been decided that a garage, if required, *(Continued overleaf)*

---

of which are the wide approach of the stairs and the oriel bay window. The bedrooms (except the main bedroom) and bathroom are approached off lobbies to the right and left of the main

BUILDING

advice on building or altering
The Director of Housing, Good toria Street, E.C.4, enclosing a envelope for reply

landing. It will be seen that three of the bedrooms will enjoy the early morning sunshine. The main bedroom is placed over the dining-room and is of the same size. A small cupboard is arranged in the fireplace recess and a second door from the room leads to the lobby off which is approached the bathroom, with linen cupboard adjoining, and w.c. allocated to this bedroom and its neighbour. This latter bedroom (13 ft. 9 in. by 9 ft. 6 in.) is intended to accommodate a single bed and has been provided with a lavatory basin.

Over the sitting-room two bedrooms have been arranged. The larger one (15 ft. by 13 ft. 6 in.) faces east and

Like a lovely night in June

Night after night last winter, when it was time to retire, you braced yourself to face the ordeal of leaving the comfortable fireside for the freezing air of the bedroom.

"Here goes," you said, and hastily dropped off your warm things to don chilly night attire and slip between icy sheets.

This year ensure a never varying summer temperature by means of 'Unity' Electric Heaters.

Tubes of steel, just 2 inches in diameter, fastened to the skirting boards, will give an atmosphere like a lovely night in June.

Write to-day for a beautifully illustrated folder, "Heating the Home." It gives you prices and full particulars of this very inexpensive yet most efficient heating system.

YOUNG, OSMOND & YOUNG LTD

47 VICTORIA STREET, WESTMINSTER
LONDON, S.W.1

Ogden's

This shows the unobtrusive "Unity," fixed to the skirting board

"Good Housekeeping" Builds a House

(Continued)

would be best placed, both with regard to the house and road, at the end of the garden and entered off the main road, Oatlands Drive. One advantage of this arrangement is that the cutting up of the garden in front of the house by a drive-in will be avoided, and it can thus be laid out to better advantage.

The dimensions and construction of a garage are also largely a matter for personal requirements contingent on the size of car kept and whether a chauffeur is employed who might require rooms over it, etc. It has therefore been decided to leave its erection to the future tenants of the house.

The plan given on this page shows the exact position of the house in relation to Oatlands Drive and the roads etc., surrounding the house, and will be of interest in this and other connections.

Further articles will be published in GOOD HOUSEKEEPING during the summer months dealing in detail with the actual building materials employed, the heating and lighting installations, and, of course, with the planning and equipping of the kitchen.

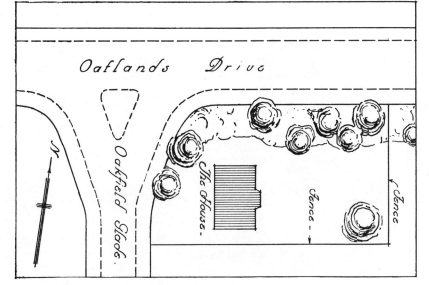

Plan of the plot showing position of house in relation to roads and existing trees

THE
20's

The Director of Good Housekeeping Institute, 49 Wellington Street, London, W.C.2, is always pleased to advise readers, free of charge, on matters relating to the planning and equipping of their homes. The Director of Housing will help readers on all matters connected with building. Send a stamped, addressed envelope for reply

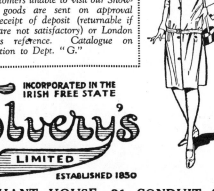

THE
20's

MR. EVERYMAN

"So your furniture terms mean over 4 Years credit Mr. Drage"

Mr. Everyman : So your furniture terms mean over four years' credit, Mr. Drage?

Mr. Drage : Four years and two months to be precise—fifty months. That's why I call it the Fifty Pay-Way. And no such terms are given anywhere else in Great Britain.

Mr. Everyman : They suit us admirably, Mr. Drage. Now my order comes to £100. I divide the £100 by 50 to get my first payment—that's 40/-.

Mr. Drage : Yes, and on payment of only 40/- now we'll deliver all the furniture to your home at once.

Mr. Everyman : That's fine. Then for 49 months afterwards I pay 40/- a month —£100 in all.

Mr. Drage : Yes, you see nothing is added to the £100 for the long credit you are taking.

Mr. Everyman : Good—you say you don't want references ?

Mr. Drage : And I mean it. I don't want a single one, but I do want to give you your Drage Protection.

Mr. Everyman : This means if I can't pay through illness or unemployment I keep what I've paid for.

Mr. Drage : Yes, less a fair reduction for use and cartage. And your Free Fire and Life Policy will be issued by the Eagle Star and British Dominions Insurance Co. and sent you at once.

Mr. Everyman : I don't wonder at your great business, Mr. Drage. But, if every one realised what liberal terms you give, your showrooms would be even more crowded than they are to-day.

DRAGES
(DRAGE'S LIMITED)

HIGH HOLBORN · LONDON · WC1
NEXT TO HOLBORN TUBE STN. PHONE: HOLBORN 3655.
OPEN 9 A.M. TO 6.30 P.M. CLOSED THURSDAYS AT 1 P.M.

OPEN ON SATURDAYS UNTIL 6.30 P.M

COUPON Please send me large Furniture Catalogue and details of your 50 Pay-Way No Deposit System for approved accounts.

NAME...................................

ADDRESS...................................

G.H.7.29 ....

Cut out and post in unsealed envelope with ½d. stamp to Drages, Limited, 230 High Holborn, London, W.C.1

THE
20's

A Song of Home

By
Ethel R. Fuller
Illustrated by Joseph M. Clement

WERE I to make a poem of a day
Of housework, I'd not write of dust and
  brooms
So much as of the sun in spotless rooms,
Of bowls of brightly glowing flowers—I'd say
Less of vegetables and kinds of bread,
Of endless dishes scraped and washed and dried,

And more of children's hunger satisfied—
I'd tell of soft, warm lips on mine instead.

OH, MORE than endless duties I would sing
Of happy hearts and of contentment, of
Ambitious dreams—yes, more than anything
I'd tally every blessing, wherein love
Is greatest of them all : is the leaven
Exalting toil, turning home to Heaven.

83

Banish household drudgery!

The "GOBLIN" gives you time to spare....

The "Goblin" Electric Vacuum Cleaner is the greatest help a woman can have. It will do what brooms and brushes can never do. The Goblin raises no dust—its powerful suction will extract deeply-embedded dirt from carpets, rugs and upholstery rapidly and thoroughly without disturbance.

The Goblin is portable, convenient, and pleasant to use. Various fittings, changed in a moment, are supplied, so that dust can be removed from every possible lurking place. The price is wonderfully low for this highest grade All British Cleaner—and it is guaranteed for five years.

Write for descriptive folder S.A.65. Can be tested in your own home without obligation. All principal London and Provincial Stores and first-class dealers can supply.

THE 20's

BEAUTY

One said to me : " You miss all beauty so,
Scrubbing on tired knees your kitchen floor ;
Outside the forest calls, the sea winds blow,
And roses toss, inviting, at your door."
Yet I know beauties other than all these,
In every room I find it, everywhere,
For as I scrub my floor on tired knees,
Ruddy and warm, the flush of brick is there.
And then, beneath my hands, the last fine gleam
Springs to the winking surfaces of brass ;
White come the linens from the clouding steam,
And fine and white I spread them on the grass.
Through all my work is beauty and to spare,
And still, each day, is " time to stand and stare."

MARGARET MARSHALL.

Illustration by Steven Spurrier, R.O.I.

Are you "Arty-crafty"

or one of the millions of our home-lovers? Whichever you are, Hall's Distemper Decoration is for you. This beautiful decoration satisfies the soul of the aesthete and the philistine, while it gives to us ordinary mortals the real "Home Sweet Home."

Arrange with your Decorator for Hall's Distemper. He will be pleased to show you tint book of the 60 beautiful colours and to help you with suggestions.

But first fill in the coupon for the Hall's Distemper Booklet. It will tell you more about this wonderful decorative material. Why it is so beautiful and yet so durable. How it is sanitary and washable. How easy it is to apply and how quick—one coat gives a beautiful finish.

HALL'S DISTEMPER
REG. TRADE MARK.
THE OIL-BOUND·WATER PAINT

Are you redecorating the Dining Room this Spring, or a Bedroom or the Entrance Hall? This Booklet will help you to decide. It is free and post free. Fill in the coupon to-day.

Sole Manufacturers:
SISSONS BROTHERS & Co., Ltd., HULL
LONDON: 203, Borough High Street, S.E.1
GLASGOW: 26-30, Montrose St., C.1   READING: 5-6, Gun St.

Please send your beautifully illustrated booklet, "Light and Colour in the Home," also Hall's Distemper Shade Card, post free.

Name...,..

Address..
G.H.2
....

Sole Proprietors and Manufacturers:
SISSONS BROTHERS & CO., LTD., HULL.

765

THE

20's

The Smokeless Labour-Saving House

NO MODERN DWELLING is complete without a Coke Boiler, which not only supplies constant abundant hot water at the minimum of cost, but also heats hall, kitchen, and adjoining rooms. A Coke Boiler consumes all dust and refuse; facilitates the use of Gas Fires and, combined with a Coke Firegrate, entirely eliminates the use of coal and incidental flue cleaning.

Full particulars of the latest types of Coke Boilers and Coke Firegrates recommended, free on application.

London Coke Committee
84 HORSEFERRY ROAD, S.W.1

Keep your Boys at home
—let them find their pleasures at home on a RILEY HOME BILLIARD TABLE

7 DAYS FREE TRIAL GIVEN

WRITE TO-NIGHT for Coloured Price List.

14/- DOWN By simply sending a postal order for 14/- you can have the 6-ft. size Riley "Home" Billiard Table—a real billiard table—delivered complete and ready for play. The balance you pay whilst you use the table. **Rileys pay the carriage and take all risk in transit . . .** and 7 days' free trial enables you to test the table before buying. Send your order to-night !

Riley's "Home" Billiard Table shown resting on ordinary dining table.

Here are the various sizes, together with cash & easy-to-pay prices

4 ft. 4 in. x 2 ft. 4 in.	..	£7 0 0	or in 8/6
5 ft. 4 in. x 2 ft. 10 in.	..	£9 0 0	18 11/-
6 ft. 4 in. x 3 ft. 4 in.	..	£11 15 0	monthly 14/-
7 ft. 4 in. x 3 ft. 10 in.	..	£15 0 0	payments 18/-
8 ft. 4 in. x 4 ft. 4 in.	..	£21 10 0	of 26/-

RILEY'S BILLIARD

COMBINE & DINING TABLE
(7 Days' Free Trial).

If your home is needing a new dining table, why not have a "Combine" Billiard and Dining Table which in a few seconds can be converted from a dining table into a perfect billiard table ? Supplied in Oak or Mahogany, various shades and designs, from £22 : 10 : 0, or in 13 or 20 monthly payments.

Rileys also make the world-famed RILEY FULL-SIZE BILLIARD TABLES.

Write for details. Estimates for repairs and accessories FREE.

E. J. RILEY LTD.,
PINE WORKS, ACCRINGTON,
and Dept. V, 147 Aldersgate Street, London, E.C.1.

This is the "Cabriole" design, 6-ft. size £34 : 10 : 0 Cash, or in 13 or 20 easy payments.

A TURN OF THE TAP

Brings Unlimited Hot Water

at as many points as you like in the house in a few seconds. When you have a CLARKHILL it's just like having Hot Water laid on at the main.

Fitted in the kitchen or the scullery, the Clarkhill leaves your bathroom clear of apparatus, and being entirely automatic, it only burns gas whilst you are actually drawing water. Directly you turn off the hot-water tap the burners are automatically extinguished, leaving a separate tiny by-pass ready to ignite the burners the next time Hot Water is required.

Wonderful economy—and no other work to do than just turn on any hot-water tap to obtain as much or as little Hot Water as you want.

You will know more about this modern system by reading "Years Ahead," a folder which we shall be pleased to send you by return of post on receipt of your request.

"CLARKHILL"
AUTOMATIC WATER HEATERS

CLARKHILLS, LTD.
13 Albemarle Street, London, W.1
Gerrard 1988

THE SECRET OF HER LOVELY CLOTHES

She always sends them to Clark's !!

and is admired for her smart appearance and practical economy.

Send CLARK'S your after-season frocks and costumes to be cleaned and dyed to the new autumn and winter colours without incurring the heavy expense of new.

FIXED CHARGES.

	Cleaned.	Dyed.
Skirts - - -	3/9	6/-
Jumpers - -	3/-	4/6
Coat and Skirt	6/6	10/6
Blanket Coat -	5/6	8/-
Raincoats - -	6/6	9/-
Men's Suits -	5/6	10/6
Hats - - -	3/6	4/6

We pay postage one way.

Write for List " G."

CLARK'S · DYE · WORKS
RETFORD

THE FIRST WIRELESS **LOUD SPEAKER** WAS A *Brown*

Hear this new *Brown*
–and no other will ever
satisfy your critical ear

THE four new *Brown* Loud Speakers—of which that illustrated on the right is one—represent a big advance in the design of these fine quality British Loud Speakers. Hitherto many wireless enthusiasts have purchased their Loud Speakers on appearance alone—only to find that a handsome and pleasing outline does not necessarily mean purity and mellowness of tone. The *Brown*, on the other hand, has invariably been bought *on actual performance*. It has achieved a wonderful reputation throughout the world solely for the naturalness of its reproduction.

In the *Brown*, external shape has always been subservient—in the interests of good music—to the actual design of the reproducer itself. But now the *Brown* Loud Speaker has been greatly improved in appearance and these four new models possess a dignity and beauty which place them in a class by themselves.

Ally this new beauty of outline to the wonderful sensitiveness of the *Brown* tuned reed movement and you possess a Loud Speaker which is a positive joy for all time.

S. G. *Brown*, Ltd., N. Acton, London, W.3

Retail Showrooms: 19 Mortimer Street, W.1.
15 Moorfields, Liverpool. 67 High Street, Southampton.
Depots (Wholesale only) · 13 Bushy Park, Bristol
Cross House, Westgate Road, Newcastle

¶ **To the Trade:** We have instituted a special Dept. to see that your orders are filled promptly. In case of special difficulty write to us at once.

The new HQ

A handsome instrument possessing the same beauty of outline as the famous *Brown* Q Loud Speaker. Gives a wonderful volume of crystal clear tone. Attractively finished in rich brown colour or a velvet black with polished nickel fittings. Height 20″. 4,000 ohms resistance. Also in 120 and 2,000 ohms.

£6

BRITISH **Brown** THROUGHOUT

These Radiants are

Inclined....

and that makes all the difference in the World!

150
different sizes and finishes
★
Cost no more than the old-fashioned vertical fire
★
Manufactured by a British firm established more than a hundred years ago

IT would have been worth it — just to have improved the old-fashioned vertical fire's appearance. But there is, in addition, a sound scientific reason for the Inclined Radiant: *more* useful heat for the *same* gas consumption.

Even the out-of-date "straight-up-and-down" gas fire had points over a coal fire. But add to these points the three immeasurable advantages of the Inclined Radiant—more comfortable warmth, more pleasing appearance, more useful heat — and it is easy to see why, to-day, modern Gas Companies instal and thoroughly recommend these New Inclined Fires.

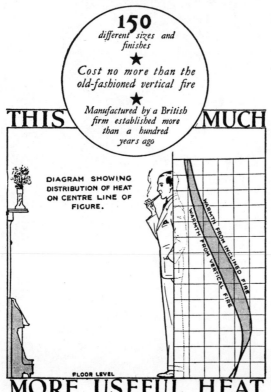

THIS MUCH

DIAGRAM SHOWING DISTRIBUTION OF HEAT ON CENTRE LINE OF FIGURE.

WARMTH FROM INCLINED FIRE

WARMTH FROM VERTICAL FIRE

FLOOR LEVEL

MORE USEFUL HEAT

CANNON
New Inclined Gas Fires

Stocked and recommended by your local gas company
Manufacturers: **CANNON IRON FOUNDRIES** Ltd., Deepfields, Nr. Bilston, **Staffs.**

HOUSING Conducted by Herbert A. Welch F.R.I.B.A.

The Tale *of a* £900 Cottage

By the Owner

MANY readers with limited incomes will doubtless have admired the plans of small houses which have appeared in GOOD HOUSEKEEPING from time to time, but regretfully put the thought of building a house aside as being too big an adventure to undertake. The fear that the final cost will largely exceed the original estimate, owing to builders' extras and other contingencies, is often the main deterrent. It may, therefore, be of interest to describe briefly how we had built a thatched cottage similar to one already described in these pages, the cost of which only exceeded the estimate by a few pounds.

For some years my wife and I had discussed building a house, but not until I had to move to another town did we arrive at a decision. During this time we had taken every opportunity to look over houses in course of erection and also to consider various plans described in this magazine and in others. Finally in March 1926, there was published in GOOD HOUSEKEEPING an article on a £900 thatched cottage, the plans of which appeared ideal for our r e q u i r e m e n t s, and when, soon afterwards, I was moved to a small town in the Midlands, I wrote to the Editor of the Housing Section, who put me in touch with the architect.

At this time I was living on the south coast and it appeared to me a difficulty to ask the architect to undertake the supervision of the building in a locality strange to us both. This did not, however, prove to be an obstacle. On his invitation, my wife and I met him and looked over one of his cottages which had just been completed in Devonshire. This cottage more than fulfilled the promise of the plans and article, and we decided it was exactly what we required.

The first thing was to find a site suitable for a thatched cottage near the town. In this we were fortunate as we found a piece of meadow land, surrounded by trees, fronting a good main road and having available company's water, electric light and main drainage. While these last may not each and all be essential, the possession of them will make things easier for the owner who is trying to budget, to spend a certain fixed sum, as the cost of these items can be foreseen and extra expense of a

It is with something of proprietary pride that we present this month's housing section, since the reader's house illustrated and described, first by himself and then by the architect, was inspired by an article in the magazine, designed by the author of that article, and fitted with equipment recommended by Good Housekeeping Institute

variable nature, as may be incurred in sinking a well, etc., cut out.

After the architect had approved the site he asked if there were any special fittings we should like, and, after deciding on these, we left things entirely in his hands. We told him what we could afford to spend and left the details to him, determining that we would not interfere. This proved to be the best thing we could have done, for the result has exceeded our expectations.

In passing it might be mentioned that, before deciding on the system for hot water, inquiries to the Director of the Good Housekeeping Institute as to these were answered by very informative and courteous letters giving full details as to fuel consumption, heating ability, ease of maintenance, etc.

But to return to the house building. After about two months from buying the land, the plans and specifications had been prepared, plans passed by the local council, the contract signed and building commenced. All the building

was done under the direct supervision of the architect. The builder took a keen interest in the cottage and to him we owe the pleasure of having old oak beams, which not only are in keeping with the old-world style of the house but are a very attractive feature of the open ceilings.

The most important matter to many people is perhaps how and when payments for the building were made. The usual contract provides for payment by four instalments; first, when up to the first floor, secondly, when the roof is on and finally, on occupation, leaving a small amount to be paid after a period of maintenance. This latter is of importance for it is during this time that small defects are put right and such things as easing doors, etc., attended to. It should not be overlooked that the architect's fees and expenses are in addition to the contract price, and that, of course, land is not included in the estimate of the cost in the original article mentioned above, but the actual cost of our cottage did not greatly exceed this amount.

There are two or three ways of paying for the house if one can only provide part of the cost. An ordinary mortgage can be obtained through the help of a solicitor, but this does not allow for paying off the amount borrowed. Another method is to take up the money through a building society mortgage, repaying capital and interest by fixed instalments. My own plan was to do this through an Insurance Company, who advanced the money required on the security of the deeds and a collateral short-term life policy for the amount advanced. The policy on maturity will repay the mortgage, leaving the profits on the insurance to be paid to the borrower, while, in the event of prior decease, the mortgage will be cancelled.

In conclusion I would say that to have the house one wants, it is necessary to build it, and it is an enjoyable adventure to do it. Make up your mind beforehand as to what you want, then give the architect a free hand within the limits imposed by the final cost, and the result will be satisfactory.

THE 30's

Illustration by Steven Spurrier R.O.I.

THE
30's

Alice Booth's

*Delicious tale
of a
Girl who discovered that
a home is not a house
after all
but
a place
in someone's heart*

IT really wasn't Anne who needed a husband—it was the house. Anne stood just as firmly on her slim little brown-Oxford feet as she had stood since she was fourteen. She managed perfectly well, alone. Her bills were all paid. She ran herself beautifully. And always she was as trim and shipshape as anything you ever saw in all your life. But the house——

Words cannot express the needs of the house. The house was battered and ragged and down-at-heel. Ivy ran all over its windows and tried to smother it. The porch roof drooped like a flag in wet weather, and it was evident that soon someone would have to take it in hand. And as for bills—why, the house's bills were never paid. No one knew that better than Anne.

She had no intention of deserting it, however. It was her orphan child. And though it was ruinously extravagant—as all children are—it repaid her for every investment in the angelic way that children do—with smiles, and a beaming face, and shining eyes.

The house was more than a house to Anne—more even than an orphan child. It was a passion and an obsession and all the years of her own lonely childhood. Naturally she wasn't going to give *them* up. It was all the reading of Robin Hood before a blazing fire on nipping winter evenings. It was all the running out in summer dawns to see just what improvements God had made in the garden over-night. It was all the blue and gold summer afternoons on green grass under old trees—all the dreams of the wide world coloured by painted sunsets. It was all the games of childhood, that house, and Anne loved it with more than human persistency and stubbornness.

It was new, too, this having a house to love and care for. Before, Anne had been only a careless, happy girl, but haunted by a persistent desire which she indulged on Saturday afternoons, and Sunday mornings when she should have been at church. The whole office knew her failing. Especially Tom, the art editor, knew it. On evenings in the week, Anne was always ready to go for a bus-ride —or to the pictures—or somewhere to dine and dance with him . . . except when she was doing those same things with Walter, who was in the legal department of the same firm. But on Saturdays and Sundays Anne was just a little girl looking for a home and never finding it.

There were no homes any more, she often decided—just things built for a period, not for people. There were millions of houses, she thought in discouragement, but no homes where you could live as people ought to live. Woodsheds for instance—why, woodsheds were what you spent all the rainy days in, and Anne looked for years without seeing even one woodshed. People kept their wood in the cellar—and every one knows that isn't right. The cellar should be kept clear

A House *needs a* H

for flower-pots, and old boxes, and cob-webs, and jam jars, and garden tools. Just as the attic was the place for old trunks full of hoopskirted dresses and tall bonnets, and grimy magazines with all the stories you had ever liked, and flower-seeds tied up in paper bags, and bathing suits, and broken furniture.

Oh, Anne knew perfectly well what she wanted. Every detail had been rankling for years in her starved and homesick heart. Through a lifetime of just one boarding school after another, through years of summer holidays, she had evolved her ideas. It took only one or two visits to some of her school-mates to teach her just what a home should be; and life in hotels—after the school-days were done—only etched the pictures deeper in her heart.

There was no compromise for Anne. No one-room-and-kitchenette cavilling with the heart's desire. A house or nothing. A home house. And on she hunted, hither and yon.

Mr. Smith helped her. Sometimes Anne became discouraged and gave up the quest for weeks and weeks. Then there was

sure to be a telephone call. Mr. Smith had another prospect—not just exactly what she wanted, of course, but still—perhaps she'd better see it. So Anne put on her hopeful face and took the first train.

And always Mr. Smith, in his bright blue car, was waiting for her—blue eyes smiling, honest yellow hair brushed in smooth, crisp crinkles. And if Anne sometimes wondered why Mr. Smith always elected to meet her at a station at least twenty miles from wherever they were going . . . why, she stopped herself firmly and reminded herself that Mr. Smith was All For Business. Never had he mentioned anything to her but business—and his success as a rising young estate agent.

And then, one day, Anne found the house. She was driving with Mr. Smith at the time—driving past new red bungalows and old grey farms, past mock Tudor and Italian villas—when she saw it first—just a glimpse down a side turning—a flash of dripping ivy, of battered fence, of a sagging porch roof—and Anne screamed—and pointed.

"I want to go there," she said. "Quick! Before it gets away! *There* —did you see it? There—round the corner! Faster! . . . Here it is! . . . I want it!"

While Mr. Smith sat in his car eyeing her disapprovingly, she leaped out and leaned on the gate and looked. There it was— *(Continued overleaf)*

usband

Three were too many. Three were a crowd. Anne got tired of them, and try as she might, she never had a minute with Tom

Its Handy Form makes Gibbs Dentifrice more popular than any tooth paste or powder

Gibbs Dentifrice is easy to use — handy to pack or carry — trim and tidy. Men, Women and Children alike are charmed with the neat little tablet in the natty aluminium case. Gibbs Dentifrice slips handily into suit-case or school-bag.

Gibbs — the British — Dentifrice cleans all the surfaces of the teeth—and all the nooks and crannies. Polishing is gentle and teeth glow with a lovely natural pearly lustre.

Keep your teeth safe and sound. Buy a case of Gibbs Dentifrice to-day.

*Your teeth are Ivory Castles
—defend them with*

GD 42 N

Gibbs
Dentifrice
BRITISH   MADE

Popular Size 7½d; Large size 1/-; De Luxe 1/6; Refills 11d. For those who prefer a paste, Gibbs Dental Cream in Tubes 6d. and 1/-. (*These prices do not apply in the Irish Free State.*)

D. & W. GIBBS, LTD., LONDON, E.1.

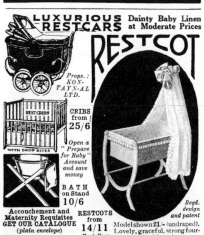

LUXURIOUS RESTCARS Dainty Baby Linen at Moderate Prices

RESTCOT

Props.: KON-TAYN-AL LTD.

CRIBS from 25/6

Open a "Prepare for Baby" Account and save money

BATH on Stand 10/6

Regd. design and patent

Accouchement and Maternity Requisites GET OUR CATALOGUE (*plain envelope*) Manageress, RESTCOTS, 208 AVON HOUSE, 16 SOUTH ROW, LONDON, W.10

RESTCOTS from 14/11 Post Free

Model shown 21/- (undraped). Lovely, graceful, strong four-posters. Pack into tiny space.

For
COMFORT, ECONOMY and CONVENIENCE
install
THE GLOW-WORM BOILER

The house that has a Glow-Worm Boiler is an *economical* house, a *comfortable* house and a *convenient* house.

It is *economical* because fuel that lasts for three months with other boilers lasts four months with the Glow-Worm. This really amounts to a free quarter's fuel every year.

It is *comfortable* because the Glow-Worm, when required, heats radiators and towel rail as well as warming the kitchen or room in which it is fitted.

And it is *convenient* because really hot water is always "on tap" for Baths, Lavatory Basins and Sinks.

No other boiler will give you equal, all-round satisfaction.

PRICES NOW FROM
£4 : 15 : 0
INCLUDING FEET AND TRAY.

Call and inspect the Glow-Worm or write for particulars.

ANTHRACITE RADIATION LIMITED
(Incorporating Glow-Worm Boiler & Fire Co., Ltd., and London Warming Co., Ltd.)
(Dept. K.1), 5 NEWMAN STREET, OXFORD STREET, LONDON, W.1

A House Needs a Husband
(Continued)

a home. A lean-to roof proclaimed something that might be possibly a woodshed —and was. Disreputable bushes, without any sense of order and restraint, spread themselves in the sun. Rotting wood gave out a pleasant odour of decay. But the front door stood open, and a stationary rocking-chair reseated with Brussels carpet tottered bravely on the porch.

"It's no use," said Mr. Smith, speaking to her back. "Old Man Barnes won't sell. Best lot in the Manor, too. Ten million people have tried to buy it. It's an eyesore to the whole place. I won't go in. The last time I was up here, with a fine chance of two thousand cash—Jones, the big soap man (owns the place above) wanted to build a pergola down here for the river view—the old man threatened to use a shot gun on me. I think he more than half meant it, too. Half crazy he is."

Anne did not hear. She glanced back once, but seeing Mr. Smith still sitting, returned to her happy musing. Her eyes embraced lovingly each detail—the weeds —the old mud-scraper by the worn steps, hollowed by feet that had come to the little old house—the torn carpet in the hall.

As she watched, an old figure tottered into sight from the back yard that—seen down the narrow passageway—was one tangle of sun-coloured blossom and light —a bent old figure that tottered on a cane, preceded by a cracked voice uttering testy commands.

"Get on away with ye now—and take that fool of an estate-agent with ye! 'Tain't no use. I won't sell. Get on with ye, now. You do as I say."

Anne's heart sank. Her face was as disappointed as a child's. "I don't suppose you do want to sell," she mourned. "I know if it was mine, I wouldn't part with it for a fortune. But mayn't I just come in and look round? Is that a woodshed out there? I haven't seen one since I was a little girl . . . And have you an old attic—with funny trunks—and old chairs? And oh, please, could I have some flowers? . . . And if you wouldn't sell, would you by any chance take boarders? I'd try not to be any trouble," she offered hopefully.

The odd figure peered at her in doubt. "Boarders? You mean ye want to *live* here?"

"Oh, I *do*!" wailed Anne, sincerity shrieking in her tone.

The odd figure came closer yet and peered into her face. "Ye don't want to pull it down and build a birdhouse or suthing?"

"Pull it *down*!" exclaimed Anne. "Why, I've spent years looking for a house like this."

She opened the gate—noting delightedly that it did not swing on its hinges; you lifted it up and set it down again, and there it stayed, sloping gracefully—and trailed after the old man.

At the door she paused in sudden remembrance. "You needn't wait," she called back to the stupefied Mr. Smith. "I don't know when I'll be going back."

And trailed absent-mindedly through the little hall to the back yard beyond.

"Look round all ye've a mind to," offered the old man magnanimously.

(Continued overleaf)

Buy a British
ELECTRIC REFRIGERATOR
The best in the long run–

Automatic in action, cheap to run, nothing to get out of order, and no expense for maintenance. Health—your most precious possession—depends largely upon pure, fresh food, and now that the use of chemical preservatives is limited by the Pure Food Act (1926), an electric refrigerator should have a place in your home. You can purchase a British Electric Refrigerator by deferred payments. Consult your local Electrical Contractor or Showroom, and write for interesting Booklet — "Is your Larder Safe?" to The British Electrical Development Association Inc., 15 Savoy Street, Strand, London, W.C.2.

AT A TOUCH OF THE SWITCH

Switch on
ELECTRICITY
Protect your Food–
Safeguard your Health!

EDA

H. P.

THE
30's

A House Needs a Husband
(Continued)

"'Twon't do ye no good, though. I ain't to be fooled so easy."

But he followed her everywhere. He listened to her exclaiming over the shells by the battered hearth, and nodded pleasantly as she listened for the roaring sea, pink shell against pink cheek. He watched her petting the flowers and the sundial submerged in the centre bed. He saw her smooth the red tablecloth, and peep into the family album on the marble-top table.

Anne was in a daze of contentment and peace and furious, passionate envy. "You don't need to wait for me," she said to Old Man Barnes exactly as she had said it earlier to Mr. Smith. "I don't know when I'm going. I like it here. I love it here. And I don't know when I'll be able to persuade myself to go home—to a hotel," she said with honest loathing.

Mr. Barnes cackled like an ancient gnome. "So ye like my house, do ye?" he suggested. "Want to buy it—an' pull it down to build a birdhouse. I know their tricks. You ain't the first that's tried to pull the wool over my eyes. But I will say I've enjoyed it," he admitted, horribly gallant.

Anne looked at him. "Look here," she said, her voice earnest. "Would you *want* to sell it if you were sure—sure it would stay just exactly as it is?"

Mr. Barnes' wrinkles gathered, then spread, in expression of two impulses. "Well, I'll tell ye the truth," he said. "I would. But I can't trust nobody. And I won't have this house tore down. And I built it myself for me and Maria, when we just got married. I'm a carpenter by trade. And the house served us well. I won't have it pulled to pieces just because a man's got money."

Anne got up and came very close. She swallowed once, then again. Her blue eyes were big with excitement. Old Man Barnes knew he was beaten at last.

"I want it just the way it is," promised Anne. "I'll never tear it down. It's a home; it isn't built in a period. There must be some way to fix things up—a promise, I mean. It could be put in the deed, couldn't it? Lawyers"—said Anne with bland innocence—"can do anything."

Mr. Barnes chewed thoughtfully on nothing. "How much money have ye got?" he snapped.

"Seven hundred and fifty-six pounds," boasted Anne.

Mr. Barnes chewed again, for a long time. "Well, for five years I've been wanting to go and live with my brother Bill. Bill's getting old," said Mr. Barnes plaintively, swaying on his cane. "Bill needs some-un to look after him," said Mr. Barnes pityingly. "He's got a good house in Sprinton—not as good as this, but comfortable. If it can be fixed legal, you can have it."

"I won't tear it down," swore Anne, her eyes shining. And then her face clouded. "But maybe I'll have to prop it up in places," she worried. "You wouldn't mind that, would you?"

Mr. Barnes' face crinkled. "Ye won't need to do any propping in fifty years," he guaranteed handsomely. "That porch —of course——" he confessed vaguely. "And maybe some new bricks. But that frame is as sound as ever it was. I laid those beams myself. Every door swings true. Not a window sticks. And you can't find a crack in the plaster anywhere—genuine hair and marble dust."

"You give me the seven hundred, and you can have the house just as it stands —furniture and all. Only I'll take the parlour organ—Bill's a master hand at the organ ("I don't play," apologised Anne.)—and the marble-top table. I always did like a marble-top table for my meals—saves washing. ("*I'm* not used to them," deprecated Anne.)

"And I'll take Maria's picture—*you* wouldn't miss her. ("But you would," guessed Anne. "And do," she suppressed immediately after.) All the rest you can have and welcome."

"But I've got more money," objected Anne. "I've got fifty-six pounds more, even after I've paid you the seven hundred pounds."

"Keep it!" said Mr. Barnes magnificently—and then, ominously, "You'll need it!"

The mournful wail of a motor horn resounded through the sunshine from far down the hill—*ah-oorah, ah-oorah*—Mr. Smith coming back.

Anne went out to meet him. She opened the gate and closed it. It was her gate now. She stood on the kerb fairly bursting with news.

Mr. Smith looked at her quizzically, pityingly. "Enjoy yourself?" he queried.

"Very much," said Anne demurely. "I've bought it! It's *mine*!" Try as she would, she could not keep her voice quiet. It soared.

Mr. Smith looked at her and lost his cigarette. "My gosh!" he said. "How much did you offer him?"

"Seven hundred," said Anne.

"My gosh!" marvelled Mr. Smith. "What a help you would be in my business!"

Anne never could have got through all the work of buying the house without Mr. Smith. He attended to deeds and titles, and did more than you would expect three men.

She saw a great deal of him in the days that followed. And of Walter and Tom nothing, for of course there was no point in dragging them through all these business formalities, and besides Mr. Smith was attending to everything anyhow.

One day it was all done. One day she no longer had seven hundred pounds in the bank. One day she packed up and left her hotel room and started for the country with all the happiness a heart can hold.

Mr. Smith met her in the bright blue car, the sun shone fair, and all the hill was green and gold with summer. Mr. Smith drew up at the gate and made a great bustle of unloading boxes and bags and putting them in the right places, while Anne subsided on the back steps, limp with happiness. She couldn't talk; she could only feel. And when Mr. Smith came out and asked whether she had ordered any groceries for over Sunday, she could only shake her head at him in blissful inertia.

In a moment he was busy with a notebook. "I'll send up some things to eat from the village," he promised. "Leave the order now as I go down the hill. I hate to hurry off like this, but I've got to meet a prospect on the three-thirty." He looked at his watch twice in quick succession. "You won't be lonesome, will you? . . . Well, good-bye . . . I'll send up everything."

And he was gone.

It was heavenly, being all alone with it. The sun shone hot. Heat-haze drifted in long veils above the river. The hollyhocks were going to seed. Crickets scraped their tiny fiddles in the long grass. Peacetime—endless time—not a tube to catch —not a tram nor a fire-engine passing. Just August sunshine and the world all yours.

It was only the sun—which grew hotter as the afternoon stole by—that ever moved

THE
30's

Stephenson's floor polish

Easy and quick to apply. Fresh and antiseptic. Labour - saving and inexpensive! Stephenson's multiplies many times the life and beauty of linoleums, parquet, etc. Its bright polish wears well. Be sure to ask for STEPHENSON'S

Tins 3d., 6d., 9d., 1/- and 1/9

Sole Manufacturers :
STEPHENSON BROTHERS, LTD.
BRADFORD

IF YOU LIKE SARDINES

YOU WILL LIKE NORWEGIAN BRISLING *better* !

NORWEGIAN BRISLING IN OLIVE OIL OR TOMATO SAUCE

NORWAY

For supper to-night

The official seal is the sign of Genuine *Norwegian* Brisling — look for it on every tin.

The Seal of   Quality.

A House Needs a Husband

(*Continued*)

Anne from the steps. She strayed into the cool shade of the little house and looked about her with an air of a queen. The little parlour with its wide brick hearth—a bright bronze square above the mantel where Maria's crayon enlargement had once hung. A bright square on the threadbare carpet where the marble-top table had once stood. Against the inside wall another bright oblong where the organ had spent its life. Bereft of their presence the room was charming. That one tiny table was perfect, with the funny little sofa pulled out beside the fireplace— and as soon as Anne's fat little coffee set was on it——

Frantically she jerked the two pieces into position and then tore out to the kitchen for her box. The coffee set was in it. She could have it unpacked and in place, in three minutes. Actually it was only two. She stood and looked at it in sheer beaming happiness.

She rushed upstairs and hung guest towels in the bathroom. Rushed down to try her lovely square of old brocade on the unfaded wall. Rushed to unpack her treasured blue bowl and fill it with a tangle of pink and lavender flowers for the middle shelf of the what-not. Her best blue tea-cloth went on the bare old table, with an old tall goblet of pink roses in the centre.

Three bedrooms upstairs. She tried them all, and immediately chose the smallest, with the sloping roof, because its gabled windows looked straight out over the blue river. "I can see it even when I sleep," she thought happily.

She hung her nightgown and her best kimono in the cupboard, arranged her twenty ivory elephants in a triumphal march across the top-heavy old bureau, and was at home.

It was just a little unfortunate that they all three came along on the first evening. It did not seem unfortunate in the beginning, but in the beginning Anne had not the least idea that they were all coming. Mr. Smith came first, just to make sure that the groceries had arrived. And as he hadn't thought to order matches, he went straight back for them in his car, leaving Anne his own box to start with. There was no telephone yet—although it had been promised two weeks ago—and besides, Anne hadn't thought of eating, until Mr. Smith's coming made her investigate the groceries.

She started off happily to make a cheese omelette—and tea—and when Mr. Smith came back, she could no less than ask him to supper. He had had his supper, but he would have a cup of tea, he said—and some cheese omelette, he said later— and just one small piece of toast—and some strawberry jam—and one of those small cakes—and shouldn't he make some coffee?

It was all perfectly natural—and Anne really couldn't have done anything else— but it was unfortunate when Walter and Tom walked in unannounced (there being no telephone) that she and Mr. Smith were sitting at supper together looking positively domestic—as she thought bitterly.

Mr. Smith made it all the worse, too, by being so hospitable. He urged them to have some supper, and dashed out after more coffee quite as if he had been doing the cooking there for years. Anne became very stiff as he became warmer. And Mr. Smith grew more and more hospitable every moment to make up for it. And what were Walter and Tom to think? Anne had never mentioned Mr. Smith in telling about the house. She had said she bought it through an estate-agent, and Tom, who had once gone house-hunting with her—and an estate-agent with one eye—had held the picture as the universal type for that profession. He was far from suspecting that this fresh young stranger in the extremely good clothes was another of the same.

Soon Walter, who never really liked anyone to get ahead of him, and Mr. Smith were hard at it, suggesting improvements and bragging about just what they could do to this house if Anne would only have the hammer and nails and a few bits of board ready the next time they came.

It sounded to Anne as if she might get a good deal of work done about the house, if only their rivalry continued. But finally, when they began elaborating on the exact technique for putting in hooks, and how many taps of a hammer ought to drive a nail, she slipped out to the kitchen on the vague plea of something to see to.

Mr. Smith was leaving, Anne found, when she went in, blinking at the light. He had a big day to-morrow, he apologised. His farewell was friendly— Had he always been as friendly as this? Anne wondered dazedly.

He swung out of the door and into the car. A wave of his hand, a long *ah-oorah* at the turn far below. And Anne was left with Tom and Walter, to explain—if she could—everything.

They wouldn't ask her anything, she soon found out wretchedly. They wanted to know, so they wouldn't ask her. She had to tell them all by herself—just like turning a back somersault.

"Isn't Mr. Smith nice!" she testified conscientiously, wanting all the while to wring his neck. "He has been so kind to me all along. He is the estate-agent from whom I bought the place."

"Nice chap!" agreed Tom—good old Tom! "His coffee was a life-saver after climbing that hill . . . Wish I could cook —or nail things . . . Twenty-one years in a flat doesn't fit a man for housework."

"You ought to be able to paint," insinuated Anne hopefully. "I should certainly think that a man who can paint a picture could paint woodwork. The house is full of it—all brown—and I want it all, every bit of it, white."

"Why, I guess I could," brightened Tom. "Count on me for the painting. I'll paint the woodwork while Walter puts hooks in the walls."

Walter became his most superior self again. "Well, you may find that painting woodwork isn't so easy," he discouraged. "There's quite a knack in painting woodwork. Perhaps I can give you a start."

"All advice thankfully received," said Tom, and for a wonder meant it.

"We'll have to step or we'll miss that train," said Walter, who was always on time as well as right.

So they stepped, and Anne was left alone with her house and the summer night.

For a moment she dropped into the sunken old rocking-chair at her window and looked out on her garden in the moonlight, on the old apple-tree that would be a bouquet of pink and white in spring. And then, all of a sudden the first warning came to Anne with a shock. She wanted someone to show it to—someone to adore it with her—someone to praise and exclaim and criticise and play with.

Not once, in her years in a crowded city had Anne been lonely. Now, safe in her own home, she suddenly realised that a house needs more than one person—and that the person her house needed was a man—to saw the dead limbs off the apple tree, to nail up her square of brocade where she had pinned it, to take up the parlour carpet, and nail the roof on the

(Continued overleaf)

"YOU MAKE THEM TOO WELL"

Testimonial No. 1095

16 INCH 43/-
14 INCH 39/-
COMPLETE WITH
MANGLING BOARD

• GUARANTEED
FOR FIVE YEARS
BRIGHTENS
A LIFETIME

ACME WRINGER
Wrings the heaviest blanket dry

Write to-day for free booklet No. V.6, "This Woman's Freedom," ACME WRINGERS LTD., David Street, GLASGOW, S.E.

". . . it has been in daily use for 10 years . . . rollers as good as new. It has many years of use still in it. I can only say you make them too well, for this one will not wear out. It's a wringer which I can recommend as the best."

Every day letters arrive saying how much drier the ACME wrings everything, from the heaviest blanket to the filmiest undies.

Work is reduced to a minimum; less ironing is necessary and there is more time for recreation. 1,500,000 women are to-day using ACME Wringers. They would not use any other, so well does it satisfy their requirements on washing day. Let your ironmonger, hardware or furnishing store show you the ACME Wringer and Table Mangle; it is adaptable for fitting almost anywhere.

THE
30's

A House Needs a Husband
(Continued)

woodshed, and prop up the porch, and polish the sixteen-inch boards which Mr. Barnes had told her were under the parlour carpet. . . .

This house was a life work for a man, Anne pondered. And suddenly another thought came to her, and at the same time thrilled her with a dreadful and delicious certainty.

"I bet you I get married," she thought with horrified decision. "I bet you I do."

Anne thought she managed very cleverly for the next Sunday. She specifically invited Walter to come up for the Sunday after next; then Friday, after the office, she and Tom went shopping happily for brushes and thinner and white enamel —pounds and pounds they bought in an orgy of enthusiasm.

Tom brought it all up with him by the first train Sunday morning, and they had breakfast together on the back steps, with the courses set out in order from top to bottom. Grapefruit first—broiled ham and eggs and piles of hot toast in covered dishes on the second—and coffee on the third—while they sat on the lowest step with their feet in the pansy bed, and the blue sky beamed down.

Never was there such a day, never such food. Full of energy—and ham—they went busily in, shoving the dishes comfortably under the stove, where they would be out of the way.

Tom started on the high part of the stairs and Anne on the low part, newspapers on the floor, newspapers on Tom for an apron, Anne in her worst smock sitting cross-legged on the floor with a newspaper in her lap. Her hair curled tighter and tighter as she worked, from heat and excitement. The smell of paint made her eyes smart, but she kept bravely on.

Tom worked with the intent gaze of an artist, slapping, slapping. A warm breeze fanned through the little hall. Anne could smell the worn matting even through the paint. She was happy, happy, happy —painting her very own house with Tom to help her.

"How am I doing it, Tom?" she asked anxiously. "Is it all right? I never painted anything in my life before."

Tom came down from the kitchen stool to look. "Wonderful!" he praised. "You're doing a better job than I am. Look—mine's lots more uneven."

Anne pulled herself up by his big, painty hand and inspected. "I believe mine *is* the best," she gloated. "But you go a lot faster, Tom. I've only done two steps, and you've done five."

"We'll both be experts by the time this job is done," Tom assured her.

As they settled to their work again, so intently that only Anne—from the corner of her eye—saw something big and dark blotting out the square of sunlight that was the front door.

She turned—if it wasn't Walter, looking very much ashamed of himself, but still brazening it out!

"Just thought I'd drop in and see how the painting was getting on," he announced loudly.

Anne fixed him with a glare, then melted because she was so eager to praise.

"Look!" she boasted.

Tom smiled down from the stool.

Walter looked—stepped up—stepped back squinted critically. "Either of you ever do any painting before?" he inquired.

"Only on canvas," Tom deprecated cheerfully.

"I thought not," condoled Walter. "You know, there's quite a knack to it. It goes this way . . ." He reached a hand.

"Lend me your brush a minute, Anne," he asked. "I think I can show Tom how it goes."

He made a long, slow, practised stroke or two. "There! See? With the grain."

"I get you," agreed Tom, and went back to his stool.

"No, *this* way," corrected Walter. "Keep your wrist like this."

Tom watched and watched. Anne sat in a chair and wished for her brush.

"Better just watch me for a while till you get the hang of it," Walter advised, painting on and on, smoothly, beautifully.

The sound of a horn cut the slapping of the brushes. Anne disappeared through the kitchen to the yard. Already she knew the sound of that horn.

It was fifteen minutes before Tom joined her.

"What's the matter?" she snapped. "Why aren't you painting? *You've* got a brush!"

Try as she might, Anne could not keep an edge of injury from her tone. Tom was lighting his pipe, slowly, reflectively.

"No, I haven't," he contradicted mildly.

"Then I'm going in and use it," threatened Anne. "I want to paint."

"I wouldn't," dissuaded Tom between puffs. "You see—Smith's got it. He's —showing Walter—how."

Anne looked at him, and then a smile painted her lips. Tom's eyes twinkled at her through pipe smoke. They laughed together.

It went right on from there. Tom, Walter, Mr. Smith—Mr. Smith, Tom, Walter—Walter, Mr. Smith, Tom. The order of their coming varied, but inevitably, if one came, they all came.

"I ought to do something to discourage them," she fretted conscientiously. "I oughtn't to let them spend so much of their time on the house, bless it!— Because of course I'm not going to marry either of them——"

"Either of them——" not "any of them." Anne caught herself up with a blush and began to plan ways to discourage people.

"Three men are too many," she repeated with conviction, and as if in answer, she heard a long *ah-oorah*, far down the hill. Mr. Smith was arriving first to-day.

Anne got up from the back steps and went hastily around to the front porch. She hoped to head him off there and keep him from seeing that a whole, long strip of guttering, eaten into lacework by the years, had parted from its moorings and swayed like a broken reed from the mouldy eaves.

But it was no use. Mr. Smith made the tour of the premises every time he came, noting the repairs and the dilapidations with a catalogue eye. It wasn't five minutes before he saw the wreck and went poking about to make sure that all the other guttering was in equally tragic ruin.

"Have to put on new guttering right away," he decided briskly for her. "Let's see—twenty feet—thirty feet—probably cost about twelve pounds. Let me know exactly what it comes to, so I can enter it in the book."

He was always doing that—entering in some unsympathetic ledger all the repairs on the poor old house, and balancing them off against some mythical compensatory column headed "Improvement value." Anne hated it. She didn't like admitting the extravagance of her home.

"Have to have a new roof, soon," Mr. Smith went on. "Perhaps you'd better do that at the same time. One winter can damage your house more than the improvement would cost."

(Continued overleaf)

THE
30's

THE
30's

A House Needs a Husband
(*Continued*)

"How much is a roof?" Anne inquired
in a small, discouraged voice.

"Oh, about fifty pounds ought to
cover it," estimated Mr. Smith cheerily.

"Fifty pounds!" Anne mourned.

"Oh, you'll have to expect that," Mr.
Smith enthused. "There are always
plenty of repair bills on these old houses."

"Perhaps you think I oughtn't to have
bought this place," Anne burst out in ex-
asperation. "Perhaps you think I was
foolish!"

Mr. Smith looked genuinely shocked. "I
should say *not*," he emphasised sincerely.
"I never said anything like that!" he denied, putting his pencil and paper away.
"I never thought anything like that. On
the contrary! Cleverest thing I ever saw,
the way you got this off the old boy. Take
it from me, *we'll make a lot of money off
this some day.*"

There was a hot, throbbing silence,
which Mr. Smith employed by turning as
red as a fair young man with good
healthy blood pressure can turn.

Anne's blue eyes blazed at him. She
said nothing—absolutely nothing—not a
single solitary word.

Mr. Smith began to stammer his way
back. "You see—this land's going up in
value all the time—and some day the house
will actually be gone—and so will Old
Man Barnes, of course—and then it'll sell
for a nice profit for you—out of which I'll
have a good commission, of course . . ."

He was almost back in his glib, young,
estate-agent manner by the time he finished.
But Anne knew—and Mr. Smith knew she
knew.

He left after a little vague conversation,
as he went, thriftily retrieving a neat
parcel he had left on the porch as he came
in, which bore a striking resemblance to
a two-pound box of chocolates.

"Well, so long," he waved in his accus-
tomed farewell, and stepped on the ac-
celerator.

The blue car turned the corner at more
than its usual speed.

Anne waited. Far down the hill the
horn sounded—*Ah-oorah*—farewell. Mr.
Smith had gone out of her life for ever.

There were just two of them, now, to
clutter up the house. It began to seem
almost big enough, again.

Tom and Walter—Walter and Tom.
Anne began to feel dreadfully conscience-
striken about Walter. He was being so
methodical in his courtship. He was doing
so much work on the house. Anne knew
he meant business.

"He wouldn't be wasting all this time
and work, if he didn't have intentions,"
Anne decided shrewdly.

After all, Walter was honest, Walter
was loyal, Walter was dependable—but
reckless philanthropy was no part of his
nature. Anne was foolish about her house
—but not about Walter. He was a dear
but not a darling—and there is all the
difference in the world between the two.

Walter kept on and kept on. Sometimes Anne wondered how he could. He
developed a proprietorial way of striding
about the place, noting the improvements
he had made and estimating the increase
in value therefrom. He expatiated on the
benefits of country life, and how fit nailing up woodsheds and flooring the porch
had made him feel.

Many a time Anne longed to tell him
she wouldn't—couldn't—ever—in a million
years—but it seemed rather presuming,
before she was sure. And then one day—
a Saturday—she was sure.

Walter never came on Saturday after-

noons. They were devoted to cultivating
the odds and ends of outside practice
which were finally to release him from
the grind at the office. Walter would
never squander a sacred Saturday without
a worthy object—and with a dreadful
sinking at the heart Anne realised that
she was it.

There was an air of suppressed triumph
about him, too, that was just a few degrees higher in temperature than his usual
bland assurance. Anne's heart fluttered.
Poor Walter! She did hate to hurt him,
so. But she would be as gentle as possible—and always be his dearest friend—
and invite him up Sundays quite often—
but nowhere near so often as he had been
coming for the last three months.

All afternoon he went about with
the same air of calm expectancy, but without a word of betrayal. It got on Anne's
nerves terribly.

The little table drawn up by the bright
coals was an irresistible invitation to
domesticity, but Walter waited. Waited
until the supper dishes were whisked away,
and the little table was folded and restored
to its kennel under the stairs, and Anne
was curled up on her big cushion on the
hearth opposite him.

For a long fifteen minutes they sat
silent, Anne's hair in bright crinkles, blue
eyes intent on the embers, her profile sweet
and girlish in the half-light.

At last Walter cleared his throat.
Walter pulled down his vest. Walter
arranged his hands. Anne could just see
him doing it to a jury. Well, why not.
If she was a jury, she would probably be
impressed. But she wasn't a jury.

"A fire-side is the ideal place for
confidences," stated Walter. "And I have
a confidence to make to you to-night,
Anne."

That much he had written out and re-
hearsed, realised Anne. Would it all be
like a speech? she wondered. She could
not look at him, but the softness of her
profile in the firelight was a temptation to
continue.

"I have not lived my life without a
plan," orated Walter. "Always I have
seen in the future—a home—a wife—
perhaps, some day—kiddies—kiddies of our
own."

This was terrible, thought Anne. What
on earth could she do? In her worst
horrors she had never imagined anything
so terrible as this.

"But I am an honest man," declaimed
Walter. "I know what is due to a woman
who blindly entrusts her future—and the
future of her kiddies—to the strength of
a man's endeavours. And I had carefully set a mark at which marriage would
be financially safe. A mark after which
I could go to any man and ask for
his daughter with integrity, saying 'Here
are my advantages, here are my disadvantages. This is the provision I can make
for a wife—not luxurious perhaps, but
firm-founded. And my prospects—as
nearly as the laws of chance can be calculated—are thus and so.'"

The tide of Walter's eloquence flowed
irresistibly on. Would it never turn?
thought Anne.

"This, I say, was my settled purpose.
I thought nothing could sway me from
it. But you, Anne, have changed my
mind."

Anne's look was horrified—but Walter
did not see it. He was caught in the
rushing current of his own oration. Soon
he would be sunk. Anne put out a hand
to stop him, but he waved her aside, and
something Hazel's grandmother had told
them long ago came to her mind now when
she needed it most.

"Never refuse a proposal until you've got it, dearies," the old lady used to tell them. "The only thing worse than refusing a gentleman when he has offered himself, is to refuse him when he hasn't."

"I have seen," perorated Walter, "how much happiness you have found even in this little home. I have experienced, myself, the simple, elemental joy in improving, repairing, decorating. It has been a vicarious joy, it is true, but I have learned from it how much pleasure I should feel in caring for my own house with my own hands.

"I have also kept careful accounts, and I see the old aphorism that two can live as cheap as one is more nearly true than I had thought. Two can live for about once and a half times the cost of one, and with infinitely more comfort. The advantages of home cooking, of shirts done exactly as one prefers them, of socks darned and buttons replaced—not to speak of the value of wifely devotion—are surely worth the slightly increased cost they would demand."

Anne's eyes began to blaze. Of all the conceit! Stop him now? Never! Let him sink. She might even push him under, herself.

"I have found—that is, Smith has found for me—a small, new bungalow with a verandah, which can be bought for a fraction of its value. The owner's wife ran away with the interior decorator, and therefore he has taken a dislike to the property and will sacrifice it for a quick sale. Payments on this will not equal my hotel bill in the city. And there is every reason to believe that appreciation in value will soon equal the small down payment which I shall make.

"With all this in mind, I have decided to delay marriage no longer—and it is you, Anne, who has made this radical change in my plans.

"I do not know whether I have ever told you—I am not by nature very communicative on my private affairs—that for some years, now, I have had an understanding with a young girl in my native town. She is the only daughter of a former mayor—beautiful, talented, a social star in every respect.

"I think the time has come to put an end to her waiting—and our happiness is all due to you, Anne. I wanted you to be the first to know—I shall write the good news to Helen, herself, to-morrow."

Anne turned red, turned white. She gasped and rose to shake hands with Walter. Relief, horror, joy, fury, shock, murder—gave a slight hysteria to her congratulations.

Walter stood beaming at her, bland, complacent, innocent.

"You'll always be our friend, Anne," he promised benevolently. "Our very best friend. I am sure I can speak for Helen as well as for myself. Oh, I've written Helen a great deal about you. There's nothing like the friendship of a good woman for a fellow alone in the city. Keeps him out of temptation, you know, and all that."

And Anne was sweet and interested and delightful. The rage boiling in her added sparkle to her blue eyes and a dangerous crimson to her lips. She questioned and approved and praised until Walter was in a transport—a dignified of self-satisfaction and complacency.

"The best friend a man ever had," he repeated solemnly when he took his leave. It was a benediction.

The wind must have caught the door. It slammed. Anne stood leaning against it, her under lip tight under her teeth.

"The idiot!" she said viciously. "I hate him!"

And then, suddenly, she found that she was crying. Damply she turned off lights

(Continued overleaf)

Letters from Mary Goodbody

Such stuff as Blues are made on

My dear Ronnie,

I hear from Peter you're in the running for your Blue. I'm so glad! We haven't had a Blue in the family since your Great-uncle James played chess for Oxford.

And to think that only a year ago one set at tennis used to tire you out! But I always did say it was largely a matter of your food, and Dr. Carter agreed. It was he who put you on to that scrunchy Vita-Weat instead of ordinary bread. Well, I know what Vita-Weat has done for me and my indigestion, and I'm delighted to know it has worked such wonders with you.

I imagine you won't ever again go stodging yourself on masses of undercooked starch. Dr. Carter says Vita-Weat contains—but there, I expect you learn all about vitamins and such-like things at Cambridge . . . .

Vita-Weat

THE BREAD OF NEW HEALTH

Cartons at 1/6 and 10d.
Packets at 6d. and 2d.

MADE BY PEEK FREAN

Makers of Famous Biscuits

THE 30's

105

THE
30's

106

A House Needs a Husband
(Continued)

and banked fires and went upstairs to the comfort of her own room. Outside, braving the rain, the little pine tree Tom had planted for her stood staunch in its place. It would always be there.

A smile broke through. So would Tom always be there. She said herself to sleep with a little refrain,

"To-morrow, Tom will be here—to-morrow—to-morrow."

It was still raining on Sunday morning, but Anne scattered sunshine through the house for Tom. November dripped down in an icy deluge that froze and glittered on the pickets and dangled in icicles from the rosebushes. But Anne did not even feel it. She was lighting a blazing fire, and placing a bowl of the last gold chrysanthemums on each of the four windowsills. She wore her best new blue and white silk dress, and matched it with a blue and white tablecloth.

This would be the day. Mr. Smith disposed of long ago—and Walter would be writing the good news to his Helen. Anne gave a vicious little poke at the fire. She had not yet begun to think Walter funny. He was too much of a blow to her conceit, to her intelligence, to her pride.

Tom usually came on the 11.36, but the taxis laboured up the hill in a slipping stream and slid gracefully back. Anne looked and looked, her nose flattened against the front window, but it was no use. He must have missed the train. No chance now until the 12.45.

Anne gave everything another twitch, poked all the pillows, and banked the fire. Nothing to do but sit down and admire her new blue shoes, which just exactly matched the blue checks in her dress and her own blue eyes.

Twelve-forty-five at last. Taxis up, taxis down—a curl of dark smoke streaking the river's grey far below—no Tom. No Tom on the 2.16—no Tom on the 3.45. No Tom on the 5.17—no Tom on the 7.53. Anne was boiling with impatience. Just like Tom—missing all those trains—just like him, the big, stupid, lazy thing!—while she slaved all day to get his dinner.

At ten o'clock the ghastly fear that she had been refusing to look at all day turned into a sickening certainty. Tom was not coming. Probably had never meant to come.

Anne looked around, and the house no longer smiled. It seemed somehow to resemble the hotel room she had left behind her in the city. Empty and cold and forbidding.

Well, it was all she had. The house, at least, had never forsaken her. It had always been there every Sunday. It always would. She could depend on it. She would never trust any man again. She would just live for her house. . . .

Anne put her head down on her knees and cried the blue-and-white silk limp.

If it killed her, Anne swore to herself, she would not let Tom know she minded. She would be fresh and frivolous. She would hint at another man. She would be sweet—she must be careful not to be too sweet—and she would just quietly and elusively never see him again.

She was late, too, and she would pretend it was because she had been out to a party somewhere last night—though it was really because she had stopped to place the order for a new roof.

She fixed her face before she went into the office—a bright, bright smile and two happy eyes. She sickened at herself even as she smirked her way down the long room.

Suddenly she stopped still. Tom's desk was vacant. Clean and clear of pictures and lay-outs. No smelly pipe balanced on the extreme corner. No hat and big coat hanging on the peg.

"Where's Tom?" Anne heard herself asking terribly, dramatically, through a determination not to say one single word.

"Oh, didn't you know?" said Miss Beeson. "He's home ill—threatened with pneumonia, I believe Walter said."

Walter—Anne flew to the little mahogany sanctum of the legal department.

"What's the matter with Tom?" she burst out. "When did you hear from him?"

Walter's smug face changed to an unaccustomed expression of self-reproach. "Oh, I say! Tom sent you a message yesterday. I forgot."

"How is he *now*?" demanded Anne. "Is he very ill? What did he say?"

"Why, he didn't come in Saturday morning," reflected Walter. "And I stopped to return an umbrella, and he couldn't speak above a whisper. I made him call a doctor, and he was ordered to stay in bed or he would have pneumonia. He told me to tell you he couldn't come Sunday—but my mind was too taken up with romance. . . ." He smiled and dismissed the subject. "I have *Her* picture in the back of my watch. Did I ever show it to you?"

Anne stared at him for a long moment. "*Oh!*" she said breathlessly. Just, "*Oh!*"

She turned and ran to the lift, was out on the street and hailing a taxi in a moment that seemed an hour to her.

"Nineteen more minutes—eighteen more minutes—seventeen more minutes——" she counted through her prayers.

Round the corner—turn again—stop.

She threw the driver the note she had been fluttering in her fingers ever since they started—tore up the steps—leaned on the bell—burst through the clicking door and dived up the stairs in a panting rush. One flight—two—and—and Tom stood at the top in an old brown dressing-gown, his hair untidy, his eyes red, a disreputable bandage around his neck riding clear to his ear on one side.

"Tom!" Anne gasped. "You haven't got pneumonia? I was scared to death!"

She held on to one of those big, comforting arms, which shoved her gently into the little living-room.

"You're sure you're all right?" she insisted. "Oughtn't you to be in bed?"

"Nonsense!" said Tom in a horrible hoarse whisper. "I'm all right. Just got a cold. Can't talk."

"I thought the house had killed you," said Anne with dreadful calmness. "I thought you had got pneumonia nailing on the roof in the rain. I was going to burn it down—give it away—never see it again. Oh, Tom!"

"If you like me better than the house, there must be hope," reasoned Tom, his arms about her. "How about it, Anne? Let's get married!"

A little smile kept twitching Anne's lips and the corners of her eyes. "Well, the house needs a husband," she tried to say demurely.

"Darn the house!" said Tom in a husky croak. "Anne—Anne!"

"And I think I do, too," she admitted.

Her head went down on the brown dressing-gown shoulder. It was just as comforting as she had always thought it would be.

Home wasn't a home after all, she thought. It was a place in someone's heart.

United for Service

What a Cheerful Room!

The heart gives a leap of pleasure as you enter—where, beneath dainty shades, gaslight in all its brilliant softness pours, and cosy warmth steals from the radiant gas fire to enfold you.

A room where you can "listen-in" in luxury, a room to work in, to rest in, to sing in—the sanctuary of family happiness.

✠   ✠   ✠

THE B.C.G.A.
representing the British Gas Industry, is at the service of the public, without charge, for advice and help on any subject, large or small, connected with the economical and efficient use of gas in home, office or factory. . . .

A letter to the Secretary of this Association will receive prompt and careful attention.

Gas Fire facts free on application.

THE
30's

THE BRITISH COMMERCIAL GAS ASSOCIATION
30, GROSVENOR GARDENS, WESTMINSTER, S.W.I.

Should we retire

Illustrations by
Arthur Wragg

"Of all the things I want most of life, I should like back my thirtieth to my thirty-fifth year and to be compelled not to work in them."

THAT remarkably brilliant hotel-keeper, Lady Honywood recently stated in an interview that she owed her success in business to the fact that she had had her fun in life first. After exhausting the pleasures of Society she found herself the better able to concentrate undividedly upon business.

Ever since I read her revelations upon this subject I have been pondering more and more upon their wisdom. The lady is perfectly right. A bold assertion— but then bold assertions were ever the mark of your convert! Never attempt to prove a dogma, wrote Cardinal Newman. Assert it. Any attempt at proof suggests the idea that the dogma needs proof. This may shake faith. Therefore—assert. Simply assert.

The usual plan of present-day *bourgeoisie,* or *booboisie,* to use Mencken's very proper version of the word, is to sacrifice the precious years of life the twenties, thirties and forties, sometimes even the fifties, to hard grinding. Then if investments have not all gone phut, or if a firm will pension one off, a last decade or so may be spent in spraying the green fly off the roses or becoming the supreme authority in the local archæological circle.

Is this good enough?

No.

All the truly wise people have told us so since the dawn of time. *Carpe diem,* sang Horace. Labour is vanity, recorded the learned writer of Ecclesiastes. Dear old Montaigne knew all about it too. Does anyone read Michel, Seigneur de Montaigne nowadays? It is a grief to me that I have not known him all my days. In his thirty-second Essay he tells us the different ways in which he ordered his life and affairs and how in his third condition he came to a sort of reformation which was that "I live at the height of my revenue . . . and content myself with having sufficient for the present." "Everyone is the hammerer of his own fortune and an uneasie, necessitous, busie man, seems to me more miserable than he that is simply poor."

Cicero knew all this long before the Sieur de Montaigne thought it out —"Not to be covetous, *is* money; not to be a spender is a positive gain," was how he expressed the matter.

Yet we go on giving our golden youths to the increase of whatever is material and spend so much energy in preparing for living that Life has gone by the time we set about living it. If Youth but knew! If Age but Could!—as the French epigram tersely sums up the problem. But the Machine of Work, of Convention, of all the myriad rules of our *booboisie* pinion us down at every moment. The glorious sun shines on river, forest, sea and mountain—all nearly empty for most of the year, whilst thousands of us sit in offices, banks and Courts of Law, listening to organised dullness; or may be heightening the dust-heap ourselves. And then by way of relaxation we do a crossword puzzle and don't win the £2,000 prize. Is it all good enough?

Reformers deluge us with plans about Utopias of various kinds. Having no ambition to join their ranks, and feeling no very acute anxiety for the future of Futility, no moral compulsion urges me to propound panaceas. If I did, it would be something of this nature. No work up to the age of seven. Work from seven to fourteen. Fun from fourteen to seventeen. Work from seventeen to twenty. Any amount of travel and recreation from twenty to thirty, with an optional break for work at twenty-six or so. Work again from thirty to thirty-five for those who have not fallen into the work at twenty-six trap. From thirty-five to forty the last long free period. Work from forty till death, with every third six-month period free from work. These periods are elastic and subject to free re-arranging in individual interests.

In that way we could take our fun whilst we had physical energy enough to appreciate it, and could lay up a stock of energy to carry through the difficult late middle years until old age.

Old age pensions could be abolished together with almost all retiring allowances. I honestly do not care one atom about the economics of this system in the

"The glorious sun shines on river, forest, sea and mountain, while thousands sit in Courts of Law listening to organised dullness . . ."

before working ?

Why not let people have leisure to enjoy their youth ? Why not let them settle down to steady work only when they reach the age of forty ? Both the individual and the nation would benefit thereby—or so in this amusingly propounded article says

HELENA NORMANTON

". . . any amount of travel and recreation from twenty to thirty."

". . . work from forty till death, with every third six-month period free."

sense that I have any preferences how it could be financed. Civilisations which can waste money as we do can easily re-allot it, once the desire arises. At present we want security by armaments or work-free old ages, or a new car every year, or a million workless people to keep, and whichever of these fads we opt for, as a community we more or less obtain them. Personally, of all the things I want most of life, I should like back my thirtieth to my thirty-fifth year and to be compelled not to work in them. Looking back at the work I did in those five years, which were hard ones, I think that the loss of what I then did would not matter now nearly as much as the having lost them matters to myself. What I do recall about them is that the hours of God's daylight were passed in some of the most hideous buildings that ever were perpetrated by the mind of any architect and the hand of any builder. Nor was I unique in that experience. Others have had some, too, and I feel for them.

"But isn't this very hard on the aged?" I can visualise an intelligent interlocutor aching to inquire. Perhaps. But why not? Why all this sentiment about age? Isn't it because we immure old people and fret them into frailty that younger people's lives have to be wasted in sacrifice to them? Why not let old people have a chance of prolonging their not-so-oldishness by feeling that there is room and use for them in the general system of industry and the professions? Then if they really become beyond work they might have the choice of a nice lethal chamber, or of living on in whatever mode they or their friends would devise—perhaps in chaperoning or companioning the young during their leisure years and in keeping well-intentioned people from worrying over the hikers. Youth, middle-age, and retired age would have some time for each other under my plan, and could get to know and appreciate each other's merits.

Necessarily it would involve putting all the hardest strain and burden of our complex of civilised work upon the middle-aged, or even on the relatively young. And so much the better. Their minds are not tired. If there is one thing which curses us to-day more than another it is the tired-mindedness of the old gentlemen who run us.

Look at our Cabinet. All seventyish. Look at our Railway Directors. Seventy-fivish. If you feel that's not so bad, turn to the financial page of your daily paper and look at the capital values of the railway stocks, and what the poor old souls have managed to lose for their shareholders. The dear old things didn't see what motor-traffic was going to do, and they don't see now what aviation is going to do. Not they. They feel that the railway improvements of the sixties were going it a bit strong. Look at the Royal Academy—and at its annual show (if you can bear to).

It is only to a body such as the House of Lords to which age is not necessarily the passport that one dare look to-day for a gleam of original thought or independence of outlook. Every other institution we have is tired, tired because it is clustered up with elderly sages, who ought to be doing merely the light routine work suited to their declining powers. If one took the Chairman and Directors away from our great industrial concerns and let them toddle round and collect the money from automatic machines, as an easy open-air activity suitable for their health, and substitute the forty to sixty group of men and women to run the big concerns, things would be infinitely better for all.

JANE FARLEY plans
A Single-handed

Scale : ¼ *in.* = 5 *ft.*

FRUIT TREES

HERBACEOUS BORDER

THE

BED

BED

HOUSE

WHAT is the ideal size of garden for a middle-aged woman to work single-handed?

The question obtruded itself as I determinedly planted out sweet-peas one glorious spring morning, firmly ignoring the claims of spinach, beetroot, and saladings clamouring to be sown, of lawns demanding the mower, and asparagus beds craving for soot and salt, even turning a reluctantly blind eye to tea-roses as yet un-pruned. A few only, these, of the tasks that crowd upon one who struggles alone with a garden planned in more spacious days. How big a garden could one cultivate entirely satisfactorily, without either calling in the help of " Edwards "—immortalised by Barry Pain—or, alternatively depriving oneself of legitimate time " for to admire and for to see," as Kipling has it ?

Gradually the garden took shape, and by the time the last sweet-pea was in position it had assumed a definite form in my mind. So, too, had the Gardener. Her name was Penelope, and she was a woman-with-a-job! The Garden was her hobby, and save for saladings and fruit trees, would be devoted to flowers. To it she was prepared to give an average of an hour's work a day, making up in spring and summer for the idle days of winter.

Running between one fence and a lawn, 39 feet by 24, I planned for Penelope a six-foot wide herbaceous border, of delphiniums, phlox, anchusas, helenium, cat-mint, Michaelmas daisies, and the like, all long-blooming, ornamental, and hardy subjects. At the end of the lawn there was to be a bed of bush roses, 15 feet by 30, backed by a fence of ramblers.

Near the house two flower-beds, for wallflowers, snap-dragons, or penste-

mons, in their season, were to be set, in a paved or gravelled space for sitting out on damp days. A three-foot path divided the lawn from a narrow border, bounded by the other long fence. This was to be devoted to annuals—misty blue love-in-the-mist, azalea-like godetia, " Queen Anne's Thimble," Virginian stock, to name a very few.

Fruit trees could be trained along the fences, and beyond the rambler roses there would be room for lettuce and reserve beds, frames, a small tool-house, and an incinerator.

Behold Penelope, then, one September morning, surveying her kingdom. During preceding weeks the beds and borders have been prepared, the path has been made, the lawn laid, and tool-house and rose fence, of larch poles, have been erected.

Probably Penelope's thoughts

will turn first to the fruit trees which are to be trained against the walls. It will save much delay at planting time in November if the holes for the trees can be prepared beforehand. They should be dug about two feet deep and the same in diameter. An iron bar about three feet long, one end tapering, the other provided with a flat head, about four inches in diameter, will be found invaluable for loosening the soil, levering out stones, and ramming earth firmly round the roots. A large flat stone may be placed at the bottom of each hole to discourage downward growth of the roots. Over this should go a layer of good soil. It is essential that the small fibrous roots should be carefully spread out, and fine soil

worked between them. No manure should be given at planting time.

The trees may be placed about eight inches from the wall, and twelve feet apart. Omitting the herbaceous border wall, there will be room for a dozen. A good selection, comprising early and late varieties, would be : dessert apples, Beauty of Bath, James Grieve, Cox's Orange Pippin, Blenheim Pippin,. Laxton's Superb; pears, Jargonelle, William's Bon Chrétien, Pitmaston Duchess; plum, Victoria, or Coe's Golden Drop (a splendid plum, given a warm autumn, but Victoria, being earlier, is more reliable).

Since the soil will not be ready till the spring for annuals and lettuces, both of which need a fine tilth, Penelope may next turn her attention to the beds near the house. Wallflowers and forget-me-nots, both hardy and reliable, will make these gay from April to June. Wallflowers should be put about two inches deeper in the soil than they were in the nursery bed. Planted nine inches apart, it will take sixteen of each to fill a bed three feet by six feet. Twelve inches is near enough in some soils, but these plants look best rather crowded.

A six-foot fence of rambler roses is suggested, both as a background for the bush roses and for a screen. Two ramblers such as Emily Gray (creamy

Wood engravings by Maud Weathered

Garden for PENELOPE

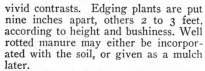

Penelope is any middle-aged woman-with-a-job and her garden is just the right size for her to run as a hobby with an average of an hour's work a day

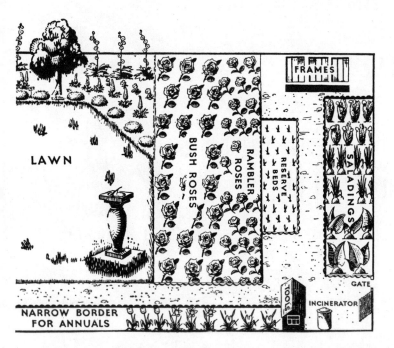

vivid contrasts. Edging plants are put nine inches apart, others 2 to 3 feet, according to height and bushiness. Well rotted manure may either be incorporated with the soil, or given as a mulch later.

Succession of bloom being the primary object, the early summer display might depend for its yellows on aquilegia Chrysantha, coreopsis Grandiflora, and geum Lady Stratheden (all about 2 to 3 feet). Later come helenium Autumnale, chrysanthemums, Florrie Wilkinson and Goldfinder (also of medium height), tall sulphur hollyhocks, and golden-rod.

Geum Mrs. Bradshaw will give a note of brilliant scarlet right up to autumn. Other good red flowers for succession are heuchera Sanguinea, sweet william Scarlet Beauty, pyrethrums James Kelway and General

French (all of medium height), with hollyhocks and red-hot-pokers to give tall spikes of bloom from August to October.

For pink tints heuchera Trevor Pink, and pink lupins might be followed by phlox Elizabeth Campbell and Jules Sandeau, chrysanthemums Normandie and Pink Profusion, hollyhocks, and Michaelmas daisies General Pershing and Barr's Pink.

Additional blue and purple tones might be supplied by columbines, and scabious Causicaa, and white by Achillea, foxgloves, candytuft, and chrysanthemum Framfield Early. Good edging plants are: catmint, with lilac flowers in profusion from May onwards, golden alyssum, violas *(Continued overleaf)*

yellow, almost evergreen), and Alberic Barbier (creamy white), alternating with one of the climbing sports, Climbing Ophelia (salmon blush), Climbing General MacArthur (crimson), will soon cover the 30-foot fence, and provide a long season of bloom.

The rosebed would hold about four dozen bush roses. Penelope, however, would be wise to start with a dozen, and add others later. Betty Uprichard, Madame Butterfly, Venus (pink hybrid teas), Christine, Golden Emblem, Rev. F. Page Roberts (yellow H.T.'s), Lady Hillingdon (apricot tea), Lieutenant Chaure, George Dickson, Red Letter Day, Kirsten Poulsen (red H.T.'s), are a representative selection. Kirsten Poulsen blooms continuously till frosts ap-

pear, and has the habit of a polyantha rose.

November is the best month for planting, and holes may be prepared as for fruit trees. They should be 1½ to 2 feet apart, and, instead of the flat stone, a generous layer of manure, well covered with good soil, should be placed over the loosened sub-soil of each hole.

The great joy of a herbaceous border is the continuous succession of bloom that it can be coaxed to give from spring onwards. Elaborate colour schemes are hardly compatible with this ideal, but it would be quite possible to have, say, a blue corner, at the farther end, where the border curves outward to the lawn. Anchusas Dropmore and Italica, blooming June and July, would make a delightful background, and if cut down after flowering will produce a number of smaller sprays in early autumn. Low growing campanula Carpatica would look well in front, and the intervening space might have campanula Persicifolia, flax, and delphiniums Lize Van Veen, Marie, and Capri. A couple of clumps of Michaelmas daisies, Feltham Blue and Climax, will keep the corner attractive till October.

For the rest, purples and crimsons must not clash, but nearly all the other colours blend happily, especially if pale flowers are introduced to soften too

THE
30's

Sweep your chimneys for the last time this Spring?
Convert your existing fireplace to a
Metro COKE FIRE
Absolutely smokeless, saves money

The "Metro" Coke Fire burns ordinary household coke such as your Gas Company supply, and is kindled without troublesome laying by a gas burner incorporated in the grate, and in about 20 minutes, when the gas is turned off, there is a glowing mass of intense heat, capped with flickering flames having all the psychological appeal of a coal fire, but burns without smoke or soot. This means clean chimneys and rooms, lower decorators' charges, and assisting in abating the smoke nuisance of England.

This shows how simply a tiled grate can be converted to a "Metro" Coke Fire, which is made in various sizes to adapt to any fireplace, and can be done at a surprisingly low cost.

38 Welbeck St. W.1 is a Permanent Exhibition of over 100 Fireplaces which you are cordially invited to inspect without obligation to purchase

Write for full particulars (and give the address of your Gas Office) to SIDNEY FLAVEL & Co., LTD., 19, The Foundries, Leamington, who manufacture and distribute the "Metro" Coke Fire for the South Metropolitan Gas Company.

FLAVELS *of* LEAMINGTON

A Single-handed Garden for Penelope

(Continued overleaf)

cornuta and Maggie Motte, thrift, pinks, and London pride. The last three have attractive winter foliage.

Expenditure will be roughly as follows:

	£	s.	d.
Tools:			
Spade, fork, rake, draw hoe, Dutch hoe, iron bar, trowel, hand-fork, shears, secateurs, pruning knife, syringe, watering-can, basket . . .	2	2	0
Fruit trees:			
11 espalier apples and pears at 10s. 6d. . . .	5	15	6
1 fan-trained plum at 7s. 6d. .		7	6
Roses:			
16 at average 1s. 4d. . .	1	1	4
Herbaceous border:			
100 plants at average 9d. .	3	15	0
Spring beds, prices vary tremendously, say		4	0
Lettuce and annual seeds . .		2	0
12-inch lawn mower and grass box	2	1	4
Wheelbarrow	1	6	0
Small incinerator . .		12	6
Garden frame, one light . .	1	14	0
	£19	1	2

This does not include preliminary outlay on the preparation of beds, tool-house, rose fence and manure, etc.

Taking the average for the year, Penelope's time will be allotted somewhat as follows:

	Hours per Week.
Herbaceous border . . .	2
Narrow border . . .	½
Lawn	½
Fruit trees	½
Roses	¾
Beds	¼
Paths, lettuces, frames, tidying .	1
Total	5¾

By
VERA
BRITTAIN

THE
30's

" If I were to explore a woman's hostel in the evening, I should encounter no bright lights and sociable games. . . . In their small rooms the girls would still be working—not at typing or book-keeping, but at ' saving ' by mending, ironing, etc."

Illustrations by J. H. Dowd

A SHORT time ago a New York doctor discovered a new disease. According to his description it was a nervous ailment, easy to diagnose, though difficult to cure by the usual methods of medicine. Its symptoms included depression, anæmia, listlessness, pallor, and insomnia, but these, its discoverer alleged, were caused not so much by poverty as by restricted, unlovely surroundings and the lack of human companionship. Because he found this disease to be specially characteristic of business girls living in one room, he christened it " one-roomitis."

Many of us who know both England and America will be surprised to find that this particular illness has been named and classified on the other side of the Atlantic. It happens far more often here than in the United States that the depressed manner and jaded appearance of shop assistant or secretary

or typist testify to the lack of some vital quality in the surroundings of nearly all young women who work away from home.

When the American delegation came to London to attend the Naval Conference a year or two ago, the girl secretaries attached to it gave rise to much wondering comment in the Press of this country. English journalists drew attention, with admiring surprise, to their expensive furs, their neat high-heeled shoes, their beautifully waved hair and well-manicured hands. Quite obviously, these young women suffered from no symptoms of inferiority complex; their poise, their self-confidence, their evident ambition, lifted them far above the shrill impertinence and the nervous obsequiousness between which, too often, the shoddily-clad English shorthand-typist alternates unhappily. The respect shown them by their employers, the opportunities offered them

by a new civilisation in which professional and social distinctions have not yet grown rigid, set no limits to the prospects before their bright, undaunted eyes. Above all, the high salaries paid to them made equally accessible their well-cut three-piece suits and the pleasant occupation of their leisure hours in the company of amusing contemporaries belonging to either sex.

It is not in New York or Chicago or San Francisco, but in London and Liverpool and Glasgow, that medical specialists in search of new diseases will discover the largest epidemics of one-roomitis. Not only, as a nation, do we who work in this island still deny the justice of equal pay; we also fail to realise the actual commercial value, in increased energy and reinvigorated spirits, of agreeable surroundings and congenial contacts. Small-scale business and professional women suffer especially from this failure in social

One Roomitis

"Lonely in the midst of a million," with only just enough money to dress, eat, and pay for their hostel cubicles, many girl workers suffer from a social disease unknown to men, since it is the outcome of the difference in conditions and salaries that still, in business, distinguishes the sexes. That such a state of affairs can and must be altered is ably demonstrated in this outspoken article

THE
30's

imagination. Struggling to make ends meet on salaries based upon the assumption that they will cook their solitary egg-suppers on their own little gas-rings, and occupy their free time in washing and mending their short-lived artificial-silk lingerie, they are unable to afford the occasional theatres and cinemas and concerts, the country expeditions and club tickets and library subscriptions, for which their domestically dependent brothers manage to save out of a "man's" rate of pay.

Not once, but many times, have I been depressed and saddened by the conditions under which the poorly-paid women workers of London spend their so-called leisure. The chill stuffiness of boarding-house bedrooms, the atrocious massacre of commonplace food which girls' hostels describe as a meal, make me understand more readily than anything else why well-qualified women, who have spent many years and much money on acquiring an education, throw away without a moment's remorse their hard-earned training in return for the unsatisfactory companionship of a limited young man which is known as marriage, and the narrowing restrictions of a four-roomed villa which can at least be described as home. When Virginia Woolf pointed out the merits of *A Room of One's Own,* she *(Continued overleaf)*

Claude Harris

Personal experiences as a V.A.D. gave Vera Brittain some insight into institutional and "community" life for women, and she believes that restrictive rules, poor pay, and poor accommodation are sapping to an unnecessary degree the health and spirits of numbers of girl workers

One Roomitis

(Continued)

wisely coupled it with five hundred a year. No doubt she realised well enough that the kind of room which can be rented out of three or four pounds a week is hardly likely to inspire original work or even to offer moderate comfort, and, in any case, is seldom one's own.

Once, being then too young to feel as strongly repelled as I now am by stewed gristle and olive-green cabbage-water, I accepted an invitation to dinner at a women's hostel in the neighbourhood of Victoria Station. Most of the inhabitants were class-teachers at secondary or small private schools, though one or two worked as secretaries or in type-writing offices. If Virginia Woolf had seen those cramped, dingy cubicles, with their wall-pegs and their inadequate little dressing-tables crowned by cracked, crazy mirrors which made the worst of each sallow face that looked into them, I think she would have agreed that the small study-bedrooms of Newnham are luxury itself when compared with the surroundings that many women workers too meekly endure. My gloom reached its depths when a peremptory gong sounded, and we perambulated downstairs in a lugubrious crocodile to a semi-lighted underground dining-room, where

One Roomitis

the self-important little woman who presided over a tepid joint from an indeterminate animal frowned disapprovingly upon every late-comer.

To find any parallel in my own life, my memory had to turn back to the War. For the greater part of those years I served abroad in military hospitals, of which the camp life, whatever its trials from wind and cold and rain, bred a cheerful camaraderie that lent humour to discomfort, and was at least free from the competitive indoor stuffiness of closed minds and unwashed curtains. But for one dreadful month between two periods of active service, I was posted to a London civilian hospital which included a few military wards. Fresh from the rough-and-ready plentifulness of Army meals, at which new French butter and green vegetables had been served without stint to the nursing staff, I realised with dismay the low valuation of equally hard-worked civilian women both by the Food Ministry which estimated their requirements, and the hospital authorities who witnessed without perturbation the ruin of the meagre rations permitted them.

The ceremony observed at these unappetising repasts wore the same character of disapproving vigilance as the dinner to which I was invited at the teachers' hostel. The ward where I worked at the extreme other end of the huge building was nearly five minutes' walk away from the dining-room, but "etiquette" and my ward Sister alike forbade me to leave it until the exact hour appointed for luncheon. We were not, however, permitted to run through the passages. At my destination the Matron, with open watch in hand, stood censoriously over the luncheon table, ready to pour a volume of sarcastic reprimand over any V.A.D. who was even half a minute late. Inevitably each luncheon-hour became, for me, a tussle with my ward Sister and an apprehensive scuttle along the corridor, followed by another and worse tussle with the Matron. Had the miserable meal been ten times as appetising as it was, I should never have been able to reach it inconspicuously or eat it with enjoyment. How I welcomed the once-a-week morning off duty, when I could take refuge in a tea-shop and eat my luncheon far from the sight of critical eyes and the sound of scolding voices!

I often wonder, without undue optimism, whether the special need of nurses for attractive and colourful surroundings to mitigate their daily fatigue and the constant nervous strain of their work is better understood and provided for in civilian hospitals to-day than during the even greater stress and anxiety of war-time. The recently-published Report of the *Lancet* Commission on Nursing suggests that in this respect the hospitals have improved very little during the past thirteen years. At the institution that I have described the Red Cross nurses were relegated without ceremony to what was considered their "place." We were housed at some distance from the hospital in the servants' quarters of an enormous mansion, of which the owners, who were seldom in London, occupied only one or two rooms. A dark basement bathroom with a very limited supply of tepid water was regarded as adequate for twenty or thirty of us, in spite of the infectious diseases and the septic wounds with which we were in contact all day.

Not one of us, I think, would have raised any objection to the servants' quarters, or even to our drab apology for a bathroom, had the rest of the house been full. Accommodation in war-time London was, as we all knew, expensive and difficult to find.

But the inescapable conclusion that we were not thought good enough to sleep in the closed empty bedrooms, or important enough to be allowed to wash our cold and weary persons in the many unused bathrooms in the upper part of the mansion, was not calculated to produce in us the gay, affirmative spirit which causes a woman to fall in love with her work.

I was once told by a girl who worked as part-time secretary in the office of a women's organisation that if I wanted an object-lesson in the results of unequal pay and conditions, I ought to take a bus ride to a certain quarter of London in which a men's club and a women's hostel stood side by side. If, she explained, I went into the men's club, I should at once find an enjoyable atmosphere free from anxiety or strain. The occupants would be smoking, talking, and playing cards or billiards with one another or with friends from outside. Others would be singing and playing the piano, or listening to some celebrated speaker on current affairs in the room set aside for a weekly lecture. Thoughts of work, of salaries, of ingenious expedients for making sixpence play the part of a shilling, would all be satisfactorily banished until the next day.

But if I explored the women's hostel, I should have quite a different story to relate. I should encounter, to begin with, no bright lights, no sociable games, no talking and no smoking—there was a rule against smoking in the corridors—and if I entered the common-room I should probably find it deserted. At length, when I had penetrated into the dimly-lit region where each young woman occupied one small bedroom, I should discover the girls still quietly working—not, it is true, at typing or ribbon-selling or book-keeping, but at "saving" out of their salaries. One would be mending gloves and stockings, a second washing and ironing collars or handkerchiefs or silk jumpers; a third—belonging to the most enterprising type of hostel-dweller—would be making herself a flimsy nightgown out of the poorest quality of crêpe de Chine. Sometimes they would gather together in twos and threes, but more often each girl would be solitary; one does not care, my secretary friend informed me, to display to a colleague the much-mended condition of one's underclothes.

As it happened, I did not need to take that bus ride in order to find my object-lesson, for I was living at the time in a Kensington upper maisonette whose windows looked straight on to one of those gloomily respectable "Girls' Clubs" which are composed of rabbit-warrens of tiny rooms inhabited by shorthand-typists and underpaid teachers. Needless to remark, this great barracks of a dwelling faced due north. Few of its depressing windows even possessed curtains with which to conceal the dreary activities of their owners. Across one or two of them little grubby pieces of torn net had been pinned, and where curtains did exist they were made out of dingy white casement cloth and hung at an infinite variety of angles.

I could not, if I would, have avoided the knowledge that nearly all the girl members of that Club spent their week-ends forlornly in their rooms, nibbling buns or washing stockings and handkerchiefs, since the products of these labours flapped on lines of string across the windows every Sunday. Occasionally—but only very occasionally—a Baby Austin drew up at the Club front door, and out of it would step one of those neat, worthy but not very prepossessing young men who are to be found in their dozens in every large bank and every big general store. In a moment

(Continued overleaf)

THE 30's

THE
30's

One Roomitis
(Continued)

or two he would be joined by one of the smarter girls from the Club, her working coat and skirt freshened up by clean blouse, scarf and gloves washed and pressed by herself the evening before in careful preparation for the great and rare event. Whenever this happened, a dozen lonely brown heads would appear at the isolated windows, and a dozen pairs of sad, envious eyes would watch the Baby Austin disappear round the corner.

How is it possible for these frustrated girls, poorly paid, monotonously worked, drearily housed, to be anything but "lonely in the midst of a million"? The need was never so great as it is to-day, when every year thousands of young women leave their homes to work "on their own" in large cities, for all men and women responsible for the care, housing and feeding of girl workers to be trained to understand the psychological value of bright, gaily decorated rooms, pleasantly served informal meals and opportunities for new companionship and stimulating experiences. Without such training, the prolonged and widespread epidemic of "one-roomitis" is likely to continue, with catastrophic effects upon the health and spirits, not only of the young women who mope in impoverished solitude, but of the new generation which they will ultimately produce.

First-rate work, an affirmative attitude towards life, the acceptance of marriage and motherhood, not as the slightly less dreary alternative to a life of monotonous routine, but as one great adventure added to another—these excellent qualities are not produced by scolding or ugliness or criticism or loneliness, by ceremonious mealtimes and unreasonable regulations. Efficiency and success blossom only out of work that is loved for its own sake, and the love of work cannot grow except in an atmosphere of freedom and serene friendliness. There is neither health nor capacity for progress in the woman or girl whose working thoughts are filled with visions of off-duty time. Neither employer nor worker profits by a task which inspires the performer only with a desire for escape.

We are slowly learning from infant psychologists that solitude, a too-strict discipline, and irksome rules made only to be broken, do not ultimately pay in the rearing of a child. In this respect the young man or woman is only a child grown up, with the old contra-suggestiveness, the old defiant reactions, barely hidden beneath an adult veneer of self-control. No profession should permit its workers to be hedged about with restrictive rules which do not directly contribute to greater efficiency. No worker should accept without protest or united demand for better conditions the poor pay which leaves no margin for a vitalising enjoyment of leisure. Above all, no guardian of youth should be content with anything less than the best accommodation that available funds can provide, the gayest rooms that cultured taste can devise, and the most stimulating companionship that benevolent ingenuity can discover.

THE
30's

There are thieves that would *enter unseen*

ROBBING YOU OF PEACE AND QUIET, AND WARMTH AND COMFORT

Locks and bolts are useless! Insulation is your only protection. Thick walls are not good enough to keep out cold, damp, and noise. You must have insulation.

Scientific tests have shown that Celotex only 1 inch thick is more effective as a heat insulator than 12 inches of brick or 25 inches of concrete.

Celotex is supplied in many forms, one of which will be most convenient for your needs.

Write to-day for interesting booklet telling more about Celotex and its wonderful properties.

Celotex products include :

**STANDARD BUILDING BOARD
ROOF INSULATION BOARD
CELOTEX CARPET LINING
ACOUSTI CELOTEX
CELOTEX LATH
LINO BASE**

IT'S QUIETER AND WARMER WITH CELOTEX

THE CELOTEX COMPANY OF GT BRITAIN LTD., AUSTRALIA HOUSE · STRAND · W·C·2

THE
30's

A MESSAGE TO ALL USERS OF GAS

The warming, short infra-red rays
of the Sun reproduced by the new "Beam" method

Greater health for the home

Everyone who has basked in the sun is conscious of the sense of physical well-being which its characteristic warmth imparts. For many years efforts have been made to ascertain the "quality" of this warmth and to reproduce it. To-day, eminent scientists are agreed that the health-giving power of the sun's warmth is largely due to the short infra-red rays. These are the rays which warm the body soothingly and healthfully. And these rays emitted by the new "Beam" gas fire now warm, in the same way, the occupants of any room in which the fire is alight.

A TRIUMPH OF 24 YEARS' RESEARCH
This vital advance in gas fire construction has not been achieved easily or quickly. For the last twenty-four years a vast store of knowledge has

been accumulated through intensive research work. Prolonged experimental work was necessary ; finally the laboratories of Radiation Limited succeeded in reproducing the short infra-red rays through the medium of a gas fire. Radiants fitted to the

new "Beam" gas fire are so made that when heated they pour into the room and upon the people therein a flood of soft, penetrating warmth similar to that in sunshine.

THE PRINCIPLE OF "PENETRATION"
The secret of the healthful property of the short infra-red rays emitted by the sun and by the "Beam" gas fire radiants lies in their penetrative power. When a ray of heat is emitted in the ordinary way by artificial means it fails to penetrate far beneath the skin; thus a dry, scorching discomfort is experienced. But the short infra-red rays of the "Beam" gas fire pass *through* the skin to the blood in the underlying capillaries, warming you through and through, mildly yet insistently, in comfort and with health.

"BEAM" GAS FIRES
TRADE MARK
MADE ONLY BY RADIATION LIMITED

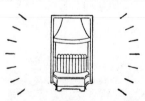

Some interesting literature regarding the beneficial properties of radiant heat from the Radiation "Beam" Gas Fire will be sent on application to Publications Dept. 212A, Radiation Ltd., 164 Queen Victoria Street, E.C.4

THE
30's

New Houses

By

Grace Noll Crowell

Illustrated by H. R. Ballinger

The echoing sound of hammers,
The scent of broken loam,
The fragrance of resined timber,
Where some one builds a home—

And I, who should be going,
Have always stayed my feet
Wherever a house is lifting
New walls beside a street.

The silver of straight nails flashing,
The gleam of a saw—and there—

A sudden new room shaping
Into a happy square:

A square so fraught with promise,
So buoyant with hope that I
Can scarcely wait for the plaster
And putty and paint to dry;

Or wait for the last clean sweeping,
For a van at the door—and then—
The things that make new houses
Homes—for the hearts of men.

121

THE
30's

THE writing table at which this is being written I bought at some period of the year 1913. It will no doubt continue to function long after I have been gathered to my fathers, for it was made in the days when wood was wood and cabinet makers were cabinet makers. Frankly I'm very tired of it, but how can I give up this faithful friend at which I've made thousands of pounds and written millions of words?

The table has now been in my service for twenty years. I write about three hundred thousands words a year. That makes a million words or so every four years. Five million words were written at this table, which if placed end to end would reach possibly from here to the moon. How ungrateful to get rid of the table; and yet change is the salt of life.

I have a most excellent suit of clothes which was made for me in 1925. The sight of the suit now bores me indescribably, though the colour, a modest grey, could not possibly offend even the most fastidious. My only grievance against the suit is that I've worn it at least once a week for nearly nine years, but how can I throw it away seeing that it looks almost as good as when new?

The trouble with us in this country seems to be that clothes, furniture, fashions, ideals, motor cars, husbands, wives, children, ideas, and morals usually endure for ages after we have begun secretly to yearn for a change. Even the secret of our declining trade might be explained by this depressing immortality of possessions and convictions. If we changed our furniture oftener we should increase trade and if we changed our minds oftener we should cause more upheavals in our lives, and no one can produce an upheaval in his or her life without spending money.

I suggest that clothes should be inexpensive and charming (whereas generally if they are inexpensive they aren't charming), so that we could throw them away frequently and buy new ones. Children should be reshuffled periodically among families, like books at a library. Both they and

" I should like to see a mild revolution in England in which might perish old clothes, old furniture, old customs, old prejudices. In this country we are continually putting up with things that endure for ages after we have secretly begun to yearn for a change

In fact—
THINGS
LAST TOO LONG"

their parents would appreciate each other better after a change for the worse. Our George drives us almost mad by beginning every sentence with " Er, well . . ." but after a month of the Smiths' Mary, who sniffs from morning till night, the prospect of George and his rambling statements will look almost rosy.

Those responsible should design light, cheap, fragile furniture and we in our

turn should indulge in it more sparsely but more frequently. I refurnished four years ago at great expense and already I long for a new scheme. What do I care to-day for my gold brocade curtains which cost me so much more than I could afford that I used to stand and gaze at them with awe? How willingly I would sell my birthright of brocade for a mess of cretonne pottage, just for a change.

L . G . I l l i n g w o r t h

By F. E. BAILY

" The average marriage allied to the average home endured daily from year's end to year's end, are what often make us neurasthenic before our time "

drawers from the village craftsman, who could only make one at a time, who was booked up with orders from year's end to year's end, whose needs were simple so that nothing on earth would make him hurry, one clung to one's chest of drawers once it had passed into one's possession, and it became an heirloom.

Nowadays miles of cloth and dozens of chests of drawers may be purchased *en masse* and delivered the same afternoon, so that durability no longer constitutes a prime virtue. I suggest that the durability of clothes, household goods, ideas, and institutions is what makes England so dull at the moment. We are constantly being tempted by fresh examples of things we have already and long for change, but the things we have already will last a lifetime, and to get rid of them involves us in accusations of extravagance, infirmity of purpose, mental instability and heaven knows what else.

Not fickleness nor extravagance but hard-wearing monotony drives respectable citizens who can't bear it any longer to pin notices on their kitchen doors: "Beware of Gas! Strike No Matches!" enter their kitchens, lock the doors behind them, turn on the taps of the gas ovens, place their heads inside, and seek what they hope will prove a less monotonous sphere.

Much, however, might be done short of putting our heads in gas ovens. Houses and flats should have interior partitions instead of interior walls so that the shapes and sizes of rooms could be altered at a moment's notice, simply by sliding back or folding up the partitions. Most certainly every husband and wife ought to enjoy two months' leave of absence from home during the year, either all in a lump or split up as preferred, and with no questions asked as to what he or she did.

" Dance joyfully in the light shed by the blazing home, already planning to buy a lovely new one out of the insurance money "

And yet I am not specially vile or light-minded. Most people, particularly women, feel as I do, if only they would admit the fact. As long as no injury or loss of life was involved, what woman wouldn't dance joyfully in the light shed by the blazing home, already planning a lovely new one out of the insurance money?

This eternity which afflicts our possessions, this invariable assertion by the salesman that the mangle will last a lifetime if kindly treated, as though a female's one ambition were to spend a lifetime with the same mangle, survive from the days that saw everything spun or constructed by hand. When the housewife spun her own cloth on a hand loom the cloth had to last, or else she could never, with her slow process, have provided enough to clothe the family. When one bought a chest of

Have you a Hearth— or just a Grate?

THE
30's

Why spoil the new harmony of your room with an old discordant fireplace? ☞ New wall-coverings, modern furniture, up-to-date lighting, are wasted on rooms with the cumbersome old mantelpiece grate.

It does not add much to the cost of your re-decorations to put in a new and harmonious fireplace and hearth— either for coal, gas, or electric fires. And it makes all the difference to the beauty of your rooms—because, **THE FIREPLACE ATTRACTS EVERY EYE.**

Artistic Brick Fireplaces
ALREADY ASSEMBLED FOR FIXING

The "IFFLEY" Brick Fireplaces have been designed by eminent Architects for the needs of the Modern Home. 27 designs, in mellow brick of harmonising colours, designed for beauty, comfort and economy as well. ☞ The natural kiln-burnt colours are Antique, Multi-colour Rustic, Cherry-Red, Dark Plum, etc., to tone with any colour scheme of yours. ☞ "IFFLEY" **FIREPLACES ARE SUPPLIED ASSEMBLED, ready for fixing.** You see the complete Fireplace as it will be, and you know exactly what to expect. No disappointment afterwards. Your builder can put in the *assembled* Fireplace inside a few hours.

SEE THE 27 BEAUTIFUL DESIGNS IN OUR BOOKLET, FREE. PLEASE COMPLETE COUPON IN PENCIL

From **£3·11·0**

BRITISH BRICK FIREPLACES
101 Gray's Inn Road
London, W.C.1

See it at
Ideal Home Exhibition STAND **160**
Nat'l Hall, Ground Floor, or at our Showrooms

Send me your Booklet, please

without any obligation to me

Name..

Address..

....

Cut this out and post in unsealed envelope (½d. stamp) to Iffley Brick Fireplaces Co. Ltd., 101 Gray's Inn Road, London, W.C.1

G.H./M.R.

124

PRAYER FOR A BRIDE'S HOUSE

By Christie Lund

Illustration by Bradshaw Crandell

SHE is so young, dear Lord, so very young;
She is so wide=eyed and naïvely sweet;
She does not dream of great rooms, draped and hung
With master paintings, rugs where some queen's feet
Have lightly trod.   She dreams of this instead:
A small, new house with freshly painted floors,
With hand=stitched curtains, and above her head
Bright dishes gleaming through wee cupboard doors.

SHE'LL learn, some day, the value of old things,
When eagerness is stiff, and she is wise—
Knowing the disillusionment time brings—
But now, there's so much springtime in her eyes,
And this is her first house—Whate'er You do,
Let everything about it, Lord, be . . . new!

THE
30's

A
Fifteen-Roomed
House
and
an Income of
£376

The old-fashioned kitchen has oak beams, whitewashed walls, and a slate floor. The room is so large that only part of it is in use

WE have lived in this old Cornish vicarage for the last eight years. It is a place of great charm, built chiefly of local Pentewan stone, with parts of the old Priory incorporated in it. The porch came from the Priory, also the coat of arms on the south side, dating back to the twelfth century. There is a large garden and drive—not many flower beds—and a tennis court. Across the road there is a large kitchen-garden, and across another road, on the north side, stabling for four horses, a cobbled yard and up a flight of steps, a drying ground.

The family consists of my husband, myself, our son aged nine years, and a wire-haired terrier. We also keep a dozen fowls. Last year we were faced with the problem of education and decided to send our son to a boarding-school. Although we were able to obtain a bursary of £30 per annum towards this, there was still another £65 to be found to cover the remainder of the fees, clothing, travelling, etc., and to meet this additional expense we decided, very regretfully, to part with our excellent cook-general, who had been with us for eight years, and whom we took over from our predecessors. I had had no practical experience at all of housework, cookery, washing or dressmaking. I have learnt all I know about cooking and management from GOOD HOUSEKEEPING, which I have taken ever since I married, eleven years ago, and from one or two women's papers which I have had lent to me lately. In spite of my inexperience, we have now managed by ourselves very

No practical articles which have appeared in GOOD HOUSEKEEPING *have aroused wider interest than the series on "How Others Live." Appreciative letters received from readers who have been helped by the efforts of other housewives, have prompted us to publish the present article. The conditions with which the writer is faced are by no means unusual, and the happy way in which she plans out the work in her home and meets her difficulties should be an inspiration to others*

happily and satisfactorily for nearly a year.

This is not a house to be tackled light-heartedly without a maid, as it consists of fifteen rooms, larder, lamp-room, hall and outside wash-house. It is very badly planned and all the rooms are very large. There are two kitchens. The main one, with range, sink, etc., measuring 26 by 16 feet, is at the extreme end of one wing and as far as possible from the living-rooms and larder. The drawing-room is enormous. Upstairs, the combined bathroom and lavatory is at the extreme end of the other wing and was converted from the landing into a bathroom about fifty years ago.

There are nine rooms upstairs and six down. Upstairs there is a central landing and two long corridors leading from it. One leads to the bathroom; and the other, which is over the kitchen, is very dark and has unexpected steps up and down, and a flight of wooden stairs leading to the kitchen. There is

gas in the house, but only in certain rooms, and a gas cooker in the kitchen. All the cooking, however, is done by the kitchen range, except breakfast and some of the meals in summer. The range which we found here when we came was huge and quite useless for heating the water, besides devouring quantities of coal, so we put in a small cottage range, which heats the water excellently and bakes well. The bath, also, of the old painted variety, was in bad condition, so a new porcelain one was installed, and a wash-basin with taps. For this, the Ecclesiastical Authorities made a loan and we are still paying it back. The amount is included in our budget under the dilapidations heading; but it is well worth it.

When we decided to run the house ourselves, we took all the furniture out of the drawing-room and the little ante-room adjoining; and as there is a separate door to that part, we closed it entirely. All the rest of the house is liable to be used, so we keep the

HOW OTHERS LIVE—VII

A view of the Cornish vicarage described in this article. Part of the house dates back to the days of the twelfth century

YEARLY BUDGET

INCOME—£376 and a Vicarage.

EXPENDITURE—	£
Housekeeping (£9 5s. monthly) . .	111
Clergy Pensions, Life Assurance, etc. .	43
Rates, taxes, dilapidations . . .	52
Gas and coal	22
Boy's school and clothes (not including a Bursary of £30)	65
Clothes, church collections and personal allowance (self and husband £1 10s. each, monthly)	36
Library, wireless, papers, outings, etc.	12
Garden, subscriptions, charity, medicine, stationery, and all extras .	35
	£376

Holidays are self-supporting—

	£	s.	d.
Rent from letting vicarage during August . . .	8	8	0
From Locum duty taken . .	10	10	0
Monthly housekeeping allowance	9	5	0
	28	3	0

How the wife of a Cornish vicar manages her household without the help of a maid

myself. To fit all this in comfortably needs a definite routine, and after many attempts, I found one which works very well. A great help is a tablet diary which I keep hanging by the kitchen table, and against each day I write the special work—meals timed to fit in with my husband's appointments, and special duties, visiting details and meetings for myself.

To save work we have turned the smaller kitchen, opening out of the main kitchen, into a breakfast room, and have put down a carpet and rug, installing an oak table and chairs, a basket-chair and gas fire, so making the room generally comfortable. The china cupboard is built into this room. We have breakfast and lunch there, and dinner when my husband is using the study all day for writing. In the winter the fire is lit in the dining-room, which is used for tea and dinner and as a sitting-room in the evening. In the summer we have most of our meals—often all of them—on the terrace on the south side of the house or in the shade of the lawn, from which we get a delightful peep of the sea.

(Continued overleaf)

two guest-rooms, maid's room, the boy's room, and playroom aired and dusted, and they are turned out when needed. The mattresses were rather a problem, so we put the three single ones on the boy's bed, and hot-water bottles are put among them two or three times a week in winter, and they are thoroughly aired in the sun in summer. The double mattress is kept under ours and all are well brushed when the room is turned out. The playroom, full of books, toys, trains, etc., is only used at holiday times, and a very special clean-

ing and scrubbing is necessary after the return to school. There are two attic rooms over the kitchen which are kept tidy and scrubbed out when necessary. One contains the hot-water tank, where household and personal linen are aired before being put in the linen cupboard in the other wing, and then aired again before using.

That disposes of nine rooms and I am still left with six rooms, larder and hall, which require daily attention and periodical turning out, in addition to cooking and washing, which I do

Redheads

THE
30's

The MAGIC CARPET comes to you by Post FREE!

THE Magic Carpet is so simple—yet so ingenious! You will enjoy it, and will soon see that this little novelty can be useful as well as amusing. A few minutes with the "Magic Carpet" will show you how you can make your home life easier, pleasanter and brighter.

Certainly, if you have a home and a family to look after, send for the "Magic Carpet." You will find it an entertaining way of learning something really worth knowing. Absolutely free—and no trouble. Just fill in the coupon below.

The Grand Prize

EUREKA
VACUUM CLEANER

EUREKA MADE IN ENGLAND

THE WORLD'S BEST VACUUM CLEANER

Highest awards at seven important International Exhibitions. Made by Reyrolle, of Hebburn-on-Tyne, England

Cash Price : **15 Guineas,** *including attachments.*
Easy terms : £1 *down.*

SEND FOR THE MAGIC CARPET TO·DAY !

To EUREKA VACUUM CLEANER CO. LTD., Eureka House, 8 Fisher Street, Southampton Row, London, W.C.1.

Please send me "The Magic Carpet" Free and Post Free, and information about the British-made Grand Prize Eureka Vacuum Cleaner.

NAME..

ADDRESS...

....DATE......................

G.H. March

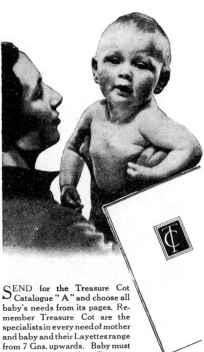
HOW OTHERS LIVE—VII
(Continued)

Plan of Work

My husband has a weekday service on most mornings at 7.30 a.m., so he is up first and lights the gas ring under my whistling kettle, which wakes me at 7.15 a.m. I make my early cup of tea. The tray and tea things are kept for that purpose and I re-lay it when I wash up the breakfast things and keep it in the larder until night, when I place it on the landing table upstairs.

7.30 a.m. Get up (7 a.m. on church mornings).
Air bed.

8 a.m. Do bathroom. Make bed and do bedroom; mop landings, running vacuum sweeper over the carpets if necessary; brush stairs.

(*N.B.*—It may seem odd to begin with this, but this part of the house is farthest from the back door and if I do it later I may miss the tradesmen or constantly be called down. As the routine is arranged, I am washing up in the kitchen at the time when most of them call.)

Sweep the hall and porch; clean brasses; mop and dust hall. Do breakfast-room and lay breakfast. Prepare and cook breakfast by 9 o'clock.

9 a.m. Breakfast.

9.30 a.m. Wash up. While I am doing this, my husband fetches coal and refills all coal scuttles from the cellar below the kitchen; clears out and lights the kitchen fire; takes the ashes from the dining-room (or study) fire, and brushes up all dust in the hearth. When I do the room, I black-lead the grate and wash the hearth, leaving the fire ready to be lighted later. After washing up, I empty the bucket under the sink and light up the incinerator outside.

9.50 a.m. Do study.

10.20 a.m. Do dining-room.

10.35 a.m. Tidy larder and sweep kitchen, then sweep away leaves and dust from the cobbles outside. I then wash over the slate floor of the part of the kitchen that I use.

I must explain about the kitchen. It is so large that I have moved the centre table and cupboard near the fire and sink. The old-fashioned tables and shelves I have covered with blue and white washable oil cloth, which is easily cleaned and always looks fresh. I have painted the cupboard blue and there are blue canisters for tea, coffee, etc., on the top. This, with the oak beams of the ceiling and white-washed walls and Cornish slate floor, looks very attractive.

11.15 a.m. I have a glass of milk or special food drink and sit at the table and plan the meals while I drink it.

11.30 a.m. Prepare lunch and as much of the evening meal as possible.

12 to 1.30 Weekly work.

1.30 p.m. Lunch—a light meal in the breakfast-room.

2.15 p.m. Wash up lunch things; fill oil lamps which are used in the hall, landings and our bed-room; also the oil heating stove. Light the lounge fire (when the study is used, it is lighted earlier in the day); wash out tea towels, dish-cloths.

2.45 p.m. Rest.

3 p.m. Pay calls—sick visiting in the Parish on some afternoons; or afternoon work, mending, dressmaking, gardening, letters.

4.30 p.m. Tea.

5.45 p.m. Wash up and prepare evening meal. Lay table in lounge; change out of woollies which I wear all day, and turn down bed. Serve meal.

7 p.m. Dinner.

7.45 p.m. Clear away, wash up and bring in coffee.

When serving a hot pudding, I have to walk ninety-six paces there and back to fetch it from the oven. I have a trolley which is a great help.

10.30 p.m. Fill hot-water bottle; take up morning tea-tray and kettle. Bath and get into bed at about 11 p.m.

We like to have our dinner in the evening if possible. It gives me a clearer morning and is very pleasant when the day's work is done. But there are very often evening meetings to attend, beginning at 7 or 7.30 in connection with the Parish or British Legion. We are both associated with the local branch of the British Legion and are keenly interested in the work. My husband is also on the Personal Service Committee for Unemployed; and I am responsible for the Mothers' Union and am on local Nursing and Girl Guide Committees. On these occasions we have dinner at midday and a high tea at 6 o'clock. This also applies during the school holidays.

Weekly Work
Monday

Washing.—I do all the washing in an old-fashioned wash-house with a copper. My husband lights the fire for me and he has also connected a large rain-water tank with the wash-house by means of a length of hose pipe with a tap. This saves me lifting the heavy baths, and he is usually about to empty them for me. I have a vacuum washer which I work up and down. When the clothes are ready to hang out, I have to carry the basket across the village street, through the stable yard and up the flight of stone steps to the drying ground. Here I hang all the big things, sheets, pillow cases, towels, woollens, etc., but the smaller things, collars, table napkins and handkerchiefs, I hang on a small line near the kitchen door. I wear coat overalls and usually have two each week. I have learnt to do them up properly. In the afternoon I fold the clothes if possible.

I also wash dusters, cleaning cloths and any brooms and brushes that require it on Mondays, and clean the candlesticks.

(Continued overleaf)

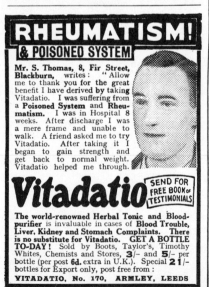
HOW OTHERS LIVE—VII
(Continued)

Tuesday

Ironing.—This often takes two hours, so I have to begin before twelve if possible.

Wednesday

First week.—Bathroom.
Second week.—Hall.
Third week.—Landings, also dust spare-rooms.

Thursday

First week.—Bedroom.
Second week.—Study.
Third week.—Dining-room. Clean silver and plate.

On Thursdays I can begin the weekly work earlier, as I have a woman who comes for three hours to scrub the kitchen and tables and larder; also alternate!y to clean the gas cooker, scrub the back stairs and clean the flues of the range.

Friday

Cake making and baking.

Saturday

Breakfast-room or any cupboard and shelves.

Sunday

I go to church at 8 a.m. and 11 a.m. on alternate Sundays and again in the evening. In the morning I do all fires and feed the fowls for my husband. Lunch is a light meal, Sunday supper after Evensong being the chief meal.

This scheme works very well indeed. I have to be careful, however, not to become a slave to routine, but be ready to alter it at short notice to suit my husband or boy. I tried to turn out each room each week, but it was too much for me. Every room is dusted and carefully gone over each day, and given a very thorough clean on turning-out day. I use methylated spirits for the windows, which reach from floor to ceiling and are made of separate diamond-shaped panes. A window-cleaner comes round about once a month and does the outside. The silver, brass and pewter are cleaned as each room is cleaned on turning-out day, and floors and all furniture polished. The study is lined with book-shelves and the walls covered with college groups and pictures and photographs of all descriptions.

I tried cake making and ironing in the afternoon, but people often call and sometimes stay to tea. A vicarage is unique in many ways, as there are constant rings at the bell at all hours of the day in this busy little village, and must be attended to. My husband has fixed up a bell from the front door connecting with the study for people who require him personally. This saves me answering the door merely to show people in; but when he is out, I have to answer this too. He has also fixed an electric light in the larder which is very large, like a room, and built like a dairy with stone and slate for shelves and white-washed walls. It faces south and is beautifully cool, but draughty.

Labour-saving Appliances and Economies

I have found many little ways of saving time and money. I make most of my own clothes, so this helps out my allowance. Then in saving labour, I have a paraffin poker, price 9d., which saves wood; or if used with a little wood and paper, the fire can be left to look after itself; a non-electric vacuum carpet sweeper; a vacuum washing-tub; a long-handled polishing mop for pictures, etc., which is washable, price

6d.; a patent ashbox, price 4s. 6d., which consists of an ashbox and sifter combined with lid which prevents dust flying about and separates the ash from the cinders. The cinders are used again on the kitchen fire, saving coal, and the ashes fill up wet and muddy places outside. A plate-rack and tea trolley also save a lot of labour.

All the tradesmen call at the door, which saves going out to shops. The grocer takes orders and delivers the goods. Dairyman and baker call every day, butcher and fish-monger call at the door and I go out and choose from the carts. The butcher only calls on Tuesday, Thursday and Saturday. I pay my books once a week and divide my monthly housekeeping money accordingly, allowing £2 each week, which leaves a little margin for renewals. These weekly bills actually come to about £1 17s. 6d. each week. The balance is spent on potatoes (4s.) and window cleaner (3s. 6d.) each once a month, also cottons, mending material, etc. There is a margin of about £1 or more each month, but out of this have to come any teas or lunches out; gifts of cakes, etc., for whist drives and parish socials; little charities to beggars, and, in fact, anything over and above ordinary house running.

There is no theatre near here, but we enjoy the cinema from time to time. We are, of course, unable to give dinner parties, but can enjoy having our friends to lunch and tea; or to Bridge in the evening, when we have sandwiches, biscuits and coffee.

It will be seen that there is no margin over and it is impossible to save anything apart from the life assurance policy. But we are able to make two ends meet, and live comfortably and very happily.

Weekly Expenditure

	£	s.	d.
Butcher		8	2
Fish		1	8
Grocery bill, which includes vegetables, fruit and all household supplies . .		13	6
Extra help		2	0
Bread		1	8
Mineral waters, etc. . .		1	9
Butter and cream . .		2	11
Eggs		1	6
Oil			10
Milk		3	6
	£1	17	6

Weekly Orderings

The local grocer sells most things, including fruit and vegetables. I buy a bag of potatoes about every six weeks at 4s. We grow our own green vegetables, and potatoes from March to October, when they are dearest.

These items occur every week:

Grocer

	s.	d.		s.	d.
Biscuits . .	5½		½-lb. slab		
Soap powder	3½		cheese .		6
2 lb. lump sugar . .	6		Cereal . .		7
2 lb. gran. sugar . .	4½		Matches .		9
			½ lb. New Zealand		
1 lb. margarine	5		butter .		6
Soap . .	5		½ lb. coffee .	1	0
Box cheese .	6		1 lb. bacon .	1	1
Apples . .	4		Tin fruit .		5
Tea . .	6½		Bananas .		6
				9	4

The following goods are ordered and
(Continued overleaf)

THE
30's

"POOR MITE, it's his gums – light the gas fire, dear"

"*Healthiest heat for bedrooms*" SAYS **Mr. THERM**

THREE A.M. Life at its lowest ebb. *Thank goodness* for a gas fire you can turn on while you soothe down baby.

A comfort for you—*but an absolute necessity for the child*. That's the whole point. A gas fire is the *healthiest* way of heating baby's room *and yours too, for that matter*. You see, a gas fire *ventilates* the room — sucks all the spent air away up the chimney, and makes the room fresh and healthy. And its cheery

rays are very like the sun's rays. That's **why Harley** Street doctors use gas fires. That's why they recommend gas fires to their patients. That's why *you* should have gas fires, too.

> ★ ONE MINER IN EVERY ELEVEN *out of those working to raise coal for this country's needs is kept at work by the gas industry. Each Sunday dinner you cook by gas, remember, is giving a miner employment.*

Issued by THE BRITISH COMMERCIAL GAS ASSOCIATION, 28 Grosvenor Gardens, London, S.W.1

132

HOW OTHERS LIVE—VII

(Continued)

spread over several weeks, large quantities being cheaper :

	s. d.		s. d.
Abrasive cleanser .	6	Cornflour .	9
Metal polish	7½	Blacklead .	9
Disinfectant	1 4	Rennet . .	1 1
Starch . .	4½	Vanilla essence .	6½
Wax polish	10½	Coconut	6
3 lb. candles	1 1½	Sultanas .	9
Cooking fat	7½	Glacé cherries .	6
Carrots and onions .	6½	Rice . . .	5
			11 3½

Butcher

	s. d.		s. d.
3½ lb. rib of beef . .	4 2	nicer than it sounds)	6
½ lb. sausages	6	Neck of mutton .	1 0
Hogs pudding (a West Country speciality		Rabbit . .	10
		Chops . .	1 2
			8 2

Fishmonger

	s. d.		s. d.
1½ lb. cod or hake . .	1 0	Smoked haddock . .	8
			1 8

Dairyman

	s. d.		s. d.
Milk . .	3 6	3 separate quarters of cream . .	
1 lb. butter	1 8		1 3
			6 5

½ lb. of New Zealand butter has also been included in the grocery order. My eggs cost me roughly 1s. 6d. a week, which covers the grain, meal and spice necessary for twelve hens.

Typical Menus for a Week in Winter

Tea is not included, but consists of bread and butter, toast or tea-cake, home-made cakes, etc. We usually drink tea with our lunch, Cornish fashion. In summer we have plenty of fresh fruit, vegetables, salad, etc., from the garden.

Breakfast

Monday, Thursday and Saturday:
Puffed wheat and cream (if any left over).
Bacon and eggs.
Toast, butter and marmalade.
Coffee.

Tuesday and Wednesday:
Puffed wheat or porridge.
Sausages and bacon.
Toast, butter and marmalade.
Coffee.

Friday:
Puffed wheat.
Eggs, boiled or scrambled.
Toast, butter and marmalade.
Coffee.

Lunches

Monday (evening meeting, so dinner midday):
Cold beef and horse-radish sauce.
Chocolate blancmange.

Tuesday:
Rabbit hot-pot (made from top half of rabbit).
Fruit.
Cheese and biscuits.

Wednesday:
Curry (a little cold meat from joint).
Fruit.
Cheese and biscuits.

Thursday:
Hogs pudding.
Fruit.
Cheese and biscuits.

Friday:
Haddock baked in milk.
Fruit.
Cheese and biscuits.

Saturday:
Macaroni Cheese.
Fruit.

Sunday:
We always have cereal, bacon and eggs, etc., as it is my husband's first meal because of Church Services.

Evening Meals

Monday (high tea at 6 p.m.):
Poached eggs.
Jam and cake.

Tuesday:
Minced beef and mashed potatoes.
Clarence pudding.
Cheese and biscuits.
Coffee.

Wednesday:
Soup.
Chops, potatoes and greens.
Cheese soufflé.
Coffee.

Thursday:
Roast rabbit (hind part of rabbit coated with flour and sprinkled with herbs).
Roast potatoes, thickened gravy.
Open jam tart.
Cheese and biscuits.
Coffee.

Friday:
White soup (made with fish and potato stock, celery, etc.).
Kedgeree.
Raspberry jam sponge pudding.
Cheese and biscuits.
Coffee.

Saturday:
Roast beef, baked potatoes, greens, Yorkshire pudding and horse-radish sauce.
Junket and cream.
Cheese and biscuits.
Coffee.

Sunday:
Soup from stock of joint bones.
Cold beef, horse-radish sauce, beetroot.
Fruit salad and cream.
Cheese and biscuits.
Coffee.

BUDGETING THE INCOME

There is a useful chapter on this subject, with information about costs of living which many people would find helpful, in GOOD HOUSEKEEPING WITH MODERN METHODS, Part I, by D. D. Cottington Taylor. Price 7s. 6d. at all booksellers, or 8s. post free from Good Housekeeping, 153 Queen Victoria St., London, E.C.4

"And it's all ready for work in no time"
says Mrs. Twenty Five

"So I see, and I do like the colour scheme"
says Mrs. Fifty Five

The world's finest wringer-mangle combined with the ideal kitchen cabinet table.

•

Patented pressed steel construction with rust-proofed non-chipping enamel — all working parts cased in steel.

•

Super-reinforced solid rubber rollers will not break buttons or fasteners.

•

Unique cantilever pressure system — will take blankets as easily as bibs.

•

This 'Cabinet' will take any size or shape of dolly tub, zinc, or enamel bath, or 'Nesta' Tubs.

•

Every machine is fully covered by a generous 10 years free replacement guarantee.

•

Obtainable of all the best ironmongers, hardware and furnishing stores.

CASH PRICE
84/-

Here, in one compact 'Cabinet' are four things without which no kitchen can be really efficient. First, the ACME Wringer — it takes the toil out of wringing and mangling. Second, complete facilities to centralise all your washday duties. Third, a steady mangling and ironing table standing firm on any floor. Finally — a most modern touch — a sparkling white enamelled kitchen table. And now you have a choice of four finishes at no extra cost — blue mottle, green mottle, grey mottle and oak finish — to suit your colour scheme.

ACME
CABINET
WRINGER-MANGLE

IF YOU ARE SHORT OF SPACE
choose either the ACME 'Folding' model at 69/6 or the ACME 'Portable' model at 43/- for the 16" size or 39/- for the 14" size. For literature giving details of all three ACMES write for booklet W.M.11, to ACME Wringers Ltd., David St., Glasgow, S.E.

CVS-30

Proper Division of Space

A narrow strip of lawn, at the front of the property, is backed by a planting of evergreen and deciduous shrubs. From the front door a flagged path leads back to the entrance to the garden —a wistaria-covered arch. Beyond the arch is the garden (a backyard)—26 feet deep by 48 feet wide—divided into three units: a flagged square, a rose garden, and a perennial border. The square flagged space is bordered with dwarf evergreen azaleas, drooping yews accenting the corners. The tiny rose garden holds only thirty bushes— hybrid, ever-blooming tea roses. The wide perennial border holds old-fashioned favourites, and is a mass of gay-coloured Darwin tulips in the early spring months

SOME of the most enchanting gardens I have ever seen are tiny gardens, and it always saddens me to hear anyone say, "Oh, my garden is too small to fuss with—you cannot make anything of that dreary space."

Oh, yes, you can! When I see a bare, dreary backyard, my fingers itch to get at it. There isn't a place so small or so shaded or so wind-swept or so dreary that it cannot be made into some kind of garden. As for our pretty, sunny backyards, they can be made into veritable bits of paradise.

If you cannot afford all the things needed for your garden the first year, you must then plan accordingly. Plan a budget for several years ahead. The

This bench offers a resting-place beneath an apple tree

first year, plan for the garden's main features; then, year by year, add the less essential items. Isn't that the way you furnished your house? Just think of your garden as you think of your house—as something you are building towards an ideal—and you will be surprised at how quickly the years pass and your garden is realised.

Plan and invest soundly. We hear a lot these days about sound investments. Sturdy peonies, old-fashioned phlox, the common lilac, and golden forsythia stand on their own merits as tried investments, against the gamble of untried novelties and hybrids. It is fun to gamble, but few of us can afford to these days; and whether you can or not, the backbone of your garden should be of plants of proved merit.

Let us start with the importance of proper division of ground. Generally prevailing is an idea that to attain a sense of space in a small area, all plants should be kept back against the boundaries. This is rarely true. A small plot, divided into skilfully arranged and related units, will seem a great deal larger and hold much more interest than the small plot enclosed with a border planting which definitely frames it, and so shows up its limitations.

The first step in any plan, whether for a house or a garden, is to decide what sort of house or garden you want. What you want will be determined largely by what you need. Most people who have small houses and plots need more living space. Therefore, the kind of garden they need is really an outdoor living-room—one that will be a place of rest, not just an added burden. A garden need not require much care, but you must plan for this. Plan it without much grass to cut and weed; use sturdy, self-reliant plants.

The plan and sketches shown with this article were chosen to illustrate proper division of ground. This garden, designed for a school-teacher, presented several problems. First of all, the

Design in the Small Garden

By
Annette Hoyt Flanders

The service path is closed with a gate of weather-seasoned wood

A wistaria-covered arch leads to the garden

owner told me she wanted a charming garden that made a lovely picture at all times of the year. Then she wanted as much privacy as possible—a place where she could sit outdoors to work or entertain her friends. She wanted plants that did not require much care or skill, plants that would not grow too big; a pool with a water lily and some goldfish; bird houses and a bird bath, for she loved birds; some roses and some flowers she could cut for the house and for her desk at school. The garden must bloom from earliest spring to hard frost, and must look well in winter. She wanted a gate she could

lock, and an arch with roses, and some attractive garden furniture. And, most of all, she wanted it peaceful and pretty, and it just could not be expensive!

Quite an order! Yes, it was. But not nearly so impossible as it would seem at first glance, for she had fulfilled the first two essential requirements: she knew what kind of garden she wanted, and she realised that all those things could not be put into any garden, large or small, without making a carefully-thought-out plan, drawn to scale, with each item allotted its proper place.

The plan and sketches show the problem solved—all fitted together as neatly as a jig-saw puzzle. When we started, we had one great asset—a lovely spreading apple tree in one corner of the backyard; and, luckily, another lovely crab apple stood in the neighbour's garden, just opposite my teacher's front door. For privacy we enclosed the garden with a tall, clipped privet hedge. The space

between the front of the house and the road was developed as a neat lawn, with a planting of shrubs, partly evergreen and partly deciduous, against the house.

From the front door a flagged path leads back to the arch at the entrance to the garden. Originally this path ran close to the hedge, as the entrance path does, but it was moved over beyond the steps so that a wider bed of planting against the hedge would screen the garden from the street. The arch to the garden is of rough-hewn, weather-stained timber to match the trim on the house, which is built of red brick and designed like a country cottage. There is too much shade for roses to grow over this arch, so wistaria was used instead.

The backyard, only 26 feet deep by 48 feet wide, was divided into three units. A square of flagstone laid on the ground with narrow, moss-grown joints, forms the largest unit and the outdoor living-room. There attractive white wicker furniture with pale-green waterproof cushions invites one to sit under the shade of the apple tree. This square is surrounded by a planting of dwarf azaleas. At one side a lily pool with a few gleaming goldfish reflects the apple tree and azaleas. A quince tree screens the end of the porch, and deep-purple lilacs, one clump on each side of the entrance arch, offer a fragrant welcome in springtime.

The flagstone square overlooks a tiny rose garden edged with dwarf box. A small stone bench is placed against the hedge; and opposite it, against the brick foundation of the porch, stands a shell-shaped lead bird bath. Climbing roses and jasmine-scented honeysuckle, which is practically evergreen, clamber over the kitchen porch. The service path to the kitchen door is closed off with a neat gate of weather-stained wood, hung on attractive wrought-iron hinges and fastened with a sturdy and good-looking wrought-iron latch.

A wide border of sweet-smelling, old-fashioned perennials, among which, in May, bloom groups of Darwin tulips, flanks the walk opposite the rose garden.

The lily pool reflects the pink azaleas that are planted round it

DEPARTMENT OF HOUSEHOLD

Good servants are made, not born, and need teaching if they are to be efficient

Good Housekeeping Institute
Conducted by D. D. Cottington Taylor
Certificate of King's College of Household and Social Science :
First Class Teaching Diplomas in Cookery, High Class
Cookery, Laundrywork, Housewifery, Dressmaking, A.R.S.I.,
49 Wellington Street, Strand, W.C.2

Everyone will have her own ideas regarding details of training a young maid, but this article, based on the actual practical experience of one of our readers, should prove helpful.

As with all successful teaching, a considerable amount of patience is demanded when training a maid, and it is here that the fussy, nervous type of mistress often fails. A reader wrote to the Institute recently complaining bitterly of her maid, but when one had finished reading the letter, one could not but sympathise with the girl. Every minute speck of dust irritated the mistress, in fact, she had stairs and all main rooms dusted twice daily, once before and once after luncheon. This is probably an extreme case, but it is an instance of the unreasonable demands sometimes made. Dissatisfaction and lack of co-operation in the household are bound to develop in such circumstances.

THOSE who had the opportunity of hearing "Martha" on the wireless some months ago will agree that maids of forty or fifty years back had no very enviable time.

Their work involved early rising, cleaning innumerable stone steps, fighting a recalcitrant stove, and the preparation of at least three heavy meals a day, apart from the "snacks" which were continually being served. Hot water had to be carried to the bedrooms, not only for hand-basins, but also for baths. Furnishings and decorations were of the most elaborate kind and involved a tremendous amount of work in cleaning and dusting—in those days there were no vacuum cleaners or other labour-saving equipment. All this meant heavy toil from morning till night, and since regular outings

The maid will probably need to be taught how to make a good cup of tea—with properly boiling water and a tea-pot that has been well warmed beforehand

No wonder girls fought against when rooms were crowded with ments. In the home of 1935 "ser

were seldom included in the routine. it is hardly surprising that domestic service went out of favour with working-class girls, who preferred to go into factory or office, where. however dull and monotonous the work, hours are. as a rule, comparatively regular and evenings free.

Nowadays, domestic service is becoming more popular again, although there are still a large number of people who experience trouble in obtaining good service. In many cases, their difficulties are increased because they do not organise the day's routine and fail to recognise the necessity of allowing a daily outing of two hours. From the health point of view alone,

ENGINEERING AND HOUSECRAFT

TRAINING A GENERAL MAID

A young maid should be taught to bring in letters, etc., on a small tray, and told that she need not knock at the door of the living-room when she enters

"going into service" furniture and orna-vice" is another matter

maids' time-tables should be so arranged as to allow this, the free time being either in the afternoon or evening to suit the convenience of the individual household; once arranged, it should be regularly adhered to as far as possible. Half a day weekly and half a day on alternate Sundays or every Sunday evening are the other free times usually allowed.

The question of free time has been commented on at some length, as at the Institute we feel very strongly that much of the dissatisfaction of work in a private household is due to the fact that there is no definite arrangement. If the mistress, for instance, has guests, she does not hesitate to alter or curtail the free time of her staff with little or no notice. That mistresses are often un-

reasonable is proved by the recent experiences of two young middle-class girls of good education who had taken domestic posts in a private house. They were looked upon askance when they requested to be allowed out for a short walk during the week. They had the usual free half-day weekly on Saturday, and were actually not expected to go beyond the confines of house and garden between Sunday night and the following Saturday afternoon.

Coming to the more practical matter of training a young maid, here again the modern mistress is often ready enough to complain of the inefficiency of her servants, but will not take the

trouble to train them as in days past. A young, intelligent maid is well worth training and with knowledge she will have an increased interest and self-respect in her work. The following hints based on practical experience gained as a result of training several young girls may be of use.

We will consider the case of a six-roomed flat or bungalow consisting of sitting-room, dining-room, bedroom, bathroom and maid's room as well as a small hall. The bungalow is occupied by a married couple, the husband going to business every day by the nine o'clock train, and returning at about 6 or 7 p.m. *(Continued overleaf)*

Good Housekeeping Diary

The Indispensable Guide for Women of Every Class

Good Housekeeping Diary

and

Household Account Book

for 1935

PREPARED AND EDITED BY
Mrs. D. D. COTTINGTON TAYLOR
DIRECTOR OF GOOD HOUSEKEEPING INSTITUTE

¶ This valuable aid for Women in the Home of every class has again been considerably revised and brought up to date, the expert knowledge of the subjects dealt with being the very best obtainable.

¶ In addition to a complete Diary for 1935 and the special Housekeeping Accounts page arranged for every week and month in the year, Mrs. Cottington Taylor contributes a series of letters at the beginning of each month to the Lady of the Household on "GOOD FOOD FOR THE MONTH," containing important advice unobtainable in any other Diary in the World.

* * * *

¶ This is in addition to the usual features which thousands of women find so useful.

THE GOOD HOUSEKEEPING DIARY
ALSO CONTAINS·

Two specially prepared Maps constituting a valuable guide to the Shopping and Amusement Centres of London, which have been revised and brought up to date,

AND OVER FIFTY SPECIAL COOKERY RECIPES — ONE FOR EACH WEEK OF THE YEAR

Bound in various shades of Cloth and Leather and packed in cardboard boxes, size 4¾ in. × 6½ in.

PRICES

Cloth Edition in cardboard box, 3/9 net;
Post Free 4/3 net.

Leather Edition in cardboard box, 5/- net;
Post Free 5/6 net.

Order at once from your Newsagent, Bookseller or Bookstall, or direct from

GOOD HOUSEKEEPING

153 Queen Victoria St., London, E.C.4

Produced in Great Britain by
LETTS QUIKREF DIARIES LTD.
160 Shaftesbury Avenue, London, W.C.2

TRAINING A GENERAL MAID

(Continued)

The Day's Routine

The maid should rise not later than half-past six or a quarter to seven, so that she can start work punctually at seven. She should open up the house, drawing blinds and curtains and opening the windows.

Her work should then be arranged more or less as follows:

Lay the fire in the dining-room.
Sweep and dust room.

7.15. Light gas stove, fill kettle and put on stove to boil for early tea. Continue dusting of dining-room, and commence sweeping and dusting of hall and passage.

7.30. Call master and mistress. Complete dusting of hall.

8.0. Lay table and cook breakfast.

8.30. Dining-room and kitchen breakfast.

9.0. Clear away, wash up; tidy and sweep kitchen. Clean front door-step, etc., if not done before breakfast. Assist mistress make beds, sweep and dust bedroom. Clean bathroom and lavatory. Sweep and dust lounge, if this is not undertaken by mistress.

11.0. Special work.

12.45. Lay the luncheon table.

1.0. Lunch.

1.45. Clear away lunch, wash up; clean and tidy kitchen.

2.30. Free time until 4.30, to go out or stay in as she pleases, but in any case not on duty.

4.30. Prepare and take in afternoon tea.

5.0. Wash up; commence preparations for dinner.

7.0. Lay table for dinner.

7.30. Dinner. Wait at table.

8.0. Bring coffee into sitting-room. Clear away and wash up. Turn down beds and fill hot-water bottles, if required.

With a new maid it is as well to superintend all the work very carefully for the first month, and the mistress will have to do most of the cooking with the exception of the preparation of breakfast. Take care to correct a young maid calmly, but on the other hand do not hesitate to give a word of praise when this is justified.

If the maid is competent and intelligent, raise her wages if possible, but do not do this because she gives you notice. It is a great mistake to ask a maid to stay on.

Work out a regular daily routine and write down all duties in detail. This helps to give the girl a feeling of confidence, as she can refer to it as often as necessary. She should be given an alarm clock and be shown how to wind it up and set it. She should also be impressed with the necessity of getting up to time in the morning.

When calling the household, she should be told to see that her hands, cap and apron are scrupulously clean. She should then knock at the door before coming in, draw the blinds and curtains, bring in the early morning tea and also any letters or papers if desired. Instruct a young girl that it is essential to bring everything in to her employers on a tray.

She should collect the boots and shoes and clean these before breakfast.

Laying the Fire

It is a good plan to give the maid a pair of gloves. She should also have a housemaid's box with everything she requires in it. She should be taught to spread a hearth cloth over the carpet or rug, and having raked out the ashes, she should be shown how to lay the fire in order that it may burn up as rapidly as possible. She should also be taught to avoid the use of a newspaper for drawing it up. A fire draw-screen constructed of metal is manufactured for the purpose.

Washing up

Few maids wash up well unless they have been given a certain amount of instruction. A little soap in the water is essential and for most things water should be used fairly hot. The silver and glass should be washed first, dried and polished, then the china, and finally, saucepans and baking tins. The maid should be taught to scrub the draining-boards, clean the sink, wash out her dish-cloth or mop after use, wring it as free as possible from water, and hang it up to dry, preferably out of doors or by an open window. Glass-cloths, cloths and tea-cloths should not be allowed to get too wet.

Care of the Gas Stove

The cooking-stove is very frequently neglected unless careful supervision is given. Special care should, therefore, be taken to impress upon a young maid the need for extreme cleanliness in this connection. She should be taught to wipe the oven out immediately after use, while it is still warm, and also to wipe over the hot-plate as soon as cooking is completed. Once a week the interior of the oven should be washed out thoroughly with plenty of hot, strong soda water, in order to remove all traces of grease.

Daily Sweeping and Dusting

Carpets and rugs should be run over with the carpet sweeper to remove all surface pieces and dust, floor surrounds should be rubbed over with a dusting mop, using, if liked, a drop or so of oil. Too much oil should not, however, be used, as this will result in a greasy, sticky floor. All surfaces and ornaments will then require thorough dusting.

In addition to the ordinary daily routine there is also the necessity for weekly turning out of rooms, cleaning of silver and brass, laundry work, etc., which, in a small house, might be arranged as follows:

Monday.—Laundry work.
Tuesday.—Turn out a bedroom. Ironing.
Wednesday.—Turn out lounge. Free half-day, 2.30 to 10.
Thursday.—Turn out dining-room.
Friday.—Clean stairs and hall.
Saturday.—Clean kitchen and scullery.

Turning Out a Room

The maid should be taught to collect everything she will require for cleaning, including the housemaid's box, pair of steps, as well as vacuum cleaner, dusters, polishing equipment, etc. If a vacuum cleaner is in use there is no necessity for a dust sheet. The attachments should be used for the cleaning of upholstery, curtains, high ledges, etc., and the cleaner then used over the carpet or rugs. All that remains is then to dust everything very thoroughly, polish the floor surround and clean the insides of the windows.

Laying the Table

If one has a highly polished table, a piece of felt or special non-conducting mats should be placed under the cloth. For lunch or dinner a tablecloth or linen mats can be used, as preferred, and in either case cork or other non-conducting mats must be used to protect the table from the hot plates and dishes. The maid will require showing in detail how to set soup spoons and knives on the right hand and forks on the left with dessert spoon and fork above.

Teach her to cover the sideboard or serving-table with a cloth and to place on this all necessary utensils for serving.

Afternoon Tea

A tray with cups, saucers, tea plates, tea knives, sugar basin, milk jug, etc., should be prepared. Show the maid how to cut thin bread and butter and also how to make tea, taking care that the teapot is properly warmed with boiling water, and that the water used is actually boiling. When all is ready she should spread the cloth on the tea table, and follow immediately with the prepared tray, unless, of course, a tea wagon is used, when everything can be wheeled in. One or two points must be impressed.

1. She must be taught to come in quickly and quietly.
2. She should not knock at the door.
3. Having arranged the table with cloth, she should bring in the tea itself as quickly as possible.

After clearing away the tea, everything should be washed up, and it is most essential to have a bottle brush for washing the insides of the small milk jugs, teapot spouts, etc., and keeping the cup handles clean.

Waiting

Where only one young maid is kept, she will not have much time for waiting at table, although it is as well, if possible, to let her wait at dinner. Tell her to hand the dishes on the left-hand side of the diners. Having handed round the vegetable dishes, she will have to attend to the dishing of the next course, coming in to clear away plates, etc., when the bell rings.

THE
30's

How much

IDEAL HOME
EXHIBITION
Mar. 26—Apl. 18
Stand No. 81

to cook
this dinner

A few pence buy the fuel for a day's cooking on the ESSE Heat Storage Cooker. The ESSE provides more appetising food, giving incomparable service and amazing economy whether cooking for a small family or for a large dinner party. The ESSE COOKER burns anthracite continuously—no daily lighting. Its fuel costs are only one-fifth to one-twentieth those of coal, electricity or gas. It has three extra large ventilated ovens, a toasting radiant, and a big, powerful boiling hot-plate.

The Auxiliary Oven gives extra cooking space as well as ample " hot-cupboard " room.

A minute or two daily is all the attention this wonderful Cooker needs.

**EXTRA LARGE CAPACITY . BIG BOILING HOT-PLATE
LARGE SIMMERING TOP . AUTOMATIC HEAT CONTROL**

COOKER . £65.   Plate-rack and back-panel . £5
COOKER AND AUXILIARY OVEN . . £80.
    Plate-rack and back-panel . £5 15s.

"No Deposit" Hire Purchase if desired.

THE
ESSE
COOKER

British Patents Nos. 370680 ; 390119 ; 390674 ; 390749 : 394177 and
Licensed under British Patents Nos. 205071 and 332444.

Full details and particulars of units with water-heater, etc., from Dept. G.H.7.

SMITH & WELLSTOOD, LTD., BONNYBRIDGE, SCOTLAND
Also at 11 LUDGATE CIRCUS, LONDON, E.C.4 ; LIVERPOOL, EDINBURGH & GLASGOW.

SERVES 100% PERFECT MEALS ... SAVES 80% OF FUEL COSTS.

Our Readers and Ourselves

A page of letters selected from the Editor's post-bag

This is *your* page, where your comments and opinions on the magazine and its contents may be given expression. The Editor will be delighted to receive your letters and afford scope for your ideas—but please keep them general in interest and worded as concisely as possible

THE
30's

FROM A READER WITH A SENSE OF HUMOUR

"I have been very interested in your series of articles, 'How Others Live.' All my life I have loved to peep through inviting windows. But I must confess that I have not read any of the articles without considerable heart-burning. Of course one must expect that in a vicarage they cultivate the ascetic life and are given 'to low living and high thinking'—but in all the seven articles I have been amazed at the frugality of the menus. Does no one nowadays ever have a square meal, I reflect?

"I am a north-country woman, but have lived in the south for ten years. We live in a small house, and have two very sturdy children, a young maid and a vacuum cleaner. We have a small salary—£400 per annum. Since an ungrateful Government reduced it by 10 per cent. I have taken a paying-guest to help to pay 'the butcher, the baker, and candlestick-maker.' I cook vast meals every day: I find your recipes most useful: I methodically plan our menus every week with one eye sternly on the calorific and vitamin value; we do all the housework to a time-table. But I cannot compete with these wonderful women who 'keep house' on so little a week, and can turn a room out in an hour and a half, 'clean all silver, polish floor and all furniture'!

"To conclude on so disgruntled a note would be ungracious, for I do want to thank you for Dorothy Whipple's delightful story, *They Knew Mr. Knight.* In my opinion, it is the best serial you have ever published, and I have read GOOD HOUSEKEEPING since its first number appeared. Her characterisation delights me with its cleverness: I love to re-read some of its subtlest bits of gentle irony. Hitherto I have been one of those readers who preferred your articles to your fiction, but the stories have improved miraculously in quality of late. And may I very greedily ask for another short story from the author of *The Heart of Mr. Pickernel?* One of the most memorable short stories I have read."

MRS. M. J. R., Reigate.

FROM A READER WHO LIKES INTELLIGENCE

"As I have been a constant reader of GOOD HOUSEKEEPING for many years, may I be permitted to send an architectural query to your Director of Housing? I should be so very grateful for his assistance and advice, before spending money —possibly in an unwise manner—on necessary alterations.

"Perhaps tributes from readers are too numerous to be appreciated, but in this, my first and probably last letter, I really would like to express my appreciation of a magazine that gives intelligent articles to housewives instead of treating them to the pitiful sentimental slush of most papers that ostensibly cater for women. I have learnt much from your 'Monthly Lessons,' and shall continue to enjoy the reading of your magazine for as many months as it appears (though it would be kinder to you to say 'for as many months as I am here,' as your work should go on for ever—and I cannot)."

MRS. A. E. H., East Horsley.

FROM A READER WHO DISLIKES "SILLY SENTIMENTALITY"

"I have taken your magazine from its very first issue and have always admired your valiant stand for better houses, better cooking, and health, but surely you can do better than this type of story:

"'*His man-face, dark with the coming need for shaving, stirred her, and his man-arm, lying over the cover, ready to awaken to strength and action.*'

"I rather think those twopenny papers for flappers could give a more interesting story.

"Sorry to be so disgruntled. I thought the Mariel Brady series were poor enough, but——!

"I do like *Mr. Knight.*"

MRS. E. M. D. P., Manchester.

FROM A READER WHOM WE ADVISED

"In September of last year, I wrote to your Medical Correspondent, asking his opinion of Tenerife's climate for a person suffering from bronchial catarrh. It may interest him to know that my husband and I came out here before Christmas. We spent the first three months in the Valley of Orotava. Unfortunately, this past winter was the worst experienced for more than twenty years. Of course, the weather was not nearly so bad as home. There was a general absence of sunshine, and this is considered unusual here. A doctor in Santa Cruz told us that Orotava was too damp and that we should have gone to Guimar on the south side of the Island. The English colony is at Orotava, where they have a delightful 'Outdoors Recreation Club' and a very fine library. No one comes to the south side of the Island, and no effort is made to attract visitors there. However, in spite of this information, we decided to risk a few weeks at Guimar. The village is just an ordinary Spanish village. The only 'hotel' where a Britisher could stay is a small house situated above the village at a height of 1,200 feet. It is run by a German as a mere 'sideline,' along with a small farm. We find that the air here is much drier and much more suitable for my husband. "We have most of our meals out of doors on the verandah, and we feel very pleased with this little hotel. It compares very favourably with the other hotels on the Island.

"After a five months' holiday, I sail for home next week. I have had GOOD HOUSE-KEEPING sent out to me each month and am now looking forward to making use of some of its publications which have appealed to me."

MRS. A. R. K., Tenerife.

FROM A READER WHO GROWS HER FAMILY'S FOOD

"Having read with interest the articles on 'How Others Live,' I am venturing to send you some details of our garden, which is worked by my husband and myself for the benefit of our family.

"Facing south, about 500 square yards of land is attached to our house. With the exception of a flower border, and a small lawn for the children, almost every foot of this land is set with vegetables and fruit. A small lean-to greenhouse at the rear is fired during the winter and early spring, and all our plants are raised from seed. To give a better idea of how we make our garden provide us profitably with vegetables throughout the year, I will give a list of the various kinds produced in each respective month of last year:

January.—Leeks, cabbages, sprouts.
February.—Leeks, cabbages, sprouts.
March.—Leeks, cabbages, sprouts, lettuce (from frame), rhubarb.
April.—Leeks, cabbages, sprouts, lettuce (from frame), rhubarb.
May.—Spring cabbages, shallots, lettuce, rhubarb.
June.—Spinach, spring cabbages, shallots, lettuce, early potatoes, turnip-tops, gooseberries.
July.—Spinach, potatoes, beet, carrots, swedes, onions, lettuce, gooseberries, strawberries.
August.—Peas, beans, cauliflowers, cabbage, beet, onions, red and black currants, tomatoes and cucumbers from greenhouse.
September.—Vegetable marrows, tomatoes, beet, potatoes, cabbage, apples.
October.—Leeks, celery, beet, potatoes (stored), cabbage, apples.
November.—Leeks, celery, sprouts, beet, potatoes (stored), cabbage.
December.—Leeks, celery, sprouts, potatoes (stored), cabbage.

"Our family consists of three children, my husband and myself, and I may say, at almost every meal, we partake of some produce of our garden. I am able to provide appetising daily meals of excellent food value mainly from our garden produce, especially during the warmer months, when meatless days are preferable. In addition we grow the various kinds of herbs, and our fruit trees and bushes provide us with jams and preserves almost throughout the year.

"The outlay is trifling, the cost of seed and fuel is amply covered by the sale of surplus plants raised in the greenhouse. There only remains the price of manures and fertilisers, which cost about 15s. to £1 annually. Our family is very healthy, and the children sturdy and strong."

MRS. E. B., Blaydon-on-Tyne.

THE IMPORTANCE OF GOOD

THE
30's

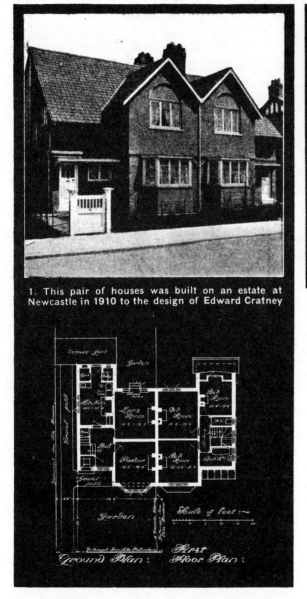

1. This pair of houses was built on an estate at Newcastle in 1910 to the design of Edward Cratney

Ground Plan : First Floor Plan :

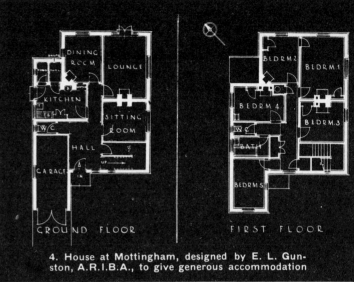

4. House at Mottingham, designed by E. L. Gunston, A.R.I.B.A., to give generous accommodation

GROUND FLOOR   FIRST FLOOR

Jessica Albery, A.R.I.B.A., discusses the past, present and future development of the semi-detached house

EVERYONE knows what a great number of houses for sale at prices varying between £500 and £900 have been built since the War. Green fields have been swallowed up, and complete new towns seem to have been built overnight. Unfortunately they are not towns of which most people feel very proud.

House-owners are usually car-owners too, and the motor-car has been developed, during the twentieth century, from an awkward imitation of a horse-drawn carriage into a highly efficient transport machine, having fine lines and a most satisfactory appearance. During this time the small house has not been developed at all! The reason for this lack of evolution is, perhaps, that there has been so great a demand for houses

3. House built in 1935 on Messrs. John Laing & Sons' estates, designed by A. W. Kenyon, F.R.I.B.A.

DESIGN IN THE SMALL HOUSE

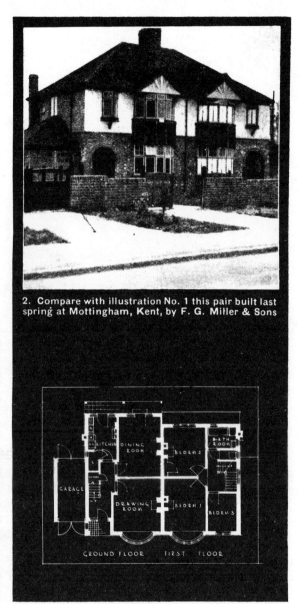

2. Compare with illustration No. 1 this pair built last spring at Mottingham, Kent, by F. G. Miller & Sons

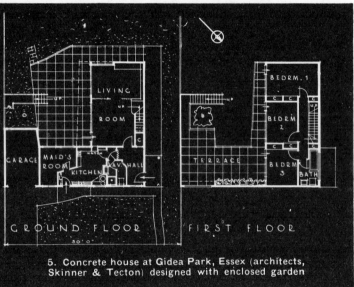

5. Concrete house at Gidea Park, Essex (architects, Skinner & Tecton) designed with enclosed garden

HOUSING

Conducted by

Joyce E. Townsend,

A.R.I.B.A.

Free advice on all housing problems will be gladly given by the Director of Housing to any reader who writes to her, c/o Good Housekeeping, 153 Queen Victoria Street, London, E.C.4. A stamped addressed envelope should always be enclosed

that any builder has been able to sell the same old design with a different coloured paint on the front door. Illustration No. 1 is of the plan and front view of a pair of houses built in 1910; the great majority of houses built since then have almost exactly this plan, while usually their appearance is much less well considered. For instance the pair shown on this page in illustration No. 2 is in plan almost identical, and was built this year.

This type of house has, of course, certain advantages: the arrangement of rooms is such that the passage-space is kept down to the minimum; there is then no wasted space, and the rooms are the largest possible for the total size of house. Moreover, the living-rooms face one in each direction, so that one of them will get some sun, whatever the aspect of the house, and this is important for the estate developer, as is

also the grouping together of the plumbing—kitchen under bathroom.

Unfortunately, owing to the expenses of road-making, the individual plots have to be long and narrow, and this makes the satisfactory planning of the house difficult; but with careful thought and determination, the various problems can be solved and much better houses built. Passages and stairs are often narrow and dark, but a little extra space in hall or passage, when properly planned, can give a feeling of "elbow room" and a pleasant atmosphere to the whole house. Variety in the shapes of the principal rooms is obviously desirable. Usually all four are of exactly the same shape, having windows at the ends in the short walls, but rooms with windows in their long sides are always much more agreeable.

BUDGETING FOR A MONTHLY SALARY OF £37 10 6

(Mother, Father and Four Children)

	£	s.	d.
Rent (mortgage repayments and interest) . .	4	10	8
Rates, including water .	1	3	10
Housekeeping (£3 7s. 6d. weekly) . .	14	12	6
Fuel and lighting (10s. weekly) . .	2	3	4
Insurances, etc. . .	1	11	2
School Fees (2 boys) .	2	6	8
Papers . . .		7	0
Clothes . . .	6	0	0
Spending allowance for husband . .	2	10	0
Allowance for doctor and dentist . .	1	0	0
	36	5	2
Balance . .	1	5	4
	£ 37	10	6

Weekly Accounts

	£	s.	d.
Groceries . .		14	5
Meat and fish . .		12	5
Greengroceries . .		8	1
Dairy . . .	1	0	3
Bread . . .		4	2
Wages—daily girl . .		5	0
Sundries, including window cleaning and bus fares		3	2
	£3	7	6

This is not an "ideal" budget drawn up by the Institute, but one evolved by a reader to suit her own family. Details are on page 51

Details are on page 51

THE
30's

P. L. GARBUTT discusses
REAL-LIFE
BUDGETS

collected from among in-terested readers during the past year

Where strict economy is essential, personal shopping goes a long way in helping to keep the household accounts within the necessary limits. Only by this means can the housewife take advantage of specially inexpensive food offers which are frequently made in the shops when there is a super-abundance of any commodity on the market

LAST year we published a number of real-life budget problems, which aroused exceptional interest. In fact, so many readers wrote asking for more that we have gone to some trouble to collect further data somewhat on the same lines. Especially at this season of New Year resolutions a study of how others manage their monetary affairs, even should one not altogether agree with their apportionments, may be of assistance in balancing one's own expenditure more wisely. Whether one's income happens to be in the hundreds or the thousands class is immaterial, for in either case careful budgeting will be of equal value in helping to ensure freedom from financial worries.

Some careful people like to plan their budget according to percentages recommended by various authorities on the subject. Such a method of budgeting has its limitations and is, perhaps, more applicable to the very moderate in-

It is always wise to check the electric meter readings at intervals, in order that any undue extravagance may be noted

The keeping of household accounts is tremendously simplified if a reliable account book is used. At this time of year our *Diary and Account Book* is in great demand, and our office boys are kept busy

come rather than to one which allows freedom as regards details of expenditure. For the majority of our readers, we feel that individual planning is more frequently called for. In working out a scheme of one's own it is hardly necessary to remind readers to make a mental list of all the special circumstances, such as whether saving is essential or not, for a point such as this obviously has a large bearing on other allocations.

Perusal of the many budgets submitted by readers from time to time indicates that, although the general scheme of expenditure is often well planned, there are one or two fairly common faults. Food expenses, for example, often reveal an exceptionally large bill for groceries. There are so many attractive prepared foods on the market to-day that this is not surprising, but where economy is needed, careful scrutiny of the grocer's account often proves really worth while. In the past the butcher's account was also often unduly heavy, but nowadays lighter meals are the rule and this criticism does not so frequently apply. On the other hand, expenditure on fresh fruit and vegetables and dairy produce is generally lower than is desirable from the health point of view.

Gas, electricity and fuel are sometimes used wastefully, and if one's quarterly bills seem very heavy it is a good plan to read the gas and electricity meters regularly for a time. If the readings obtained are compared with those of a similar period in previous years, any undue extravagance, possibly on the part of a new maid, will soon be noticed and can be checked.

The tendency to extravagant use of cleaning materials is also fairly frequent, for maids are very apt to think that elbow grease and personal effort can be saved in this way. They are, of course, quite mistaken, as apart from the actual wastage, in many cases unnecessary wear and tear is caused by the lavish use of certain cleansing agents, notably those of the abrasive type. Actually, also, far greater energy is required to polish a surface when too much wax or furniture cream has been applied than when it is used sparingly.

It is hardly necessary to go over item by item in this way, for extravagances vary, and it is for the individual to whom economy is essential, to scrutinise her expenditure as impersonally and critically as possible. She will probably have little difficulty in laying her finger on any leakage there may be and she can then take steps to find a remedy.

How other people face their problems is always a fascinating and interesting study, and it is hoped that the budgets published here, all of which have been submitted by readers, will prove of help to others. We do not necessarily consider them exceptionally well-balanced, but have refrained from adjusting them, as we think that other readers will prefer to see the actual figures which, if not theoretically ideal, have at least passed the test of practical experience. Some are more or less complete budgets, but others only give details of the housekeeping expenditure, the latter obviously being of special interest to GOOD HOUSEKEEPING readers.

Before passing on to these, we would remind readers of the *Good Housekeeping Diary and Account Book,* which is planned to simplify the keeping of household and personal accounts. We should also like to say how glad we are to give individual advice to any readers who write to us for assistance.

The budget on the opposite page was received at the Institute just as this article was being prepared for press, with the accompanying letter:

"After you so kindly interviewed and 'lectured' me last August at Good Housekeeping Institute, you asked me to send *(Continued overleaf)*

REAL LIFE BUDGETS
(Continued)

**THE
30's**

you particulars of our budget and here it is. I should be so very obliged for any comments.

"Since seeing you I have made drastic reductions in my housekeeping, but find great difficulty in finding a varied collection of cheaper dishes, particularly for midday dinners. I have your *A.B.C. of Cookery*, but wonder if menus are published which would be suitable for our slender allowance. In case you have forgotten particulars of our family, it consists of husband and wife, three boys—ages 13, 11 and 9 years, one baby girl—1½ years, one daily girl for midday meal and tea.

"I am enclosing sheets with details of budget (see page 50) and you will see I have made a big effort to live on our income. However, I still feel there should be a larger margin, but where and how to cut down now I do not know. As you will note, there is no allowance for renewals to house and home, nor for holidays other than the £1 5s. 4d. per month."

The Institute feels that this reader has now worked out a very creditable budget and makes the following suggestions:

"It will obviously be necessary to amend the budget slightly to make any appreciable provision for renewals, holidays, etc. Try to cut down expenditure on fuel a little, keeping the total to not more than £2 per month. You may also care to cut down a little on clothes, say 5s. or so per month, and perhaps your husband could also manage a small reduction of his personal allowance of 5s. In this way it should be possible to effect a saving of about £8 per annum which, together with the balance of £1 5s. per month or approximately £15 per annum, would make a total of £23. This would only allow of a very economical holiday, but perhaps you could rent a small furnished cottage in a country district for a few guineas per week. Food, etc., for the holiday period would be covered by the ordinary housekeeping allowance."

Five other budgets sent in to us by readers now follow.

Budget No. 1
A Vicarage

Income: £650 and a house.
Family: Two adults, four children (aged 13, 11, 5, 3), daily help and woman two days a week.

My husband is the Vicar of a pleasant seaside parish. We pay no rent, but rates etc., amount to a considerable sum, and upkeep expenses, such as heating, lighting, are rather heavy.

The house is convenient and only just large enough for our family, so that we have only outside help. We have sitting-room (coal fire), dining-room and study (gas fires) and kitchens with gas cooker and independent boiler. Upstairs are five bedrooms and a bathroom. We pay an annual charge to Queen Anne's Bounty for external repairs to the house, and this is included under "Vicarage" in our budget. We have a car and our holiday charges are low because, although we have a month, we usually exchange house and duty with another parson and make all our excursions in our car. School fees for our three elder children are not heavy, although the second (a boy) attends a small public school and the two older girls an excellent private school. This and the absence of medical fees is due to generous special arrangement. Income tax is low also because of allowances for children, car and professional expenditures. I care for the family, cook and do a certain amount of washing. All cleaning is

left to my helpers whose only fault is that they do not live in, so that I have to stay at home most evenings. The item called "Sundries" includes presents, postages, medicines, bus and tram fares, newspapers and periodicals, part telephone and amusements. Our food is, of necessity, of the simplest, but we use many eggs and as practically all jams, cakes, etc., are home-made we all have plenty of varied plain food and are blessed with good health.

Yearly Budget

	£	s.	d.
Income tax . . .	14	0	0
Insurances . . .	30	0	0
Vicarage (rates and dilapidations) . . .	65	0	0
Fuel and light . . .	37	0	0
Housekeeping (11 months) .	213	0	0
School fees . . .	40	0	0
Household repairs . .	10	0	0
Religious and charitable clubs .	56	0	0
Sundries	36	0	0
Personal £20 (self), £20 (husband), £25 (family) . .	65	0	0
Holidays	37	0	0
Car	37	0	0
Savings	10	0	0
	£650	**0**	**0**

Weekly Budget

	£	s.	d.
Wages	1	8	9
Laundry	0	2	6
Milk and eggs . .	0	13	6
Meat	0	10	4½
Greengrocer . . .	0	6	0
Grocer (including butter) .	1	1	6½
Fishmonger . . .	0	3	3½
Baker	0	2	9½
	£2	**17**	**6**
Total	**£4**	**8**	**9**

Budget No. 2
A Doctor's House

Family: Two adults, three children, maid and nurse.

I have yet to see a budget in which the wife has an allowance on which to run the home, excluding rent, rates, insurances, telephone, car expenses and holidays. These last are all heavy items with us, and my husband deals with them, allowing me £500 per annum. I am not expected to save, merely to keep out of debt. I might mention that I am one of the thousands of doctors' wives trying to make one penny do the work of two and run an efficient establishment, including the practice side of it, on one young maid and one young nurse. I have three children, aged 6, 4½ and 6 months. I have kept strict accounts for five years, and find things run smoothly with a small margin with the following arrangements:

Monthly Budget

	£	s.	d.
Food: This includes drinks, entertaining, cleaning materials. We feed well on about 14s. 7d. for adults, 9s. 6d. children, 4s. 6d. baby weekly	19	10	0
Lighting and Heating: This includes gas, coal, coke for boiler, wood, electricity. (£5 winter, £3 summer.) .	4	0	0
Laundry: Only children's and oddments done at home .	3	0	0
Wages: Maid, nurse, windows, occasional help, insurance stamps	6	13	4

REAL LIFE BUDGETS

Monthly Budget (continued)

	£	s.	d.
Personal: Clothes for self and children (I make all children's, including coats, and sell when outgrown). Presents (quite a large item), plants for two gardens, photographic expenses (for snapshots)	5	0	0
Household: Replacements, linen, curtains and loose covers, (which I make), maids' and nurses' uniform, wallpaper and paint, furniture, etc.	2	10	0
Papers, etc.: For house and two waiting-rooms, stamps, stationery	1	0	0
	£41	13	4

Budget No. 3
A Business Man's House

Income: £263.
Family: Two adults, two children.

Our income is not large, we are of those who have suffered and had to "mark-time" during the industrial depression, but we hope that my husband's position and income will improve in time to give the children the higher education and start in life they may need.

We live on one of the housing estates and have a good house of three bedrooms, bathroom, 2 living-rooms, scullery and garden. There is a good elementary school on the estate. I do all my own work, cleaning, cooking and washing (all with the aid of as modern equipment as I can afford), and knit and sew for myself and the children and still have time to read and keep up-to-date so as to be a companion to my husband.

Yearly Budget

	£	s.	d.
Rent and rates	35	0	0
Coal and logs	10	0	0
Electric light and power	5	0	0
Housekeeping	117	0	0
Insurances	26	0	0
Subscriptions	3	10	0
Clothes and renewals	30	0	0
Holidays	20	0	0
Doctor and dentist	4	0	0
Husband's pocket expenses	12	10	0
	£263	0	0

Weekly Budget

	£	s.	d.
Grocer	0	16	0
Greengrocer and fruit	0	6	0
Butcher	0	8	0
Milk and eggs	0	8	0
Fish	0	2	0
Laundry	0	1	0
Newspapers and library	0	2	6
Chemist	0	1	6
	£2	5	0

Budget No. 4
Two Doctors—(Husband and Wife)

Income: £1,000 (approx.).
Family: Two adults.

Both my husband and I are doctors living in the heart of the country, and so, on account of my work, I have no time for helping in the household duties, but must rely on efficient servants. Such servants are not too easy to obtain in the country, but by careful selection and by having a detailed knowledge of what one wants done, suitable staff can be found. Naturally they must be given comfortable quarters and good wages. We employ a married couple, the wife does the cooking and lighter housework, while the man, in the morning, takes on the heavy housework, windows, etc.; in the afternoon, on four days a week, he does odd carpentering or painting jobs, while on the fifth afternoon he presses my husband's clothes. He is free from 4.30 to 7.30 (his wife is free in the afternoon) and then at 8 o'clock he waits at dinner.

After breakfast I inspect the larder, criticise or praise yesterday's menus, write out the menus for the next twenty-four hours, do the necessary ordering by telephone, and then leave the servants to carry on for the rest of the day while I attend to my own work.

Our joint income is just over £1,000 a year, after income tax has been paid. On this sum we are able to live very comfortably, afford a month's holiday abroad every year, have a number of visitors staying with us during the summer, and save £65 a year by life insurance.

Yearly Budget

	£	s.	d.
Wages (married couple)	116	0	0
Wages (gardener, part time)	48	0	0
Rates	25	16	0
Insurances	8	0	0
Housekeeping	198	10	0
Laundry	22	4	0
Coalite, anthracite, logs, paraffin	32	10	0
Petrol for car and lighting plant	64	10	0
Money placed on deposit towards cost of new car	60	0	0
Replacements	24	9	0
Repairs to house	43	0	0
Telephone	12	14	0
Library and club subscription	10	0	0
Amusements	26	0	0
Holiday	100	0	0
Clothes	110	0	0
Gifts and sundries	34	0	0
Life insurance	65	0	0
	£1,000	13	0

No. 5
A Budget from the Wilderness

We live in the midst of a howling wilderness—picturesque and healthy certainly but far from civilisation—hence I am glad to pay one shilling weekly to a girl who is kind enough to do my shopping.

The family consists of husband, self and three children aged respectively five, seven and eight. I teach them myself, make all their clothes and do my own washing with the exception of bed and table linen. The house is modern with six rooms, and I do all the housework. The children do not eat meat, but have plenty of milk and butter. They are remarkably strong and healthy, very rarely suffering from so much as a cold. My husband pays the rent, rates and coal bill. We cannot afford newspapers and magazines—good friends pass these on to me. For clothing for myself I am thankful to accept "cast-offs" from my sister's wardrobe. Here is my weekly budget:

Weekly Budget

	£	s.	d.
Meat	0	4	3
Bread	0	2	0
Milk	0	6	9
Eggs	0	2	0
Vegetables	0	1	6
Groceries	0	15	3
	£1	11	9

THE 30's

147

A Convenient Country House

THE
30's

Left : the exterior, appropriately treated in Sussex style. Note the brick margin to the lawn and the flagged pathway. Below : the dining-room taken from the stairs, showing sideboard in the recess, and a general view of the living-room

Architects :
Minoprio and Spencely, AA.R.I.B.A.

Described by Baseden Butt

NO matter what our taste may be, and apart from the extent to which individual requirements may vary, it is of increasing importance that a country house should be planned so that it is easy and convenient to run, and so that it provides pleasant comfort for everyone. Moreover, it must make the most of the site selected, so that wherever fine views exist they may be enjoyed to the full.

It is also essential for the house to incorporate up-to-date practical and decorative features while at the same time conforming with the architecture associated with the neighbourhood. One would not, for example, build a Cotswold stone cottage in Suffolk, nor an Essex brick house in the Cotswolds. There is almost as much to be said to-day for employing, so far as possible, materials which are obtained locally as there was years ago when transport was more difficult. This, of course, comes under the head of making the most of one's site, for it means that the house

Built in Sussex at an inclusive cost of £2,000

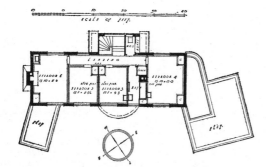

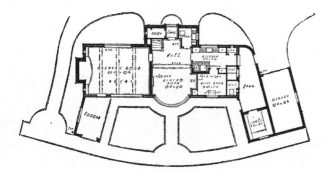

HOUSING

Conducted by

Joyce E. Townsend,
F.R.I.B.A.

Free advice on all housing problems will be gladly given by the Director of Housing to any reader who writes to her, c/o Good Housekeeping, 153 Queen Victoria Street, London, E.C.4. A stamped addressed envelope should always be enclosed

The kitchen is well equipped with built-in fitments and is decorated in primrose yellow. The upper storey of the house is hung with red tiles, which also roof the bay-window of the dining-room. The brick-built loggia outside the living-room has an outlook to south and east

must be designed in a way which is courteous to the neighbourhood as well as enabling those who live there to go on enjoying the rural scene without any feeling of displeasure at the advent of a "new house."

These several requirements have been fulfilled in the house here illustrated with a degree of thoroughness which, it must reluctantly be confessed, is not always found. It combines extreme practical efficiency and many modern features with an architectural style appropriate to its locality, and its windows are placed so that the noble views surrounding the house can be enjoyed fully *(Continued overleaf)*

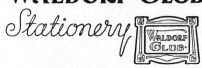

150

A CONVENIENT COUNTRY HOUSE
(Continued)

from indoors. In addition to its practical fitness, the plan betrays the quality of having been visualised and worked out to a fine result.

The site chosen for this house was midway on a steep slope at Kingsley Green, near Haslemere, on the borders of Surrey and Sussex. There is a particularly fine view towards the north, and for this reason, the architects have provided wide windows on both the long sides of the living-room, with an outlook north and south, thereby making the most of both sun and country-side. The whole south elevation really forms an extensive sun-trap. The house was originally planned with a brick-built loggia on the west, looking south and east, admirably balanced by the tool house and garage forming a wing over which a future extension could be built. This extension is now being carried out, by the addition of two extra bedrooms. A broad stone pathway runs the entire length of this front, and in the centre is the wide bow window of the dining-room which, again, is a feature taking fullest advantage of both sun and landscape.

Although treated in a modern way, the exterior is in traditional Sussex style, the upper storey being hung with red tiles similar to the red roofing tiles. All windows are metal casements set in limed oak window frames, and multi-coloured bricks in brown, red and purple are used for the main walls and chimney stacks. The front door is of oak with a decorative surround of shaped bricks which were made specially for this purpose.

The interior woodwork, including the floors, is for the most part in pine, slightly darkened by staining, and wax polished. The plaster of the walls is grit finished, and in the principal interiors, and hall, staircase and landing, is a pinkish parchment colour, this being sufficiently neutral to serve as a background for a variety of colour schemes while at the same time suggesting appropriate similarity of character.

The living-room, which is the largest interior in the house, has a wide fireplace with a raised brick hearth and cosy corner seats, and has stout wooden beams running across the ceiling. The dining-room is divided from the hall by heavy hanging curtains fixed along another beam which forms an architrave. This room is charmingly equipped with mahogany furniture in the style of Hepplewhite.

While the living-rooms all enjoy a south aspect, the hall with its entrance lobby, cloak room and wardrobe, is on the north. The kitchen, too, has north windows, and there is a tradesmen's entrance on the east opening on to an enclosed yard. Adjoining the kitchen is a servants' sitting-room, which has a south aspect.

The various kitchen fitments are up-to-date and remarkably efficient in their manner of arrangement, having been installed so that the utmost possible accommodation and service is available in a small space. There are abundant cupboards and a built-in kitchen cabinet, all with "flush" doors, and a dresser with glazed sliding doors. The sink is beneath the windows, the interior window shelf being protected with white tiles, and draining boards and a plate rack are on either side. The kitchen colour scheme is simple but effective—pale sunshine yellow walls and ceiling, green linoleum and green and white chintz curtains. A gas cooker and an independent boiler occupy a tiled recess.

There are four bedrooms, each of which has its fitted wardrobe cupboard. All the bedrooms have windows on the south. There is a linen cupboard on the land-

ing and storage space for trunks and boxes. The bathroom is situated between the third and fourth bedrooms and has a green bath and lavatory basin. The bathroom walls and ceiling are silver grey, and the bath itself is in an arched recess at the back of which is a modern, simply conceived mural decoration in pale yellow and white, which was painted by Anthony Minoprio. This, almost in monochrome, is an interesting example of a style of wall decoration which is highly effective without being too insistent. It often happens with wall paintings that the greater the realism and the more elaborate the wealth of detail, the more quickly is the eye wearied, but a simplified treatment, being much more truly decorative, is a source of constant charm. In the present case, the decorative character of the painting is emphasised by the fact that the design is reminiscent of eighteenth century *chinoiserie* and the willow pattern plate.

The bathroom is decorated with a simple mural in yellow and white on silver grey

The heating is allowed for in several ways which have been chosen for efficiency and convenience. There is an open coal fireplace in the living-room and a second in the bedroom immediately over it, the flues being carried up in the same chimney stack. The living-room has also a hot water radiator beneath the north window which is heated from the kitchen boiler, and there are similar radiators in the hall and on the upper landing. The dining-room has an electric fire, and there are electric fires in the second and third bedrooms. The fourth has a gas fire. There are thus three different methods of artificial heating in the four bedrooms, and it is possible for each member of the family to enjoy the kind of artificial warmth they most prefer. There is also the minimum of inconvenience in the event of a breakdown, and owing to the existence of the hot-water radiators there is no necessity to light the coal fires except in really cold weather.

The cost of the house was £2,000, including the drive, gates, paths, paving, terracing, drainage, decoration, and a number of the electric fittings. It is at once admirably suited to its site, charmingly reminiscent of the traditional domestic architecture of Sussex, and extremely modern from the point of view of practical efficiency, comfort, and convenient arrangement.

Christmas at the Chesters

THEY'VE done some wise spending—sending cheer to the old folks—useful gifts to the bright young things.

Economy in their own household is seen in their adoption of a Metro Coke Fire—which permits immediate economy in fuel and ultimate saving in the elimination of chimney-sweeps, and a reduction in spring cleaning costs.

The dish warmer is from Jim and Mary—it plugs in to their special gas holder.

THE CHAREES METRO COKE FIRE

This Grate is specially designed and con‗structed to burn household coke—a cheap smokeless fuel.

Coke burned this way makes a brightly glowing fire, capped with flickering flames, having all the psychological appeal of a coal fire.

The design of this Grate with its hammered iron effect gives it a style of the Tudor Period—that old‗world atmosphere so sought after to‗day.

12″ Fire, price in Rough Armour Bright Finish, **£4 19s.**—Catalogue showing many other models, Free on request.

THE METRO GAS DISH WARMER

Constructed of a polished aluminium plate, stainless steel legs fitted with Bakelite toes and handles.

Complete with gas burner of special design, having 4′ of silk covered flexible gas piping $\frac{1}{4}$″ diameter, connected to burner with a union joint and fitted with an automatic bayonet jointed tap, which is made with a floor plate suitable for making good to any gas‗point, or the tap may have an attachment for connecting to an existing gas bracket.

Uses 2 cubic feet of gas per hour.

Size 1 6$\frac{1}{2}$″ wide, 1 2$\frac{1}{2}$″ deep, 4″ high. **Price 37/6.**

Write for full particulars (and give the address of your Gas Office) to SIDNEY FLAVEL & CO., LTD., 43 The Foundries, Leamington.

When in London call and see the whole range of models at the Flavel Galleries, 38 Welbeck Street, W.1.—a permanent Exhibition, covering over 5,000 sq. ft. floor space.

FLAVELS of LEAMINGTON

& 38 WELBECK ST., W.1

Manufacturers and Distributors of the Metro Coke Fire for the South Metropolitan Gas Co.

151

THE
30's

THE ITCH

*Speaking as an old-established
her reactions to those ruth*

THAT remarkable woman, Winifred Holtby (now, unhappily, no longer with us), said once that there was no itch in the world more exasperating, no impulse more commanding, than that felt by efficient people to take hold of the affairs of the inefficient and put them right by force. She was herself efficient in a dozen ways, and this sounds like a cry from the heart. How numerous are the muddlers, how avoidable their muddles, and how easily a very little common sense, ruthlessly applied at the right moment, could straighten out their lives for them! Thus must sensible persons muse; and their dreams at night must be troubled horribly by the thought that, given a free hand, they could so easily and quickly set the world to rights.

But I am (at heart) one of the muddlers, and I know that it may not, after all, be quite so easy as that. I know

my own sensations when a competent friend tries to set me to rights. They are a murky compound of inner resentment, outward compliance, and a dogged, or rather mulish stubbornness.

Take, for example, competence as applied in the nursery. I lead the friend, full of theories and the best will in the world to help me, up to the nursery to say good night to my daughter, who is discovered trying to stand on her head under the bedclothes. The bed itself presents an odd appearance, having apparently been made the wrong way round. After rather tempestuous good nights have been exchanged we retire to more civilised quarters, and my friend says crisply:

"I suppose you know that child's head and shoulders are in a through draught?"

I admit that this may be so, and proffer something feeble about the nursery being such an odd-shaped room.

"If you turned the bed round, so that her head was against the wall, it would be all right," says the friends. "If I were you, that's what I should do."

"Of course, you're quite right."

"Let's run up and do it before she goes to sleep," says the friend, zealous in well-doing. "She may easily get a disgusting head-cold, the way it is now."

"Yes, but——"

How is the muddler, involved in a net of other people's wills and won'ts, to give a true account of the inner history of this business of the bed? If it is

Illustrations by Clixby Watson

OF EFFICIENCY

muddler, the author describes lessly competent people

by HELEN SIMPSON

turned the other way, as the friend suggests, a peeling patch of paper becomes dangerously accessible to idle hands. No child can resist a peeling patch of paper, it is the strongest of nursery temptations, and the only thing is to put the child out of its way. Otherwise there will be succumbings, and subsequent punishments, not wholly deserved. The efficient thing to do would be to have the room repapered; but at once that problem crops up which gets in the way of slum clearances: what to do with the inhabitants in the meanwhile? Send them away for a couple of days would be the efficient solution. But school can't be missed, and paper-hangers won't work, and can't be expected to work, on Sundays.

Additional difficulties pile up. The bed's present position has become a formidable magic, protecting its occupant against bears, snakes, and the things that go bump in the night; to change it will bring down nobody knows what terrors. We all of us have these private magics, from Dr. Johnson down; numbers, attitudes, rules which we must keep for our own mental comfort: there is no arguing against them, and to punish for holding to them is barbarous. It is all very absurd, and at the same time very real. Psychologists utter grim warnings about interfering with such fantasies. What to do?

The end of it all is, that I resist my friend's sensible impulse, giving no reason, since I cannot hope to present her with anything sufficiently convinc-

ing, but fobbing her off and distracting her mind with offers of refreshment. Meanwhile I privately determine that the bed must stay as it is until December, when school ends and a holiday can be arranged; the child meanwhile doing all in its power—happily she enjoys gargling—to prevent and rebut that cold in the head to which my pusillanimity has exposed it.

From this single example, which has its parallel in a dozen other situations, all equally idiotic, and pressing equally insistent claims upon the attention of the muddler, it will be seen that logic is not always the solvent. The incompetent is a person for whom two and two never make, quite neatly, four. His arithmetic is for ever subject to the shocks of Wonderland mathematics; Ambition, Distraction, Uglification and Derision beset all efforts to make the ends of his problem meet. Indeed, the Mock Turtle's world is, taking it all round, the only one in which the incompetent can move with a sense of ease. There, fantasy and the unexpected always come off best. There, the tyranny of two and two is ended.

But the Mock Turtle's world is, alas! for the muddler, only a beautiful dream. He can retire into it now and then, for brief blissful periods, but sooner or later an efficient person will discover and drag him out into the light of common day. He comes quietly, knowing it to be a fair cop, and that there is not much use in resistance; life, he tells himself drearily, is real, life is earnest.

Let us then, he resolves, set about living it, and see if we cannot work up some interest in efficiency too.

With this he—it is more usually she—decides to do the thing that's nearest, and demands to be shown the household books, neglected for weeks in the vague but baseless hope that if left long enough they will settle themselves. At once, feeling adequate, the householder perceives, and demands an explanation of, a mysterious sign, rather like a starfish, opposite the item " 1 lb. toms." This means, it appears, that two of the tomatoes were bad, and were taken back to the shop. The credit due on them, *2d.*, was expended there and then on a bunch of watercress; so that neither this nor the watercress makes any appearance in the book at all, the transaction having somehow and inexplicably taken on the status of a cash payment. A trifle bewildered, the householder remarks:

" Oh ! "

And setting a business-like tick against the starfish, proceeds with the investigation. The books seem all right, as checked by a memory quite unable to recall the details of any meal previous to yesterday's luncheon; but at last there occurs an item (for fish) which looks suspicious. The memory, taxed and backed by an engagement book, pays up at once. On Saturday week there were no dining-room meals, that was a week-end visit; whence, then, this expensive sole?

" I'm sorry to say, madam, that was pussy."

Dover sole, at heaven knows what a pound, for cats to eat! What next? The householder pretends to be shocked; likes cats very much, but really must draw the line—

" Oh, not for him, exactly, madam. That is—well, you know what a bad boy he is. That was the day he went next door, and the housekeeper there told me you could have knocked her down with a feather when she saw my lord up on the table."

" Did he steal it ? "

" It was *(Continued overleaf)*

153

THE
30's

" **...** my considered opinion is that
"a coal fire burning in a modern
"grate of the Triplex type is
"generally the most comfortable and
"most desirable form of room heating,
"and that food cooked in a coal-heated
"oven is more wholesome and more
"delicious in flavour than that with
"which the gaseous products of com-
"bustion have been allowed to come
"into contact.

PROFESSOR A.M.LOW.
The Great Scientific Authority in a report entitled "The Comfort of Coal" writes as above···

There is one room in the house more than another that always draws you. The room with a coal fire where the light from the dancing flames flickers lovingly on ceiling and walls. And in a Triplex Open Grate coal gives of its best. It has a scientifically designed system of ventilation which ensures a smokeless, fumeless fire that warms you, cooks for you and gives you a plentiful supply of hot water in bathroom and kitchen.

There is no food so healthful and nourishing, science says, as food cooked in a well-regulated Coal oven. It is more delicious cooked the Triplex Way. There are no fumes and no smoke with a Triplex Grate. No soot and flying smuts. No drying up of the air. It is easy to clean and very inexpensive to run.

The Triplex Grate
TRIPLEX FOUNDRY LTD.
Great Bridge - Staffs.

Showrooms:
LONDON - - - 12 Newman St., W.1
BIRMINGHAM - - 3 Stephenson Place
MANCHESTER - - 33 Princess Street

154

THE ITCH OF EFFICIENCY
(Continued)

next door's dinner fish, yes, madam. Not stole it exactly, but she saw him breathe on it, and the Doctor's very particular, so away it had to go. Of course I told her you'd make it good."

The householder once more can find no better comment than:

"Oh!"

And so the tale told by the tradesmen's books goes on, a romantic and vivid tissue of incident, stirring up resentments, partisanships, despairs, and conjectures. From the money side they do not get properly dealt with, of course. All those slips of paper, vilely written, stained with steak and fish and tomato juices—how is it possible for the muddler, dependent on her fingers as the Chinese merchant upon his abacus, to tot them up, and allot them totals, and compare these totals with those arrived at by the tradesmen? "Do them weekly," impatiently says the efficient person; "then there won't be so many, and you can easily cope with them." But weekly there are so many other, and more entrancing, things to see and do; walks in the parks; writing novels; bookstalls in the Farringdon Road; composing, by means of canvas and coloured wool, flowers that never were on sea or land; cooking; chattering; broadcasting; playing with children and cats . . .

"How can I help you," demands the efficient person, by now genuinely enraged, "if you won't make the effort? You simply won't try. It's so simple, everything's so easy, if only you'll use common sense and some sort of method. I could solve all your ridiculous problems on my head, in five minutes. Use your wits! I believe"—this with infinite scorn—"I believe you *like* muddle!"

There is no answer to this accusation, for the good reason that (speaking now as an old-established muddler, resentful of competence, wedded to the craven and roundabout methods by which unpleasantness is avoided) it happens to be true.

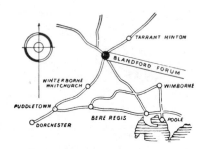
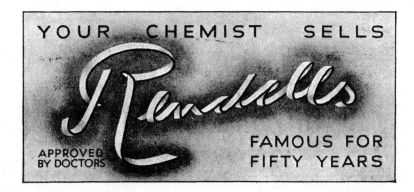

THE 30's

Half-Time Home Life

In this plea for the woman who runs a job as well as a house, it is the love and thought, rather than the actual time we put into a place, that makes the home, says

IRENE STILES

MODERN marriages are more remarkable for their spirit of comradeship than were the marriages of yesterday. Not that we need pat ourselves on the back about it. Modern conditions make it possible for us to be comrades in every sense of the word. Men and women of to-day meet on more or less level ground. There is every incentive towards good companionship.

One of the finest comradeships I know exists between a husband and wife who share what some of the more critical of their friends are pleased to call a half-time home life, a make-shift marriage. And all because the wife "runs" a job as well as a home!

"I'm sorry for Peter," these well-meaning critics say, "getting home to an empty flat" (as he does very rarely), "and always eating restaurant food" (which is worse than an exaggeration).

Actually this so-called half-time home is more efficiently managed and infinitely more comfortable than many which are run by whole-time housewives. There is really no room for criticism or comparison, but the critics in this case judge not so much by results as by the amount of time wisely or unwisely expended in achieving those results.

Peter's mother, one of the severest critics, was born of a generation of women who found all the interest and happiness they required in the then more various and complicated aspects of housekeeping and homekeeping. Her early married life was a peaceful country affair. As the wife of a country town solicitor she had her share of entertaining to do. Butter-making, extensive preserving and pickling of orchard and garden produce played no small part in the household activities. Naturally enough she found it was as much as she could manage to be out of kitchens or garden and into a different frock in time for dinner at night.

She has to admit when she goes to Peter's home that everything *looks* all right and Peter seems well enough. The food appears to be good; is astonishingly well cooked and pleasantly served. In fact the whole atmosphere of Peter's home is friendly and restful, and everyone, including two growing children, seems very happy in it. Peter's mother looks on incredulously and with a certain half-grudging admiration, quite convinced that there is a catch somewhere. She is, so to speak, always half-expecting to meet some housekeeping skeleton whenever she happens to go to the linen cupboard or the larder.

She forgets that the old-fashioned house in which Peter was born was a place of many stairs and difficulties. She forgets that those were the days of still rooms and oil lamps, of obstinate kitchen ranges, wash-hand stands and constant cold water. Moreover, families were larger then and large houses were needed to accommodate them. It is worse than foolish to compare her own case with that of Peter's wife who, in her home life at least, has only to contend with the conveniences of a well-equipped, modern, labour-saving flat.

Peter's wife, being a tolerant and good-humoured woman, suffers her mother-in-law's unspoken censure and the not unspoken criticisms of her friends with a smile and the firm conviction that it does not really matter. Peter, however, takes it all rather more to heart. Only he, after all, knows what an essentially good manager his wife is. For has she not contrived to be a good worker and earner outside the home and a good wife and mother at the same time? Have they not with their joint savings been able to give their children a far better education than would have been possible had there been only his earnings to draw from?

The busy woman, like the busy man, finds time for everything. It is invariably the inefficient housewife who complains drearily that she has no time to read, answer her friends' letters or darn her husband's socks, let alone try to earn some money in her spare time. Admittedly a half-time home life needs careful organisation if it is also to be a happy and comfortable home life. But then, any full life needs a good deal of organisation, whether it be the crowded life of a film star or member of Parliament.

Obviously certain privileges and concessions must be accorded to the woman who earns her living and runs a home at the same time. She will, if she can, wisely suit her home to her present needs. A good deal must of necessity depend upon whether she is married or single.

If she is married with a young and growing family and lack of funds is no obstacle, she may prefer to live in the country that lies less than fifty miles from town. I know one family who do this very successfully. The family consists of wife, husband, the wife's brother, who is in business with the husband, and two young children not yet ready for the schoolroom proper.

The original idea was that the small country house was purchased for the benefit of the children in order that they could grow up in plenty of space, light and fresh air. In practice, however, the grown-ups derive almost as much enjoyment and healthy benefit from the place as the children do. Long summer evenings away from noise, dust and petrol fumes, and week-ends in the garden all the year round prove themselves well worth working for, and because there are three bread-winners backing this establishment in various ways the little extra expenditure of time and money involved in travelling to and from town is more than justified. Health is and should be of first consideration, and change of scene is possibly almost as important to the mental worker as change of air.

In this particular household there is a staff of three: a trained nurse for the children (who does all the preparing and cooking of food for the nursery), a cook-housemaid, and a chauffeur-gardener (who also does a few odd jobs in the house). This may seem a large staff for a smallish

HALF-TIME HOME LIFE

house, but a good deal of simple week-end entertaining is done and living out of town would not be practical without a chauffeur.

Many people in similar circumstances prefer a fast train service to a drive to town in the face of increasing traffic difficulties. For the only alternative to keeping a chauffeur waiting about in town all day for the return journey, is to drive oneself, and this is hardly a good preparation for a strenuous day's work. Even if the fast train service is patronised there is the problem of getting to the station, and here the chauffeur-gardener or chauffeur-secretary comes to the rescue. In the case I have quoted the chauffeur-gardener drives the three bread-winners to the station in the morning and fetches them from there at night. In spite of a full, hard-working and incidentally very happy life, the wife and mother in this establishment makes time for quite a number of household and nursery duties, and always does the household accounts and supervises the menus. Most working women, however, are concerned with a flat or small house and possibly one maid, or even, as in my own case, with a small flat and a very little daily help. Here, perhaps, we may start talking about the concessions and privileges!

The half-time housewife, if she is to live in a flat, will naturally prefer one of the labour-saving varieties, complete with central heating, constant hot water and refrigerating system. If she is already settled in a small house or converted flat without these conveniences, she will choose gas or electric fires for most of her rooms in preference to coal. Should she or her husband prefer a coal fire in one room, she certainly will not feel it her duty to clean her own grate or lay her own fire, for she knows that her earnings warrant her paying someone else to do the rough work.

She will find it very necessary to practise economy in the time as well as the money she spends on her housekeeping, and there is absolutely no need for the home to suffer because of it. Indeed professional women, by very reason of the organisation they must of necessity put into their housekeeping, often become the best and most systematic housekeepers. Unless rigid economy must be observed a telephone cannot be regarded as an extravagance, especially now that rentals have been reduced. The telephone allied to a weekly account with one good "all-in all" store will prove of great assistance. A weekly survey of supplies and accounts and a weekly provisional compiling of menus are great time-savers and will also eliminate too many afterthought telephone orders.

I know one woman (without a telephone) who sends a weekly postcard to her provision merchant with her daily needs written clearly on it. Each day, or every other day as the case may be, her orders are delivered at the time requested. Even with the telephone two or more days' orders may be given in one call. For if you have decided, more or less, what you are going to eat during the week a good deal of ordering may be done at once, and more than one dinner may be prepared and cooked at the same time. Quite apart from one's own inspirations in these matters, there are cooking stoves and cookery books especially designed to meet the needs of busy women.

Where there is no help the chores of the half-time home life should obviously be shared by the family or members of the establishment more or less equally. If the wife should cook and prepare the evening meal, husband and children should

wash up and clear away, but since this is often the mode of procedure in an ordinary household, it is perhaps unnecessary to stress or even suggest this. Obviously again, so far as married people are concerned, the half-time home life would be neither possible nor practicable during the whole of married life. A new baby changes everything and most existing conditions have to be altered because of the newcomer, for the time being at least. Moreover, few mothers will wish to go out and earn a living while small babies need the care which only mothers can give.

When the children are growing up it is a different matter and nowadays, hard and cynical as this may sound, a little extra money may prove far more helpful than a lot of love and care. It is, after all, the old story of a little (practical) help being worth a lot of pity. And once a child is past babyhood it is easy enough for a clever mother to ensure that neither child nor husband suffers in any way because of a half-time home life. Indeed, when we consider that most children are away at school all day and many away for the whole term, it is difficult to see how and where the children of professional women suffer at the expense of their mother's career.

The clever manager of a famous firm of beauty preparation manufacturers could tell you a strange and interesting story if he were writing this article. With his permission I shall tell it instead. Some of his earliest recollections are of being taken to a crèche in New York every morning and being fetched every evening. The pretty creature who took him and fetched him was his mother. Left a widow by the young husband who had taken her to America, she set out to earn her living as best she could. First of all she worked in a hat shop and then at a hair-dressing establishment, which sold its own beauty preparations as a side-line. Working there also was an analytical chemist interested in herbal dyes and remedies. She used to talk to him sometimes about the creams and lotions her own grandmother made from the flowers and fruits of an old Gloucestershire garden. In due course these two, already bound together by the common interest of their work, fell in love and married.

Of this second marriage there were two more children. With each the mother gave up her work until the child could be safely entrusted to the care of others. Apart from these respites that woman continues to be to this day a very successful half-time home maker. Those who criticise her for working when she no longer needs the money receive the very satisfactory explanation that this business which she has helped to build up, not only gives employment to herself, her husband and three grown children, but also to the children of many other mothers and fathers and to the fathers and mothers of many other children!

More interesting than all this, however, are the clever young manager's stories of the small rented room that was once his home. Short as his waking hours with his mother were, the details of that shabby room impressed themselves on his young mind as the details of his later and more comfortable homes did not. It was a poor enough place in which to try to rear a small boy. For him it was a quarter-time rather than a half-time home life, but love and determined cheerfulness in the face of tremendous odds made of it something which he will always remember with tenderness and gratitude. For it is the love and thought, rather than the actual time which we put into a place, that make the home.

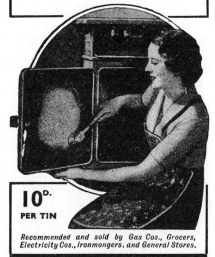
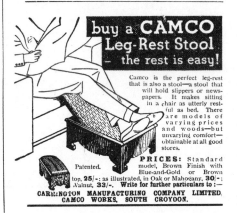

ASHLEY

Owed to Spring

How searchingly the young Spring sunlight pries into the house! How it shows up faded curtains and dingy loose covers, and makes you long for new ones! Why not? Waiting in the shops are all Sundour's new Spring fabrics — crisp and gay as a bunch of fresh tulips. Go and see them. Go and revel in the bright, inex-pensive Sundour prints, the dainty cretonnes, the linens of buttercup, rose, and periwinkle blue, the delicate satins and silks. Choose whichever you will — Sundour fabrics are all practical, all fadeless. They will put sunshine into your house, and keep it there, not only for this Spring, but for years to come.

Sundour {furnishing fabrics

' Sundour' is the registered trademark of Morton Sundour Fabrics Limited, Carlisle, who guarantee Sundour fabrics unfadable

The Cross-Word Garden
A new idea for planning a garden

Described by Gerald Wynne Rushton

A DEFINITELY new note in garden-design is not an easy thing to achieve. The Dutch garden— the Tudor garden —the Parterre garden—the Wild garden—all give one opportunities; but, unless they are supremely well done, the Dutch garden is a muddle, and the parterre is apt to recall the worst moments of the geranium-cum-lobelia-cum-marguerite era; while the wild garden is as often as not more wild than garden, and less garden than bare.

Thinking over this matter of originality of design—I was concerned primarily with a piece of ground that I wanted to look "different"—I found myself staring, fascinated, at a cross-word puzzle. In a flash I saw it in terms of design for a garden. Now, there are two great advantages about the designs illustrating this article; or, if it comes to that, about any cross-word puzzle that lends itself as a basis for garden design. The two advantages are, formality and irregular charm. If one studies either of the two designs given here, the formality is obvious; but the irregular design is not so obvious. Yet it is in the design before ever a single plant is set out in the beds.

Take, for example, the design above. The black spaces correspond to beds. The white is paving, or grass, or gravel. Incidentally, in gardens of this sort paving or gravel subsequently give the least amount of trouble to keep in order. The centre of the design is a swastika. Immediately, centrally, above, below, to right and left of it, are long narrow beds, as it were dividing the design into four quarters. If we examine each one of these quarters they all differ, though each is made up of eight beds. But the beds are so arranged as to give an air at once formal and irregular to the whole.

Now let us deal with the treatment of these beds. One can, of course, please oneself in the matter, but I propose to follow the charming effects afforded us by the example of Spanish gardens, where the planting follows the usual Eastern plan of using one, or at most two, flowering plants to each little square, or small bed.

Anyone who has seen the Court of Cypresses in the Alhambra will remember how fascinating the flower-beds were there. In this way, I would fill the long narrow central beds on each side of the swastika with delphiniums and Michaelmas daisies. The swastika itself could be planted with flowering-cherries, under-planted with pink monthly roses and lavender. The other beds could be planted with annuals; great masses of mallows, or clarkias, sweet sultans and cornflowers; the shifting blues of nigella, stocks, flaunting poppies and pansies; gorgeous African marigolds or stiffly splendid zinnias. If the beds were edged with violas, or the silvery lamb's ears (*Stachys Lanata*), the effect would be charming. Or, if one likes, one can edge the beds with dwarf lavender, or rosemary kept clipped to a foot to eighteen inches in height. This latter makes a really charming edging. It is cheapest to raise the plants quickly from seed, sowing each seed in April or May, six inches apart where the plants are ultimately to grow. Or one can put in rosemary cuttings, taking care the "heel" of the cutting rests on sand and is firmly planted. Alternatively, one could use the same design for a garden of flowering shrubs. The swastika and the dividing narrow beds could be planted with flowering trees; crabs, laburnum, cherries, almonds, snowy mespilus, halesia tetraptera, judas trees, etc.—and each of the remaining beds confined to some one shrub, so grown as to give its individual beauty room to show off the "line" of the plant, which brings me to the question of dimensions. If the paths are three to four feet wide, which is a comfortable width to walk in, one can, with a little thought, work out the size of the beds for oneself. In any case, it depends on the size of the plot you intend to allot to the cross-word garden. I have in mind a piece of land not quite a quarter of an acre in size for the experiment.

The design on the opposite page gives one some really magnificent opportunities for decorative effect. For instance, the large corner beds could be planted with almond trees under-planted with Persian lilacs, and deutzias, or philadelphus. In the very centre of the garden a single "blue" cypress such as cupressus Lawsoniana var. Rosenthali, or cupressus Fletcheri would be handsome, uncommon and altogether less obvious than a sundial. The eight beds around the cypress could be filled with border carnations, lilies and roses— reminiscent of the famous picture "Carnation—Lily; Lily—Rose." On the outside the sixteen square beds, between the corner beds of lilac and almond etc., could hold a single double-flowering cherry tree in each bed; under-planted with azaleas, lilies, irises or annuals.

Or one could, returning to the Spanish tradition, have a Moslem garden. But this confines one in the choice of plants.

(*Continued overleaf*)

THE 30's

(Continued)

On the other hand the choice includes pink roses, lilies, irises and jasmine. It also permits bay trees and cypresses. And above all it permits, nay demands, the "glorieta," a characteristic feature peculiar to Spanish and Arab gardens. The "glorieta" is an arbour made of roses and jasmine, or bay trees interwoven and trained to a great height, or even treillage (as at San Roquela in Majorca). The arbours are round in shape, and eight in number, and each stands at the crossing of any paths in the garden. Their obvious position, if one were using this design would be between each of the eight beds around the cypress in the centre. They are derived from the eight pearl pavilions of the true believer's vision, where eight lovely houris await their master in the Moslem paradise.

This garden gives us the choice, in flowers, of all the lilies (white, yellow, orange, pink), all the irises, all the pink roses, *but no others;* the lovely red jasmine Beesianum from China, which is perfectly hardy, as well as the yellow and the old white jasmines; not to mention the stately decorative quality of the bay laurel. If one can add the charm of water to one's garden one can also enjoy the delights of Japanese irises and water-lilies. Failing a water supply (always

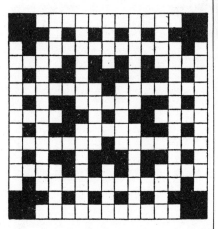

rather an expensive luxury to do well as tubs of stagnant water, let into the ground, are apt to collect scum and become a breeding place for flies and, in any case, are never the same as pools fed from a running or laid-on water supply) the Moslem motif can be used in a cross-word design—and adds the halo of antiquity to what is essentially a modern invention, since cross-word puzzles, per se, are definitely post-war in date! Thus will the age of Mahomet and the age of Mustapha Kemal meet in your garden—and thus will you yourself earn a reputation for quite unexpected originality.

FOR THE BUSY HOUSEWIFE

Useful hints on all aspects of housework, including cookery, laundry-work, cleaning and repairs, save you much unnecessary worry and irritation. Send for *The Housekeeper's Dictionary of Facts,* 1s. 2d., post free, from GOOD HOUSEKEEPING, 153 Queen Victoria St., London, E.C.4

Illustrations by   Franke Rogers

BEDTIME BOAT

I have a little tiger whose name is Tawny Ted;
He's so scudgelly and woofelly I take him into bed.

And I have an alligator whose name is Alastair;
He's nobbly and pobbly, so he sits on the chair.

I have a little porcupine whose name is Peterkin;
He's so prickly and tickly that he cannot come in.

I have a little camel whose name is Cautious Claude;
But he's humpy and he's bumpy, so I don't take him aboard.

For my bed's a ship at night=time to sail a starlit sea
And no one who is awkward can come on board with me.

So I sail until the morning with Tawny Ted as mate,
But we're always back in harbour punctually at eight.

Then, after we have breakfasted, Tawny Ted and I,
When Peterkin and Alastair and Cautious Claude are by,

I tell them all the things we saw, as we sailed our starlit sea,
With Tawny Ted for Master's Mate, and for the captain, ME.

M. T.

DO YOU KNOW

by P. L. GARBUTT, A.I.C.

The first of a practical series of hints which will appear from time to time

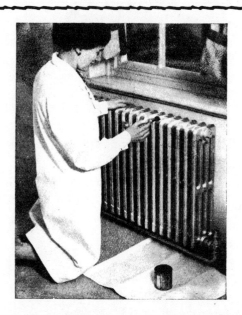

. . . that it is a very simple matter to renovate hot-water radiators which have become shabby, or alternatively to alter their colour, if this does not coincide with the decorations of the room?

As with other decorating jobs, careful preparatory treatment to remove dirt, dust and grease is demanded, and the radiator or radiators should first of all be washed thoroughly with strong soda-water, using a brush to get into all the interstices. When they are quite dry, a stiff wire brush will ensure removal of all signs of flaking, traces of rust, etc. Suitable metal paints can now be obtained for treating metal surfaces which must withstand heat, and in addition to the more usual aluminium, silver, bronze and gold shades, blue, green, red and mauve colours are also available. After applying the paint, it is an advantage also to apply a protective varnish, which will guard against tarnish and result in a smoother and more easily cleaned finish.

. . . that when fabrics, including net, are washed, any shrinkage is invariably greater the selvedge way of the material, rather than the weft? Anyone sufficiently interested can easily ascertain this for herself, by cutting a square of fabric, measuring carefully and washing. When dry, measurements will sometimes reveal quite a spectacular difference between the length or selvedge way of the material and the width or weft. A big study of shrinkage problems has been made lately, and by suitable manufacturing treatment it is possible to reduce or eliminate shrinkage altogether. There are, however, still fabrics on the market which exhibit a fairly considerable amount of shrinkage on laundering, and although we have discovered nets which hardly shrink at all, net curtains are often an example. Little can be more exasperating than after laundering to have to unpick, lengthen and restitch hems. With a little care, this can be avoided. The curtains should be carefully measured before washing, and afterwards gently pulled into shape and back to their original measurements. They can then be laid out flat or pinned to dry, on a large table or suitable rack, or if there appears to be much tendency to excessive selvedge shrinkage, this can be counteracted by pressing, etc., and then inserting a smooth wooden rod through the top and a heavier bar through the bottom hem of the curtain while still wet. Two open cupboard doors a suitable distance apart make a convenient support for the curtains and rods while drying.

. . . **that** the current consumed by electrical appliances of a mechanical nature is practically negligible? It is surprising how many people think that to use a vacuum cleaner or washing machine for any length of time must result in the consumption of a fairly considerable amount of current. Nothing, however, could be further from the truth, for such machines can be used for four or five hours with a consumption of only about one unit of electricity, an amount out of all proportion to the work done. Thus, a really heavy wash, for instance, can be accomplished by a domestic washing machine for a mere fraction of a penny, since electricity is now available in most parts of the country for a penny or twopence per unit or less, and the consumption only amounts to $\frac{1}{4}$–$\frac{1}{5}$ unit per hour. Other labour-saving tools, such as a vacuum cleaner or polisher, can be used equally economically. Why not, therefore, make full use of them at very little cost to oneself, other than the initial outlay?

Large organisations, such as up-to-date hotels and steamship companies, invariably appreciate the economy of mechanical labour-saving appliances. The photograph on this page was taken on board the *Queen Mary*, where vacuum cleaner models identical with those supplied for ordinary domestic purposes are in daily use. In addition to the long-handled machine shown, which is used for carpets and floors generally, small portable dusting machines are used for cleaning upholstery, cushions, etc.

. . . **that** the surface of a trolley table, or other article of furniture exposed to heavy usage and required to withstand hot plates and dishes, can be protected from damage by applying a suitable clear lacquer or varnish preparation? Before doing so all traces of grease, polish, etc., must be removed from the surfaces to be treated. In the case of a trolley already stained, and to which wax polish has possibly been applied from time to time, rubbing with a cloth dipped in turpentine or a turpentine substitute such as white spirit will be a suitable way of doing this. Strong washing soda or caustic solutions should be avoided unless it is also desired to strip the wood of the existing stain. After thorough preparation, the varnish should be applied evenly over the surface and allowed to dry and harden thoroughly before the trolley is taken into use again.

It should be remembered that varnishing is one of those jobs which should be undertaken on a dry day, as the presence of dampness or moisture tends to dull and spoil the finish, often giving it an unsightly " bloom."

. . . **that** many people spoil their furniture (1) by applying polish far too lavishly, (2) by marking with hot plates, (3) by spilling scent?

A very sparing application of polish, followed by a quick " rub up," gives more satisfactory results and leaves a hard polish which will not smear or finger-mark so readily as when polish is used extravagantly. With the exception of the dining-table and other articles of furniture subjected to exceedingly hard usage, it should only be necessary to use polish once a month or even less frequently.

Small whitish marks occurring on polished wood, as the result of the effect of hot plates or dishes, or the spilling of a few drops of perfume, can as a rule be removed by applying one or two drops of methylated spirits on a soft cloth, covering with a single layer of material or piece of folded muslin and rubbing on and around the mark. It is important to remember that literally a drop or so only of spirit is required and that too much will do more harm than good. Used correctly, the spirit works by removing from the undamaged part of the wood surface traces of stain and polish which serve to colour and revive the injured part. This method of treatment is, however, only suitable for smallish marks, and where fairly extensive areas are damaged, rubbing down, re-French polishing and more drastic treatment altogether is usually demanded.

THE
30's

"The Pantiles"
at
Oakfield Glade, Oatlands Park,
Weybridge.

FOR SALE

Apply

Good Housekeeping

153, Queen Victoria St., London E.C.4.

THE HOUSE
THAT
Good Housekeeping
BUILT

Realising that practical experience is essential to those who would give reliable information on home-making, Good Housekeeping Institute has co-operated with the Architectural Editor in building a house which incorporates its ideals of materials and equipment. The house is now complete, and a large number of readers have expressed their satisfaction. Provision has been made for the installation of all types of electrical equipment, and the house is centrally heated. Downstairs there are a large kitchen, hall, lounge, dining-room, and sitting-work room ; upstairs, two bathrooms and five bedrooms. The purpose of the Magazine being achieved, the house is offered for sale at its cost price.

In a Modern Flat

THE illustrations show two of the rooms in one of the Dolphin Square flats decorated by the Institute. Below is a view of the nursery, furnished in peach and blue. The curtains are made of a new material, resembling glazed chintz, which does not lose its glaze when laundered In the sitting-room (left) the fitted carpet, woodwork, walls, fireplace surround, and damask curtains are in off-white, and the upholstery and curtain-borders in colour. An article describing the flat will be found on the next page.

FURNISHING
& DECORATION

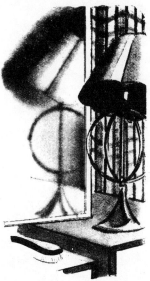

The colour scheme of the bedroom is rust, cream and green, which shows the sycamore furniture to the best advantage

THE INSTITUTE

—and discovers a

novelties to intro

MARCH proved an outstandingly interesting month for Good Housekeeping Institute, for in addition to our daily routine work at 49 Wellington Street, we came into close contact with large numbers of readers at the flats we had decorated, equipped and furnished at Howard House, Dolphin Square.

Meeting our readers is no new experience, because they are always welcome at the Institute, but the flats provided an unusual opportunity to show

modern trends in hangings, wall decorations, furniture and floor coverings, as well as in the equipping of kitchens where space is limited.

For the benefit of those who were not able to visit Dolphin Square personally, we are describing and illustrating one of the flats this month, and are looking

The nursery in peach and blue (left) proved very popular with visitors, special interest being centred on the new unit furniture for small people

THE
30's

Supplementary heating is provided by a gas fire of new design. The woodwork, walls and fireplace surround are all decorated in off-white, and the chairs and settee upholstered in green

furnishes **A FLAT**

number of decorating

duce to our readers

forward to discussing the others later.

No. 207 Howard House consists of two bedrooms, a sitting-room, a small kitchen and bathroom, and a hall of moderate size, and in common with the whole of the block it is centrally heated, and provided with lavish quantities of hot water. In contrast to the other two

flats, in which we installed electrical equipment, gas appliances were chosen for No. 207, and included the latest type of gas cooker, built-in refrigerator and an entirely new type of gas fire.

The decoration throughout is light in tone. The colour scheme chosen for the bedroom is cream, for the sitting-room off-white, for the second bedroom, which we furnished for a small girl, peach, and for the kitchen blue.

Weathered oak furniture was chosen for the dining-room-lounge (right), and off-white, crush-proof carpet laid throughout the flat

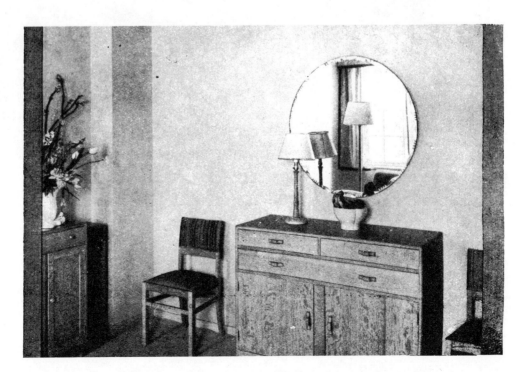

Above and on opposite page : two views of Dolphin Square, where readers may see the three flats decorated and furnished by the Institute.   Left is a plan showing how to reach Dolphin Square, which is situated on the Embankment, overlooking the river

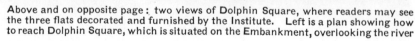

The Institute shows furniture and fabrics in homelike settings

Good Housekeeping extends a Cordial Invitation to its readers

IT has always been the aim of GOOD HOUSEKEEPING to be more than a magazine, and readers who regularly or occasionally utilise the services of the Institute appreciate the value of our work, and in particular, the thoroughness with which the testing of domestic appliances is carried on.

With the desire to be of still further help in 1937 we have planned to equip, decorate and furnish three livable and practical homes in the centre of London, and we extend a pressing invitation to readers and their friends, not merely to inspect them, but to make the fullest possible use of the services of the Institute staff. The invitation extends from Monday, March 1st, to Wednesday, March 31st, and members of the staff will be available on weekdays, including Saturdays, from 11 a.m. to 7 p.m.

We have been fortunate in securing the co-operation of the owners of Dolphin Square—Europe's largest block of self-contained flats—who, two months ago, put three adjoining flats, Nos. 205, 206 and 207 in Howard House, at our disposal to treat as we wished. Nothing beyond walls, floors, doors and windows were provided, so we were free to create homes which, we venture to hope, will provide inspiration, and offer suggestions of ways and means by which your own home can be made more convenient, labour-saving and attractive.

Furnished show houses there are in plenty, but GOOD HOUSEKEEPING homes are different, for they are equipped throughout with our Approved Appliances, and with fabrics, furniture and bedding which we have proved are reliable, and which are covered by our guarantee. Moreover, the homes will be in actual use; cooking and housekeeping will be in progress, and answers will be given to any domestic query, whether it concerns the cooking of puff pastry or sweetbreads, the making, laundering or cost of net curtains, or the furnishing of a not too costly Regency bedroom. Advice on the choice of floor coverings for bedrooms, nurseries, bathrooms, kitchens, etc., the making of chair covers, colour schemes, or on catering, will all be dealt with in a homely atmosphere. Readers who

want help with special problems are asked to make an appointment by writing to me at Good Housekeeping Institute, 49 Wellington Street, Strand, W.C.2, so that the person best qualified to deal with the particular enquiry will be in attendance for the interview.

In brief, it is our wish during the month of March to transfer many of the activities of Good Housekeeping Institute to Dolphin Square, where, in fact, we shall be doing the same work, but in a home where our ideas and theories have been put into practice.

Readers who are not yet acquainted with Dolphin Square will find it an impressive building in Grosvenor Road, facing the Thames, between Chelsea and Vauxhall Bridge. The accompanying map will show its relationship to other important centres such as the Houses of Parliament, the West End, St. James's Park and Victoria Station.

River-front wharves are being dismantled to give an uninterrupted view of the Thames. Three acres of garden, a restaurant, and free telephone calls to tradespeople, are some of its features which, whilst undoubtedly of great attraction, are insignificant compared with the domestic amenities which are available to residents. Sound-insulation, a children's boarding centre, cleaning service by the hour or week, and a central tradesman's delivery arrangement will appeal particularly to the practically minded woman who sees no virtue in unnecessary housework.

The children's boarding centre is an outstandingly unique service, which makes life possible and congenial for the parents of young children. No description of the facilities which Dolphin Square provides in this direction will give a true impression; a visit, a few words with the Matron, a glimpse of the toddlers' dining-room, the day and night nurseries, older children's play-room will prove that it is no mere term to attract tenants. Children from ten days to seven years can be accommodated for as short a time as one hour, or even for a single meal, or they may take up permanent residence, so whether the mother wants freedom from the responsibility of looking after a tiny infant or toddler for an odd hour, a day or a week-end, she can at very reason-

able cost transfer her duty to the Matron, who is assisted by a staff of trained Nannies. A daily time-table from rising until bed-time, and afternoon walks under the supervision of a Nanny, make the children's lives happy and full.

One of many nursery details which I noticed was the infant's wardrobe provided at the foot of each cot, so that there is no risk of one baby's belongings becoming mixed with another's. A small point, but one which will appeal to mothers, is that the temperature of each child is taken when it is received at the Centre, even if the visit is to be of the briefest. The object is, of course, to guard against the danger of any child carrying infection.

It was with pleasure that I noticed the Matron had selected GOOD HOUSEKEEPING approved enquipment, and she was proud to show me the washing machine with which all the babies' laundry was done within the nursery wing, sheets only being sent away.

Residents at Dolphin Square can if they wish dismiss all domestic details, and leave them in the hands of the competent Housekeeper who is in charge of a uniformed staff of domestic workers. Fixed prices are charged, according to the size of the flat, and the services given, vary from as little as 6s. 6d. per week, which comprises the daily washing-up and making of beds, and vacuum cleaning and dusting three times a week.

Unique and delightful though the Dolphin Square flats are, we are not only inviting those who are house-hunting to visit us, but more especially readers of GOOD HOUSEKEEPING, and their friends, who are interested in up-to-date household decoration and equipment. The Institute devotes much of its time to the testing of household appliances of all kinds, from refrigerators to kitchen ranges, but, while our premises are ideal for the trying out of cooking stoves and equipment, washing machines, ironers, water softeners, etc., we have not before had an opportunity of displaying furniture, fabrics, and interior decorations, which can only be shown to advantage in a complete home.

D. D. COTTINGTON TAYLOR.

ANNE ORR *Needlework* DESIGNS

A Round Flower-bag in Canvas

IF you want to make a present for a friend who has a garden full of flowers and loves to cut and arrange them in vases, the simple flower-bag illustrated on the right is a splendid choice. It consists merely of a circular piece of strong awning canvas, bound with coloured bias binding and supplied with handles. Laid out flat to receive the cut flowers, it picks up easily and holds the blooms without crushing them or breaking the stems.

A rich blue canvas was chosen for the original, and a circle was cut 24 in. in diameter. The edge was bound by machine with green binding, with a row of white and a row of red applied at half-inch intervals inside this. Two handles each ten inches long are plaited from the three differently coloured bindings and sewn opposite each other on either edge.

As a decoration, a formal flower spray in American cloth is applied to one side. The pattern is given full-size on page 126, and from this readers can trace the necessary shapes. The two flowers are white and also the scroll-like leaf. The stems, narrow-shaped leaf and round flower-centre are green, the pointed flower-centre red. Trace on to one side of the bag the outline of the design and glue the American cloth patches in their appropriate places.

If American cloth is not available, coloured felt might be used, or even odd scraps of material. The latter, however, would have to be hand-sewn in place, a somewhat troublesome task on the thick canvas, and likely to look a little clumsy.

The same colour scheme and materials might be used for garden cushion covers or seats for metal-frame chairs of the folding type.

At the top of the page is a useful garden bag, very easy to make from a circle of awning canvas, with a decoration of American cloth. Below is the working diagram for the amusing cross-stitched nursery or beach-hut tea-cosy on the right

A Cross-stitched Tea-set for Beach-hut or Nursery

THE well-worn old tea-pot rhyme appears here in an amusing guise. The embroidery is simple cross-stitch, and children would find it quite within their powers to make a cloth and cosy for the nursery or the holiday beach-hut all by themselves. Cream Old Bleach linen should be used, with Peri-Lusta stranded cotton for the embroidery, which should be deep blue, green or any rich colour to harmonise with the tea things. Cut out the tea-cosy to the size and shape desired and tack a piece of canvas of about 14 meshes to the inch in the centre of one side. Cross-stitch the pattern from the diagram on the left, using two strands of floss in the needle. Extend the centre lines by cross-stitching these right up to the seam. For the *(Continued overleaf)*

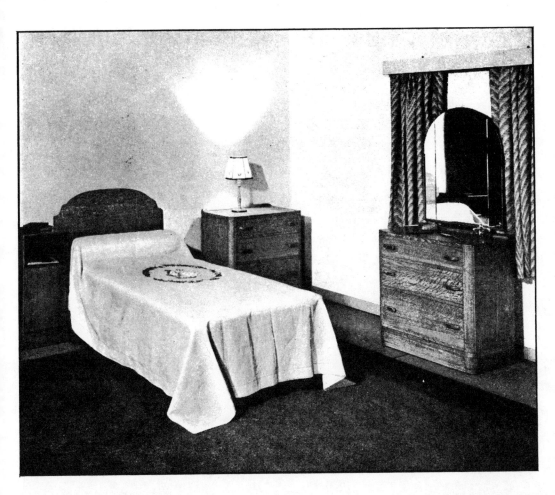

A Bedspread with Floral Wreath Design

A BOLD wreath of flowers, worked in embroidery wool if a quick and strong effect is required, or in stranded cottons for a more subtle result, is always popular for bedspread decoration. In this case the wreath is also a frame for a quaint Victorian pair, who walk sedately through it, dressed in colours that pick up and blend with the colours of the flowers. The design is available as a transfer, design No. 2, price 1s., post free from Good Housekeeping Needlework Dept., 28/30, Grosvenor Gardens, London, S.W.1. It is about 22 inches deep by 18 inches wide, there being more space between the wreath and the head and feet of the Victorian pair than is shown in the diagram on the right. The transfer, of course, carries a complete wreath, not half as shown. Portions of it might well be used for matching runners, mats, etc., for the bedroom.

The linen bedspread in the photograph was bought ready hemstitched from Messrs. Robinson & Cleaver, and is shown in a setting kindly arranged for us by Bowman Bros. The transfer was stamped slightly above the centre of the spread, so that when laid on the bed the design falls well in the middle.

The following are the stitches and colours that were used:

Victorian Pair

Man. Hat: Black outline st., brim black satin st. Face and hands: Flesh outline st., eyes and hair brown satin st., mouth red. Bow: Black satin st. Collar and Cravat: Black outline st. Coat: Purple outline st., collar purple satin st. Stick: Black satin st. Trousers: Grey satin st. Shoes: Black outline st.

Woman. Hat: Brown outline st., ribbon blue satin st., flowers rose wheat st., with yellow French knot centres and green lazy-daisy st. leaves. Parasol: Rose outline st., with border of satin st., handle brown satin st. Face and arms: Flesh outline st. Bodice and crinoline: Rose outline st. Petticoat: Blue outline st. Shoes and pantalettes: Black outline st. Skirt flowers: like hat. (Continued overleaf)

171

THE
30's

WE SAW THE IDEA IN THE SANDERSON BOOK

"We used to think that wallpaper was, well, just wallpaper—until we saw the Sanderson Book. The idea you see here of using a patterned paper only for part of the walls, leaving the frieze, ceiling and fireplace section plain— that idea (and many others for our new home) came from the Sanderson Book."

★ *The Sanderson Wallpaper Book is not just a collection of patterns and prices, but is really a complete guide to wall treatment for the home and is packed with ideas from cover to cover. Any good decorator will be delighted to lend you the Sanderson Book at any time.*

SANDERSON WALLPAPERS

There are also SANDERSON Indecolor FABRICS — Sun-resisting and washproof. Ask to see them at Furnishers & Stores throughout the country, they are made by the makers of the World's most famous Wallpapers. *Arthur Sanderson & Sons, Ltd., Showrooms: 52 & 53, Berners St., London, W.1, and 6 & 7, Newton Terrace, Glasgow, C.3*

172

ANNE ORR NEEDLEWORK DESIGNS
(Continued)

matching cloth, turn an inch hem on the chosen size of linen and sew this down with herringbone stitch on the right side. Then about 2 in. above the hem in the centre of one side tack a piece of canvas measuring 10 meshes to the inch and cross-stitch the design in the diagram given above, using six strands of floss in the needle.

This is the full-size diagram for the motif on the flower-bag on page 48.

A Bedspread with Floral Wreath Design

Wreath
(Reading from one side of diagram upwards to centre.)

Leaves and Stems: Green throughout.
Bell Flower: Light mauve satin st. with deep rose veins in back st.
Spray (same throughout): Deep blue detached chain sts. on green stem.
Seven-petaled Flower: Light blue button-hole st., with centre of yellow French knots.
Daisy: Yellow lazy-daisy sts., with centre of mauve French knots.
Five-petaled Flower: Light rose satin st., with deep rose centre.
Rounded Flowers: One light mauve button-hole st. with dark mauve centre, one dark mauve with yellow centre and one yellow with light mauve centre.
Bell Flower: Deep rose satin st., with veins light mauve back st.
Daisy: Light blue lazy-daisy sts. with yellow centre.

Five-petaled Flower: Light rose button-hole st., with yellow centre.
Seven-petaled Flower: Yellow satin st., with deep rose centre.
Rounded Flowers: One deep rose button-hole st. with yellow centre, one light rose with deep rose centre, one yellow with light rose centre.
Bell Flower: Light mauve satin st., with veins light rose back st.
Seven-petaled Flower: Light mauve button-hole st., with light rose centre.
Daisy: Yellow lazy-daisy st. with light blue centre.
Centre Five-petaled Flower: Light rose satin st. with deep rose centre.
Centre Bell Flower: Light blue satin st. with veins deep mauve back st.

This completes one quarter of the wreath. Work the other sections similarly.

HOME PLANNING AT THE

THE
30's

Glasgow offers something for every-

The front view of the house designed for the Glasgow Exhibition by Basil Spence, A.R.I.B.A.

TRADITION—Scottish tradition, of course—enters into the design of the Ideal Scottish House by Basil Spence in the Empire Exhibition. Mr. Spence was architect of the Scottish Everyday Art Exhibition described in GOOD HOUSEKEEPING in June, 1936; since then he has designed the Scottish pavilion in the Johannesburg Exhibition and also the Scottish and Imperial Chemical Industries Pavilions in Glasgow this summer, so he must be accepted as one of the foremost young architects in Scotland. His Scottish house is just traditional enough to make it take kindly to the Scottish landscape—a very slight Doric accent which could easily be dropped in other surroundings. Its chief national features are the old red farmhouse pantiles of its spreading roof, its modest-sized windows with painted surrounds and the walls of white-washed " harl." Those window surrounds are what I like particularly: they are usually a cottage feature in the north, and they give this most efficient suburban villa exactly that air of welcome and cosiness which beams, say, from the little white houses by the burns in the Isle of Arran. A monumental chimney towering above the roof belongs to quite a different spirit, but it is really a clever trick to bring the house into scale with the broad effects of the Exhibition as a

whole. The canopied entrance is well placed at the base of this chimney, and its bright colours give it due importance.

Colour is the dominant note inside. Those responsible will be accused of breaking with all Scottish—and perhaps English—tradition here, but they have made a splendid effort to put an end to what remains of the " drab colours for

a drab climate " school in favour of a more Scandinavian attitude. The fabrics are superb. Take the dining-room: a simply-designed suite includes chairs upholstered in a Glamis material with bold leaf-and-ribbon pattern by Marion Dorn carried out in colours which suppress any tendency in the pattern to " jump off the cloth." In this room I

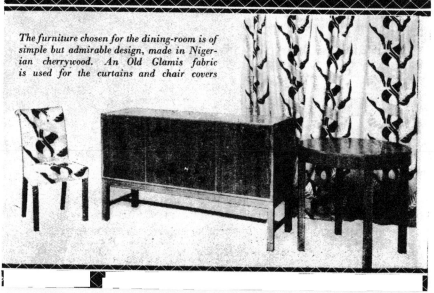

The furniture chosen for the dining-room is of simple but admirable design, made in Nigerian cherrywood. An Old Glamis fabric is used for the curtains and chair covers

Matthew Pollock

EMPIRE EXHIBITION

by MORAY MACBETH

one, not least the home-lover

The back view of the house designed by Basil Spence, showing the water garden

should like to pay a special tribute to the sideboard, because I think it comes as near the perfect 1938 style as could be—a simple chest with cupboards, on four plain legs joined by a plain stretcher, undecorated but most decorative because of the subtle relationship between its parts.

The living-room is a pleasant place —a golden room. Oatmeal and cream walls set off a floor of squares of birch with the grain running now one way and now the other, and the fireplace is fitted with figured tiles in the Dutch manner, but Scottish-made. Indian laurel is the wood chosen for the furniture, and it is upholstered in a Glamis fabric with leafy pattern. Fitted book-

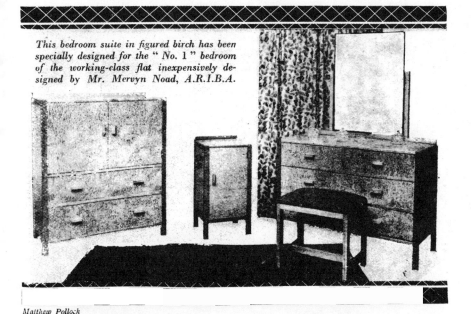

This bedroom suite in figured birch has been specially designed for the "No. 1" bedroom of the working-class flat inexpensively designed by Mr. Mervyn Noad, A.R.I.B.A.

cases occupy an end wall. The curtains are of "Torridon" fabric, a coarse-textured, soft-coloured stuff with a simple check of buff, silvery-grey and brown. Several pictures have been lent by the Society of Scottish Artists. Of the other rooms, the nursery and the largest bedroom attract me most. Duck-egg blue is the finish of the nursery furniture, and the curtains are printed with a delightful nursery-rhyme pattern by Morton Sundour. The bedroom —it has a south exposure—is a symphony in cool silver-greens with pale silver-grey walls and furniture of light sycamore veneer. Upholstery is in a shot mulberry fabric, which tones subtly with the rest of the room. The furnishings are a clever blend of the ingenuous and sophisticated.

Blue is my favourite colour for a bathroom: this one is tiled to the ceiling with a wonderful clear, pale turquoise, there is deep blue linoleum on the floor, and the curtains strike a medium tone. The kitchen breaks away from the cellulose-finish tradition—all furniture is of wax-polished oak, reverted to because of its lasting qualities. A feature beside the window is a little dining-alcove for the maid.

Matthew Pollock

BACHELORS' Homes

by WINIFRED JAMES

THREE EXPERIMENTS

Though the individual items vary greatly, it will be seen that the totals are much the same for the three types of accommodation

C OMING from Australia a few years before the War to try my luck in London as an utterly unknown and inexperienced writer, I decided at once, on such small capital as I possessed, to have a place of my own. From the dawning of infant desires when we made wigwams out of shawls and chairs, this has been the ruling passion of my existence, and every penny I made later went to feed it.

My first flat in Chelsea sounds now like a pipe dream from the point of view of floor space. A newly built affair, but no skyscraper, for I was at the top of the building which, as far as I remember, was the third floor. There was a good-sized living-room fourteen feet square, a small bedroom, a large kitchen and a fairly spacious

bathroom. This, with a little hall and your own front door, costs forty pounds a year with an extra two pounds for the care of the stairs. Every room was airy, with a bright outlook, and the

This was originally the kitchen in the Kentish cottage mentioned in the article, but with a book-surrounded ingle-nook replacing the old range, it became a most attractive living-room for a writer to work and rest in

living-room had two windows where the others had only one. There was a tidy porter in a neat uniform for every so many blocks. The bus to Piccadilly pulled up outside the door! And a stone's-throw away was every kind of shop that the most exacting housewife could want.

They were not exactly smart flats, and in competition with the wonderfully equipped places that have ousted them, they must take a back seat, but they were a great scoop then. And even now they command a price. Out of curiosity a little while ago I inquired at a house agent's the rent of one like mine. It was on their books at a hundred pounds—or offer!

Because of the romance and wonder of my own beginnings in Lon-

COUNTRY COTTAGE

Rent £20
Service 25
Heating &
    Hot Water 26
Expenses to
    London,
    Marble Arch or
    Hyde Park Corner
        Approx 20
Garden & Repairs 20
        Total £111

FLAT IN LONDON

Rent £87
Service 12
Expenses to
    London,
    Marble Arch or
    Hyde Park Corner
        Approx . . . 6
    Total £105

THE
30's

IN ECONOMIC HOUSING

don, the single individual seeking to make a home will always hold first place in my interest. There is something gallant and defenceless about youth starting out alone to battle with life. Raising the umbrella, the tent, the roof, over its unsuspecting head and having no protection against adversity except the inexperience it takes to the encounter.

In spite of the many towering blocks of flats that are rising all over and around London, the bachelor male and female is very inadequately catered for. The increase in the cost of land, labour and materials does not permit of building at pre-war prices. But sometimes, when I come upon the attractive-looking houses that the County Council are erecting for the artisan at moderate rentals, I wish that something along the same lines could be done for the artist, who is many times not as well off as the artisan, and who has expenses to do with his work that the artisan has not.

Some years ago, after a long absence in America, I came to take up life again in London, and looked around me for the best and most economical way to

settle myself in. I could not imagine being without some sort of a place of my own. But things were very different from what they had been in the days when I had come, ignorant and unhampered by experience, to conquer the world. The puppy days were gone. I had been so long out of my world—my writing world—that it looked, in this new world, as if I would have to begin all over again. This would mean spartan living in more ways than one. With labour so hard to get and so untrained when you got it, there would be much one would have to do oneself, and little time for house-dalliance if I were to make up for the years I had lost away from work.

Out of these necessities came three experiences which were so paradoxical and so unexpected that they cannot fail to be a source of illumination on the path of those who, without experience, are to-day faced with the same problems that faced me when I returned. They have also this value, that the budgets were done after and not before the hap-

pening. Those of us who have been through the mill know that the difference between the appearance of an income on a budget sheet before and after experimenting, is just about the difference between a lovely new hat that had gone to the Derby in the sunshine and returned on the top of a coach in the rain.

But all that has to be learned.

The first venture was to do with one of the new housing schemes, for women by women, on the outskirts of London. A member of my club had taken one before the building was finished and she professed herself very satisfied. I made investigation. It sounded quite good except for the fact that, with the exception of one house which allowed for married couples, it was for women only. I am against any plan which makes any division of sex. In some way or other it seems to turn houses into institutions. But the argument for it was fair. Women were seeking to find some solution of the housing problem for *themselves*; not *(Continued overleaf)*

177

THE
30's

178

BACHELORS' HOMES

(Continued)

as a business venture. A commission had gone to Europe to study the latest building schemes there, in a country which had specialised in economic and labour-saving housing.

The building design seemed good and the scheme worked out an extremely low basis of rentals. For the smallest flat one had to take up twenty-five pounds worth of shares. And more for the larger ones.

When I came in upon this, there was already a waiting list, and when my turn arrived I had to make up my mind immediately between the choice of two at forty-five pounds a year. The building was nice-looking and the gardens were simply and well laid out. It was a sort of communal living without interference and seemed interesting. The design of the bed-sitting-rooms was simple. Hardwood floors, white walls, and wrought iron casement windows with red-tiled sills. The rooms were well ventilated, and the toilet, which unfortunately was shared by two flats, was built under cover on a small communicating balcony which also gave each tenant a space for growing plants.

As well, each tenant had the right to a tiny allotment at the foot of the garden where she could grow things out in the open. A fascinating game, that, to grow your own herbs or salads! And these joys all included in a rental of forty-five pounds a year!

But things did not work out quite so well—for me, at any rate. Warmth, physical warmth, and friends are two supports without which I cannot exist. The English Commission visiting Europe must have cut down on the original cost of European building by dispensing with the heating apparatus. The block where I was housed stood on a windswept common bounded on one side by a road like a river in spate, on another by a corridor, and on the remaining two by wide open spaces. An error of judgment from the tenants' point of view had given fireplaces to the inside flats, and only gas fires to the corner ones, which were so mercilessly exposed. There was, as I have said, no central heating as there certainly would have been in the original houses. The corridors were tiled and the casement windows were always open. The dividing doors between the different corridors worked on a two-way hinge and swung open with every gust and blast.

For many the place must be a godsend. Women who go away to their jobs at eight o'clock or eight-thirty in the morning and do not return until six or seven at night would find gas fires both adequate and inexpensive. But I who write most of the day at home, and whose blood has been

chilled in tropic countries, had to add a guinea or more a week to my rent for heating. It would be impossible for the average Englishwoman to understand this, for death by freezing is not within the range of possibility for any home-grown English. You could burn an Englishman to death, or chop him to death, or shoot him to death, but you couldn't freeze him to death because he simply wouldn't freeze.

And none of my friends would come to see me. For them I had gone off the map. When I met them in town they seemed as affectionate as ever, but until I returned they simply grumbled and continued to love me at a distance.

Another flaw in the building plan was the kitchenette-bath. A bed-sitting-room is a practical utility, but a kitchenette-bath is a pure horror. Sometimes in one's life one has had to "make do" temporarily with a corner rigged in a bathroom. But Beau Brummell's differentiation between a darn and a hole in the stocking applies equally well to the kitchenette-bath: "A hole," said the arrogant Brummell, "is an accident, but a darn is premeditated." The premeditated kitchenette-bath is a sin against decent living. It means bath salts in the butter and bacon in the bath. When it is being a kitchenette it takes on all the elements of a bathroom, and when it's a bathroom you seem to bump into food every time you move. The same space with a ventilated bath cabinet opening into the living-room, and a smaller kitchenette with a separate ventilation would deal with the matter of floor space and keep fastidiousness well served.

At the end of a few months I was able to get a working idea of the cost of my economy and I gave it up. I repeat that it was an excellent plan for some, but the individual needs have always to be reckoned with.

On page 26 is the budget worked out at a yearly cost which shows that a small rental is not always the best economy. A small gas fire will not heat a room which has two sides exposed to the elements. The corridor which flanked one side might just as well have been entirely open with the winds that blew down it. And the extra expense of living so far out added £15 a year to the rent, for this allowance only carried one as far into the city as Marble Arch or Hyde Park Corner, where the ordinary fares about the city proper began. It meant that if one had two appointments in a day and one was in the morning and the other in the afternoon one must stay in town cooling the heels between, or else take the tedious journey twice, losing both time and energy doing it and duplicating

(Continued overleaf)

It's newer . . .
It's better . . .
It's bigger . . .

'COLDSPOT'
—no finer refrigerator under the sun

More efficient, more economical, more beautiful than any you have ever seen, the 'Coldspot' has arrived. Created by one of the world's most famous industrial designers, its graceful modern cabinet conceals a host of exclusive features. Every refinement, every little extra convenience, every intriguing ingenuity you have admired singly in other refrigerators — only 'Coldspot' has them all. Yet a 'Coldspot' need cost you very little indeed. For only 6d. a day a 'Coldspot' is yours !

The 'Coldspot' is acknowledged by engineers to be the safest, quietest, simplest electric refrigerator yet devised. Vibration is eliminated and absolute silence achieved. The 'Coldspot' is guaranteed for 4 years.

Read the list of special features in the model illustrated. Post the coupon for " The Seven Wonders of Refrigeration "—a book that will really open your eyes. Then see the range of 'Coldspot' models to suit all households, at your nearest dealer.

For only **6^D a day**—*a 'COLDSPOT' is yours*

THE 30's

COLDSPOT

" The Puffin as a Northern Creature appreciates each 'Coldspot' feature"

ANON

"TOUCH - A - BAR" DOOR OPENER — equal to an extra hand. When both hands are full, a slight touch with the elbow and the refrigerator door swings open. Saves endless journeys in a day.

AUTOMATIC INTERIOR LIGHT. Recessed dome-light goes on automatically when the door is opened ; goes off when door is closed. Lights up the whole inside of the cabinet perfectly.

REFRIGERATED ROLLING PIN. Filled with chilled water it prevents dough from sticking during rolling. Also useful for keeping ready-mixed cocktails in.

ALL 'COLDSPOT' REFRIGERATORS are fully automatic and thermostatically controlled.

LEMONADE OR WATER COOLER. You can draw off a drink without removing the glass cooler from its shelf. Heavily chromium-plated tap. Holds 3 pints.

9 FREEZING SPEEDS. Allows extra fast freezing when required. Saves current when on " slow." Semi-automatic de-frosting.

VEGETABLE BASKETS and Vegetable Reviver. For crisping salads.

MORE ICE CUBES. Largest model gives 138 cubes at one freezing. Quick release trays—no need for pick.

LIFETIME PORCELAIN ENAMEL. Acid and stain-proof. Seamless for easy cleaning. Rounded corners. Rustless aluminium shelves.

EASY PAYMENTS UP TO 4 YEARS.

Keep food fresh in a
'COLDSPOT'

Searsint PRODUCT

To SEARSINT LIMITED (Dept. G.H.), I Thames House, Millbank, London, S.W.I
Please send me by return of post a copy of your booklet "The Seven Wonders of Refrigeration" and the name of my local 'Coldspot' Agent.

NAME .... ADDRESS ....

RA/2.A

179

For SKIN FITNESS
in the SUN !

Sport makes and keeps your body healthy—NIVEA does this for your skin.

NIVEA CREME and NIVEA SKIN OIL both contain 'Eucerite,' which penetrates deeply and strengthens and conditions the skin tissues.

Application of NIVEA before sun-bathing reduces the danger of painful sunburn. Your skin will then tan quickly and smoothly even when the sky is cloudy.

NIVEA also protects the skin from cooling off too quickly, and is therefore helpful in preventing chills.

NIVEA CREME or NIVEA SKIN OIL is indispensable for those engaged in all forms of sport and outdoor exercise.

NIVEA CREME is obtainable in tins at 6d., 1/- and 1/9.
Tubes: 7½d. and 1/3. Jars: 1/9.
NIVEA SKIN OIL in bottles 1/3 and 2/-.

"NIVEA"
"EUCERITE"
Trade Marks.

" Treasure Island right ahead, Captain, with a damsel waving to us."

" A Treasure it is—that Mansion Polish shines the floors until they look like a glassy sea."

The bright, clean, and beautiful floors which are to-day a feature of so many homes are due to the use of Mansion Polish. It requires so little rubbing to obtain a brilliant and lasting finish. And ' Mansion ' also ensures a healthier home, because its antiseptic properties destroy dust germs.

Tins 3d., 6d. and larger sizes.

Mansion WAX Polish
FOR FLOORS, FURNITURE & LINOLEUM

MP/FK/17

BACHELORS' HOMES
(Continued)

the fares. Not till one budgets truly on a small income does one realise what an increase of even one shilling a week makes. One shilling a week means two pounds twelve a year. Quite a nibble.

Dinners and evening theatres dropped out. Indeed, everything seemed to drop out. And with the dropping out a listlessness settled in. It is not good for man to be alone.

Rent	£45 a year
Service . . .	£20 ,,
Heat and hot water (average on summer and winter) .	£45 ,,
Fares into London once a day	£15 ,,
	£125 a year

There came a heavenly interlude. At the moment when I was wondering how I should dispose of the body a cottage in the country materialised. Australian children are reminded every year of a romantic and unseen world which is England, through the medium of Christmas cards. Those of my childhood established a dream world of gabled cottages sparkling with frosty snow and glowing with warm firelight which, by a trick of red gelatine window panes,, shed its radiance out upon the snow. If you wanted to get the zenith of entrancement you stuck a light behind the card.

When the cottage came my way the young adoration was stirred afresh. Here was a dream materialising at last at the price of eight shillings a week, taxes included. A motor-bus passed the gate three times a day for London, which was fifty miles away. The fare was seven-and-six return. If I were to go up even as often as once a week—which I wouldn't do—it would be little more cost than living on the outskirts of London and going in every day. At this distance there would be no daily hankering after companions. New interests would arise. And as there would be a spare room in the cottage friends could come down to me for week-ends.

The cottage was, frankly speaking, a wreck when I went into it. Built about 1730, it had good oak ribs to it, and with money to spend one could have done wonders with it. It consisted of four large, light rooms, two up and two down, with a roomy attic on top and a little staircase of eight steps in the wall. The front door opened right out of the room on to a garden, and the space generally occupied in such rooms by a kitchen range had been turned into an ingle-nook with an open fireplace.

But the rain poured in through the kitchen roof and the windows hung on broken hinges, and many of the panes were broken. There was no light except by lamps, no inside sanitation, and the brick floors, which slanted all ways, were laid straight on to the soil. The ceilings in places were coming down, and the garden was a rubbish heap from which everything in the nature of a plant had been removed by the neighbours before I took possession. Perhaps it was the blood of pioneers that worked in me, but I was stirred rather than daunted by the drawbacks. Certainly I would have been very glad if some of the major drawbacks had been missing, but what couldn't be cured must be endured. And there was so much of joy in the other things I was content to take the rough with the smooth.

I lived in it for two years and got great happiness out of it. When I left it it was a habitable and attractive place.

THE 30's

Do You Know...

... How to Wash Blankets and Protect from Moth During the Summer Months?

MANY people shirk washing blankets, having the idea that the work is difficult and arduous. Provided, however, that one possesses either a washing machine—and this of course ensures thorough washing with the least expenditure of energy—or a large sink or tub in which blankets can be cleansed by kneading or squeezing or by means of a vacuum washer, the work can be accomplished without undue fatigue or trouble. It is, however, very essential to choose a bright, windy day when the blankets can be hung out of doors to dry and air after washing. For washing, a soap jelly prepared from a reliable make of laundry soap should be used, or, alternatively, soap flakes, sufficient of either of the above being added to warm soapy water at a temperature of about 100° F. to make and maintain a good lather. With new blankets it will be found that a good deal of soap is required and if the lather does not persist on immersing the blankets for a minute or so, more should be added. Washing should be by gentle kneading and squeezing, as already mentioned. Rubbing should be avoided at all costs, as nothing tends to felt and shrink wool to a greater extent. When the blankets are quite clean they should be passed through a wringer, and incidentally there is no difficulty about passing a full-sized blanket through a 14-in. or 16-in. rubber wringer, provided it is roughly folded once or twice lengthwise before passing through the rollers. After wringing, the blanket or blankets should be rinsed thoroughly in one or two rinsing waters at about the same temperature as that used for washing. After being passed through the wringer again they should be hung out of doors to dry and shaken now and again in order to loosen the pile. When they are really dry it is quite a good plan to run over the surface lightly with a fine wire brush to raise the pile.

If the blankets are not of a make with a prolonged guarantee against damage caused by moth, and are to be put away for the summer months, they should be sprinkled with a reliable moth-repellent such as para-dichlorobenzene, and made up into airtight parcels, care being taken to paste down the seams so that there is no chance of a stray insect entering.

by

P. L. GARBUTT, A.I.C.

First Class Diploma King's College of Household and Social Science : late staff Battersea Polytechnic

... How to Renovate a Bath?

WITH sufficient patience, the average person can renovate an old, shabby bath very successfully, and provided cleaning methods are wisely selected afterwards and care is taken to run a little cold water into the bath before the hot, a reasonably durable finish can be achieved. For successful results it is essential to use a really hard bath enamel, to prepare the surface thoroughly and carefully, and to allow ample time for the enamel to dry before using the bath again.

The preparation required includes first of all thorough removal of all traces of grease and soap by washing thoroughly in hot, strong soda water, after which the bath should be scoured well with pumice powder or a prepared abrasive block. After rinsing and drying the enamel, the surface should be rubbed down with fine No. 0 glass-paper. After removing dust and all loose particles it is advisable to apply a coat of anti-rust priming if there should be any bare places where the underlying metal is exposed. Leave for twenty-four hours and then apply a thin undercoating. When this is quite dry—a matter of at least twenty-four hours—it should be rubbed down with fine and partly worn glass-paper, and carefully dusted again. Another undercoating should be given if this appears necessary, and allowed to dry, after which the final coat of bath enamel should be carefully brushed on. While the work is in progress it is important to avoid spoiling the surface by drips from the tap, and small pans should be hung underneath each of these.

... That Impregnated Cleaning and Polishing Cloths are available?

THESE eliminate the need for collecting separate polishing cloths, polish, and other paraphernalia for cleaning metal ware of all kinds, mirrors, windows, and furniture. Some of these useful cloths are illustrated. The household series includes a cloth impregnated with suitable ingredients for cleaning mirrors and windows, another for silver, chromium and electro plate, a third for furniture, woodwork and leather articles and a fourth for brass, copper and other metals. The housewife who does her own work will be specially interested in these cloths, which are by no means new, but the convenience of which is sometimes overlooked when spring cleaning, at which time they prove quite invaluable for rubbing up and polishing with the minimum of effort and trouble. In addition to the household series the woman motorist will appreciate the set designed for the car owner. These include a cloth for cleaning and polishing windscreens and windows, as well as others for chromium plate and other parts, for polishing cellulose bodies, and a fourth for cleaning plated parts which may be badly weather-soiled.

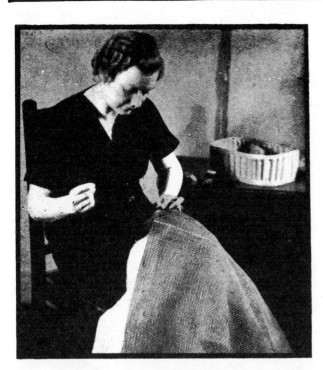

. . . How to Prevent Rugs Slipping on Polished Floors?

WHERE there are young children and animals, rugs are very apt to slip about over polished floors unless preventive measures are taken. The prepared rubberised canvas illustrated is designed for stitching to the under side of rugs, and will be found to hold the most refractory rug firmly in position. The price of this useful material is very moderate.

. . . How to Clean a Discoloured Brick Fireplace?

AFTER the winter, many people find with dismay that the spring sunshine reveals a very discoloured brick fireplace, which resists ordinary cleaning methods. The best way of removing soot and other discoloration is to treat with a diluted solution of hydrochloric acid, often sold as " spirit of salts," using five or six parts of water with one of acid. This should be applied by means of an old cloth or brush, taking care only to rub over the bricks themselves and not to allow the acid to come in contact with the cement between them, on which it is likely to have a slight solvent action. Afterwards all traces of the acid should be very thoroughly rinsed away with plenty of warm water. Rags and brushes used will probably become rotted and should be thrown away, after rinsing thoroughly, as, of course, this acid is extremely poisonous as well as corrosive.

If any soot marks should be apparent on the rug or carpet in part of the fireplace, these might be dealt with at the same time. They can generally be removed quickly and easily by rubbing over with a cloth dipped in carbon tetrachloride, and care should be taken, as we have often warned readers before, to avoid inhaling the vapour from this liquid.

. . . How to Treat a Dusty Cement Floor?

MANY people suffer the inconvenience of a dusty cement floor year after year simply because they do not realise that it is possible to treat it successfully. Such a floor can, however, be improved tremendously by sweeping and then applying a solution of sodium silicate. A prepared sodium silicate designed for waterproofing and hardening concrete can be purchased, or the ordinary

preparation used for preserving eggs can be utilised. If the special preparation is used the manufacturers suggest diluting one gallon of the silicate, which is supplied in a syrupy form, with four gallons of water, using, however, more water when the weather is very hot. The above will make sufficient mixture to treat about 350 square feet of concrete.

A kitchen floor which may be slightly greasy should be scrubbed thoroughly with plenty of hot strong soda water before treatment, as it is imperative for all surfaces to be free from grease as well as perfectly dry. The easiest way of applying the liquid is by means of a watering-can, after which the floor should be brushed over with a mop or soft broom. The treatment should be repeated two or three times, or until the cement will absorb no more liquid.

Another satisfactory way of treating a cement or concrete floor, especially if it is desired to colour it, is to apply a coloured wax polish which, with repeated application, usually gives a very satisfactory finish.

. . . That Good Housekeeping Now Guarantees All Domestic Equipment to which the Institute's Seal of Approval Has Been Given?

READERS should make full use of this new service, and make a point of filling up a guarantee card or the form in the magazine in respect of any tested domestic equipment which they may purchase. The particulars required include the purchaser's name and address, date of purchase, and retailer's or manufacturer's name. With this information the card or form should be posted to Good Housekeeping Institute, 49 Wellington Street, Strand, London, W.C.2, in order that the transaction may be registered and the guarantee take effect. We feel that readers purchasing domestic equipment, particularly the more expensive appliances such as stoves, refrigerators, washing machines, vacuum cleaners, etc., will appreciate this guarantee, which is an assurance of the efficiency and reliability of the article purchased. In the unlikely event of an appliance proving inefficient or of its being faulty in any way, the Institute's backing is often found an invaluable aid in getting matters rectified satisfactorily and expeditiously.

Hints of special value at Spring-cleaning time

THE
30's

An Englishman's HOME

R. BEVERLEY METCALFE tapped the barometer in the back hall and noted with satisfaction that it had fallen several points during the night. He was by nature a sun-loving man, but he believed it was one of the marks of a true countryman to be eternally in need of rain. He had made a study and noted the points of true countrymen. Had he been of literary habit and of an earlier generation, his observations might have formed a little book of aphorisms. The true countryman wore a dark suit on Sundays unlike the flannelled tripper from the cities; he loved a bargain and would go to any expense to do his marketing by private treaty instead of through the normal channels of retail trade; while ostensibly sceptical and conservative he was readily fascinated by mechanical gadgets; he was genial but inhospitable, willing to gossip for hours across a fence with any passing stranger, but reluctant to allow his closest friends into his house. . . . These and a hundred other characteristics Mr. Metcalfe noted for emulation.

"That's what we need—rain," he said to himself, and opening the garden door stepped into the balmy morning air. There was no threat in the cloudless heavens. His gardener passed, pushing the water barrow.

"Good morning, Burns. The glass has dropped, I'm glad to say."

"Ur."

"Means rain."

"Noa."

"Down quite low."

"Ah!"

"Pity to spend a lot of time watering."

"Them'll burn up else."

"Not if it rains."

"Ain't agoin to rain. Don't never rain round heres except you can see clear down-over."

"See clear down-over?"

"Ur. Can always see Pilbury Steeple when rain's a-coming."

Mr. Metcalfe accepted this statement gravely. "These old fellows know a thing or two that the scientists don't," he would often remark, simulating an air of patronage which was far from sincere. Burns, the gardener, was not particularly old and he knew very little; the seeds he planted seldom grew; he wrought stark havoc whenever he was allowed to use the pruning knife; his ambition in horticulture went no farther than the fattening of the largest possible pumpkin; but Mr. Metcalfe regarded him with the simple reverence of peasant for priest. For Mr. Metcalfe was but lately initiated into the cult of the countryside, and every feature of it still claimed his devotion—its agricultural processes, its social structure, its vocabulary, its recreations; the aspect of it, glittering now under the cool May sunshine,

"Mr. Westmacott's sold his field," said Burns. "Sold it! Good heavens! Who to?" his master asked. "Gentleman from London. Paid a tidy price for 'er, too, I've a heard said," replied the gardener

THE
30's

Threaten it, and
you get some very curious results

by EVELYN WAUGH

fruit trees in flower, chestnut in full leaf, the ash budding; the sound and smell of it—Mr. Westmacott calling his cows at dawn, the scent of wet earth and Burns splashing clumsily among the wallflowers; the heart of it—or what Mr. Metcalfe took to be its heart—pulsing all round him; his own heart beating time, for was he not part of it, a true countryman, a landowner?

He was, it is true, a landowner in rather a small way, but, as he stood on his terrace and surveyed the untroubled valley below him, he congratulated himself that he had not been led away by the house agents into the multitudinous cares of a wider territory. He owned

seven acres, more or less, and it seemed to him exactly the right amount; they comprised the policies of the house and a paddock; sixty further acres of farmland had also been available and for a day or two he had toyed with the rather inebriating idea of acquiring them. He could well have afforded it, of course, but to his habit of mind there was something perverse and downright wrong in an investment which showed a bare two per cent. yield on his capital. He wanted a home, not a "seat," and he reflected on the irony of that word; he thought of Lord Brakehurst, with whose property he sometimes liked to say that his own "marched"—there was indeed a

(Continued overleaf)

(Continued)

hundred yards of ha-ha between his paddock and one of Lord Brakehurst's pastures. What could be less sedentary than Lord Brakehurst's life, every day of which was agitated by the cares of his great possessions? No, seven acres, judiciously chosen, was the ideal property, and Mr. Metcalfe *had* chosen judiciously. The house-agent had spoken no more than the truth when he described Much Malcock as one of the most unspoilt Cotswold villages. It was exactly such a place as Mr. Metcalfe had dreamed of in the long years in the cotton trade in Alexandria. Mr. Metcalfe's own residence, known for generations by the singular name of Grumps, had been re-christened by a previous owner as Much Malcock Hall. It bore the new name pretty well. It was " a dignified Georgian house of mellowed Cotswold stone; four recep., six principal bed- and dressing-rooms, replete with period features." The villagers, Mr. Metcalfe observed with regret, could not be induced to speak of it as " The Hall." Burns always said that he worked " up to Grumps," but the name was not of Mr. Metcalfe's choosing and it looked well on his notepaper.

It suggested a primacy in the village that was not undisputed.

Lord Brakehurst, of course, was in a class apart; he was Lord - Lieutenant of the County with property in fifty parishes. Lady Brakehurst had not, in fact, called on Mrs. Metcalfe, living as she did in a world where card-leaving had lost its importance, but, of the calling class, there were two other households in Much Malcock, and a border-line case, besides the vicar, who had a plebeian accent and was apt to preach against bankers.

The rival gentry were Lady Peabury and Colonel Hodge, both, to the villagers, newcomers, but residents of some twenty years' priority to Mr. Metcalfe.

Lady Peabury lived at Much Malcock House, whose chimneys, soon to be hidden in the full foliage of summer, could still be seen among its budding limes on the opposite slope of the valley. Four acres of meadowland lay between her property and Mr. Metcalfe's, where Westmacott's plump herd enriched the landscape and counterbalanced the slightly suburban

splendour of her flower gardens. She was a widow and, like Mr. Metcalfe, had come to Much Malcock from abroad. She was rich and kind and rather greedy, a diligent reader of fiction, mistress of many Cairn terriers and of five steady old maid-servants who never broke the Crown Derby.

Colonel Hodge lived at the Manor, a fine gabled house in the village street, whose gardens, too, backed on to Westmacott's meadow. He was impecunious but active in the affairs of the British Legion and the Boy Scouts; he accepted Mr. Metcalfe's

" *I cannot help feeling,*" *said Mr. Metcalfe,* " *that if this young man were tactfully approached he might be induced to resell at a profit* "

**Illustrations by
H. A. Seabright**

invitations to dinner, but spoke of him, in his family circle, as " the cotton wallah."

These neighbours were of unequivocal position; the Hornbeams at the Old Mill were a childless, middle-aged couple who devoted themselves to craftsmanship. Mr. Hornbeam senior was a genuine, commercial potter in Staffordshire; he supported them reluctantly and rather exiguously, but this backing of unearned quarterly cheques placed them definitely in an upper strata of local society. Mrs. Hornbeam attended

church and Mr. Hornbeam was quite knowledgeable about vegetables. In fact, had they preferred a tennis court to their herb garden, and had Mr. Hornbeam possessed an evening suit, they might easily have mixed with their neighbours on terms of ostensible equality. At the time of the Peace Ballot, Mrs. Hornbeam had canvassed every cottage in bicycling distance, but she eschewed the Women's Institute and in Lady Peabury's opinion failed to pull her weight in the village. Mr. Metcalfe thought Mr. Hornbeam Bohemian, and Mr. Hornbeam thought Mr. Metcalfe Philistine. Colonel Hodge had fallen out with them some time back, on a question relating to his Airedale, and cut them year in, year out, three or four times a day.

Under their stone-tiled roofs the villagers derived substantial comfort from all these aliens. Foreign visitors, impressed by the charges of London restaurants and the splendour of the more accessible ducal palaces, often express wonder at the wealth of England. A half has not been told them. It is in remote hamlets like Much Malcock that the great reservoirs of national wealth seep back to the soil. The villagers had their Memorial Hall and their club. In the rafters of their church the death-watch beetle had been expensively exterminated for them; their Scouts had a bell tent and silver bugles; the district nurse drove her own car; at Christmas their children were surfeited with trees and parties and the cottagers loaded with hampers; if one of them was indisposed, port and soup and grapes and tickets for the seaside arrived in profusion; at evening their men folk returned from work laden with perquisites, and all the year round they feasted on forced vegetables. The vicar found it impossible to interest them in the Left Book Club.

"God gave all men all earth to love," Mr. Metcalfe quoted, dimly remembering the lines from a calendar which had hung in his office in Alexandria. "But since our hearts are small, Ordained for each one spot should prove, Belovèd over all."

He pottered round to the engine house where his chauffeur was brooding over the batteries. He popped his head into another outbuilding and saw that no harm had befallen the lawn-mower during the night. He paused in the kitchen garden to nip the blossom off some newly planted black-currant bushes which must not be allowed to fruit that summer. Then, his round finished, he pottered in to breakfast. *(Continued overleaf)*

An Englishman's Home
(Continued)

His wife was already there.

"I've done my round," he said.

"Yes, dear."

"Everything coming along very nicely."

"Yes, dear."

"You can't see Pilbury Steeple though."

"Good gracious, Beverley, why should you want to do that?"

"It's a sign of rain when you can."

"What a lot of nonsense. You've been listening to Burns again."

She rose and left him with his papers. She had to see the cook. Servants seemed to take up so much time in England; she thought wistfully of the white-gowned Berber boys who had pattered about the cool, tiled floors of her house in Alexandria.

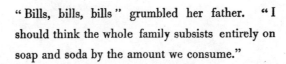
188

Mr. Metcalfe finished his breakfast and retired to his study with pipe and papers. The *Gazette* came out that morning. A true countryman always reads his "local rag" first, so Mr. Metcalfe patiently toiled through the columns of Women's Institute doings and the reports of a Council meeting on the subject of sewage, before he allowed himself to open *The Times*.

Serene opening of a day of wrath!

Towards eleven o'clock Mr. Metcalfe put aside the crossword. In the lobby, by the garden door, he kept a variety of garden implements specially designed for use by the elderly. Selecting from among them one which had newly arrived, he sauntered out into the sunshine and addressed himself to the plantains on the lawn. The tool had a handsomely bound leather grip, a spliced cane handle and a head of stainless steel; it worked admirably, and with a minimum of effort Mr. Metcalfe had soon scarred a large area with neat little pits.

He paused and called towards the house, "Sophie, Sophie, come and see what I've done."

His wife's head emerged from an upper window. "Very pretty, dear," she said.

Encouraged, he set to work again: Burns passed.

"Useful little tool this, Burns."

"Ur."

"Think we ought to sow some seed in the bare patches?"

"Noa."

"You think the grass will grow over them?"

"Noa. Plantains'll come up again."

"You don't think I've killed the roots?"

"Noa. Makes the roots powerful strong topping 'em off same as you've done."

"Well, what ought I to do?"

"Bain't nothing you can do with plantains. They do always come up again."

Burns passed. Mr. Metcalfe looked at his gadget with sudden distaste, propped it petulantly against the sundial, and with his hands in his pockets stared out across the valley. Even at this distance Lady Peabury's aubrietias struck a discordant note. His eyes dropped and he noticed, casually at first, then with growing curiosity, two unfamiliar figures among Westmacott's cows. They were young men in dark, urban clothes and they were very busy about something. They had papers in their hands which they constantly consulted; they paced up and down the field as though measuring it; they squatted on their haunches as though roughly taking a level; they pointed into the air, to the ground and to the horizon.

"Burns," said Mr. Metcalfe sharply, "come here a minute."

"Ur."

"Do you see two men in Mr. Westmacott's field?"

"Noa."

"You don't?"

"Er bain't Mr. Westmacott's field. 'E've a sold of 'er."

"Sold it! Good heavens! Who to?"

"Couldn't rightly say who e've a sold 'er to. Gentleman from London staying at the Brakehurst. Paid a tidy price for 'er, too, I've a heard said."

"What on earth for?"

"Couldn't rightly say, but I reckon it be to build hisself a house."

Build. It was a word so hideous that no one in Much Malcock dared use it above a whisper. "Housing scheme," "Development," "Clearance," "Council houses," "Planning"—these obscene words had been expunged from the polite vocabulary of the district, only to be used now and then, with the licence allowed to anthologists, of the fierce tribes beyond the parish boundary. And now the horror was

An Englishman's Home

in their midst, the mark of the Plague in the court of the Decameron.

After the first moment of shock, Mr. Metcalfe rallied for action, hesitated for a moment whether or not to plunge down the hill and challenge the enemy on his own ground, and decided against it; this was the moment to act with circumspection. He must consult Lady Peabury.

It was three-quarters of a mile to The House; the lane ran past the gate which gave access to Westmacott's field; a crazily hung elm gate and deep, cow-trodden mud, soon, in Mr. Metcalfe's imagination, to give place to golden privet and red gravel. Mr. Metcalfe could see the heads of the intruders bobbing beyond the hedge; they bore urban, purposeful black hats. He drove on, miserably.

Lady Peabury was in the morning-room reading a novel; early training gave a guilty spice to this recreation, for she had been brought up to believe that to read a novel before luncheon was one of the gravest sins it was possible for a gentlewoman to commit. She slipped the book under a cushion and rose to greet Mr. Metcalfe.

"I was just getting ready to go out," she explained.

Mr. Metcalfe had no time for politeness.

"Lady Peabury," he began at once, "I have very terrible news."

"Oh dear. Is poor Mr. Cruttwell having trouble with the Wolf Cub accounts again?"

"No, at least he is; there's another four-pence gone astray; on the credit side this time, which makes it more worrying. But that isn't what I came about. It is something that threatens our whole lives. They are going to build in Westmacott's field." Briefly, but with emotion, he told Lady Peabury what he had seen.

She listened gravely. When he had finished there was silence in the morning-room; six little clocks ticked among the chintzes and the potted azaleas. At last Lady Peabury spoke:

"Westmacott has done very wrong," she said.

"I suppose you can't blame him."

"I do blame him, Mr. Metcalfe, very severely. I can't understand it at all. He always seemed a very decent man.... I was thinking of making Mrs. Westmacott secretary of the Women's Institute. He had no right to do a thing like that without consulting us. Why, I look right on to that field from my bedroom windows. I could never understand why you didn't buy the field yourself."

It was let for £3 18s.; they had asked £170 for it; there was tithe and property tax on top of that. Lady Peabury knew this.

"Any of us could have bought it at the time of sale," said Mr. Metcalfe rather sharply.

"It always went with your house."

In another minute, Mr. Metcalfe felt, she would be telling him that *he* had done very wrong; that *he* had always seemed a very decent man.

She was, in fact, thinking on just those lines at the moment. "I daresay it's not too late even now for you to make an offer," she said.

"We are all equally threatened," said Mr. Metcalfe. "I think we ought to act together. Hodge won't be any too pleased when he hears the news."

Colonel Hodge had heard, and he was none too pleased. He was waiting at The Hall when Mr. Metcalfe got back.

"Do you know what that scoundrel Westmacott has done?"

"Yes," said Mr. Metcalfe rather wearily, "I know." The interview with Lady Pea-

bury had not gone off quite as he had hoped. She had shown no enthusiasm for common action.

"Sold his field to a lot of jerry builders."

"Yes, I know."

"Funny, I always thought it was *your* field."

"No," said Mr. Metcalfe, "never."

"It always used to go with this house."

"Yes, I know, but I didn't happen to want it."

"Well, it's put us all in a pretty nasty fix, I must say. D'you suppose they'd sell it back to you now?"

"I don't know that I want to buy it. Why, they'll probably want a building land price—a hundred and fifty pounds an acre."

"More, I daresay. But, good heavens, man, you wouldn't let that stop you. Think how it would depreciate your property having a whole town of bungalows right under your windows."

"Come, come, Hodge. We've no reason to suppose that it will be bungalows."

"Well, villas then. You surely aren't sticking up for the fellows?"

"Certainly not. We shall all suffer very much from any development there. My belief is that it can be stopped by laws; there's the Society for the Protection of Rural England. We could interest them in it. The County Council could be approached. We could write letters to the papers and petition the Office of Works. The great thing is that we must all stand together over this."

"Fat lot of change we shall get out of that. Think of the building that's gone on over Metbury."

Mr. Metcalfe thought, and shuddered.

"I should say that this was one of the times when money talked loudest. Have you tried Lady Peabury?"

For the first time in their acquaintance Mr. Metcalfe detected a distinctly coarse strain in Colonel Hodge. "I have discussed it with her. She is naturally very much concerned."

"That field has always been known as Lower Grumps," said the Colonel, reverting to his former and doubly offensive line of thought. "It's not really her chicken."

"It is all our chickens," said Mr. Metcalfe, getting confused with the metaphor.

"Well, I don't know what you expect me to do about it," said Colonel Hodge. "You know how I'm placed. It all comes of that parson preaching Bolshevism Sunday after Sunday."

"We ought to get together and discuss it."

"Oh, we'll discuss it all right. I don't suppose we shall discuss anything else for the next three months."

No one in Much Malcock took the crisis harder than the Hornbeams. News of it reached them at midday by means of the village charwoman, who dropped in twice a week to despoil their larder. She told them with some pride, innocently assuming that all city gentlemen—as she continued to regard Mr. Hornbeam in spite of his homespuns and his beard—would welcome an addition to their numbers.

Nervous gloom descended on the Old Mill. There was no explosion of wrath as there had been at The Manor; no moral condemnation as at The House; no call to action as had come from The Hall. Hopeless sorrow reigned unrelieved. Mrs. Hornbeam's potting went to pieces. Mr. Hornbeam sat listless at the loom. It was their working hour; they sat at opposite ends of the raftered granary. Often, on other afternoons, they sang to one another catches and refrains of folk music as their busy fingers muddled with the clay and the shuttles. To-day they sat in silence,

each, according to a Japanese mystical practice, attempting to drive the new peril in the World of Unbeing. It had worked well enough with Colonel Hodge and the Airedale, with the Abyssinian War and with Mr. Hornbeam senior's yearly visit, but by sunset the new peril remained obstinately concrete.

Mrs. Hornbeam set their simple meal of milk, raisins and raw turnip; Mr. Hornbeam turned away from his elm platter. "There is no place for the Artist in the Modern World," he said. "We ask nothing of their brutish civilisation except to be left alone, to be given one little corner of land, an inch or two of sky where we can live at peace and occupy ourselves with making seemly and beautiful things. You wouldn't think it was too much to ask. We give them the entire globe for their machines. But it is not enough. They have to hunt us out and harry us. They know that as long as there is one spot of loveliness and decency left it is a standing reproach to them."

It was growing dark; Mrs. Hornbeam struck a flint and lit the rush lights. She wandered to the harp and plucked a few poignant notes. "Perhaps Mr. Metcalfe will stop it," she said.

"That we should be dependent for the essentials of life upon a vulgarian like that . . ."

It was in this mood that he received an invitation from Mr. Metcalfe to confer with his neighbours at Much Malcock House on the following afternoon.

The choice of meeting-place had been a delicate one, for Lady Peabury was loth to abdicate her position of general leadership or to appear as leader in this particular matter; on the other hand it touched her too closely for her to be able to ignore it. Accordingly the invitations were issued by Mr. Metcalfe, who thereby accepted responsibility for the agenda, while the presence of the meeting in her morning-room gave something of the atmosphere of a Cabinet meeting at the Palace.

Opinion had hardened during the day and there was general agreement with Colonel's Hodge's judgment: "Metcalfe has got us into this hole by not buying the field in the first place; it's up to him to get us out of it." Though nothing as uncompromising as this was said in front of Mr. Metcalfe, he could feel it in the air. He was the last to arrive. Lady Peabury's welcome to her guests had been lukewarm. "It is very kind of you to come. I really cannot think that it is necessary, but Mr. Metcalfe particularly wished it. I suppose he intends telling us what he is going to do." To Mr. Metcalfe she said, "We are full of curiosity."

"Sorry to be late. I've had a day of it, I can tell you. Been to all the local offices, got on to all the Societies and I may as well tell you at once, there's nothing doing from that end. We are not even scheduled as a rural area."

"No," said Colonel Hodge, "I saw to that. Halves the potential value of one's property."

"*Schedules*," moaned Mr. Hornbeam, "that is what we have become. We must be *scheduled* to lead a free life."

". . . And so," persisted Mr. Metcalfe, in his board-room manner, "we are left to find the solution ourselves. Now this young man has no particular reason, I imagine, for preferring this district above any other in the country. The building has not yet begun; he has no commitments. I cannot help feeling that if he were tactfully approached and offered a reasonable profit on the transaction, he might be induced to resell."

"I am sure," said Lady Peabury, "we

189

(Continued overleaf)

Given Flavourable Conditions...

Seasoning! Now there's a word which either means exactly what it's meant to mean—or just nothing at all!

Time was when housewives had their own blends of spices for seasoning ragouts and savoury stews. I remember receiving from an old woman a cherished mixed spice family recipe. She gave it to me, " not," as she said, " because it is so useful to-day, but rather to show you what my mother's idea of a spice blend was."

Well, I mixed the lot and added a pinch of the concoction here and there to casserole dishes, but I soon went back to my old tried and tested way of seasoning—because I get a softer and more mellow spiced flavour by using Lea & Perrins Sauce.

There's a very good reason for this. In Lea & Perrins, you have a true flavouring-seasoning essence made by the maturing of a wide variety of spices, herbs, fruits and vegetables in vinegar and soy. The process under which Lea & Perrins is made produces a concentrated extract of the goodness of the various ingredients.

It's simply another instance of a manufacturer producing for us an indispensable commodity which we would like to make, but could not possibly succeed in making, for ourselves—and at amazingly small cost to us.

Take a bottle of Lea & Perrins. Do you know, you can get one for as little as sixpence! If you could buy the ingredients of that bottle (and you couldn't) they would cost you many more times what you pay for them in their assembled form.

I look on Lea & Perrins as the most economical of all seasoning agents. I use it in so many dishes, to which it adds delicious piquancy and zest at next-to-nothing cost. Always I have a bottle at hand for kitchen use—and another one, for table use, in the sideboard of my dining-room.

Try adding anything from a half teaspoonful to a dessertspoonful in all but milk soups, the amount depending, of course, on the quantity of soup itself. Add Lea & Perrins, too, to clear or slightly thick brown gravies. For Sauce

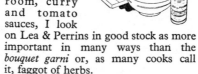

Piquante and Robert, mushroom, curry and tomato sauces, I look on Lea & Perrins in good stock as more important in many ways than the *bouquet garni* or, as many cooks call it, faggot of herbs.

It's always on hand, always (after a shake of the bottle) ready for use—and, to tell the truth, it's much more economical, much more practical and *much more flavorous.*

While I use Lea & Perrins most frequently in " wet dishes "—that is, soups, sauces, casseroles, etc.—I find that in what I call " dry cooking " it can do more than any other seasoning to add that touch of piquancy such " dry cooked " dishes often lack.

Take, for instance, fried fillets of fish. Add a drop or two of Lea & Perrins on each fillet. Rub the seasoning well in. Pass the fillets through salted flour, then egg and bread-crumb them and fry them in the usual way. Judge the improvement for yourselves!

I have a special Spanish cheese recipe—simply wedges of Gruyère cheese, with a drop of Lea & Perrins rubbed over them, floured, egg and bread-crumbed, then deep-fat fried. Before I tried Lea & Perrins with this savoury, the cheeses were very good. Now they're twice as good!

Next time you have a mixed grill, pour off most of the fat from the grill-pan. Add a teaspoonful of Lea & Perrins, heat it through, pour it over the grill—and serve a better dish!

I have a trick with thin slices of fillet steak, which I suggest you try. I melt a little butter in a frying-pan, add a good teaspoonful of Lea & Perrins and dry off the liquid from the sauce, leaving the zestful flavour there. I add a little more butter and fry my thin steaks in it—not too quickly or the butter will burn. I serve the steaks at once with the flavoured butter poured over them.

Flavorous! It's what I've told you—Lea & Perrins Sauce!

★　　★　　★　　★　　★　　★　　★　　★

(Continued)

shall all owe a deep debt of gratitude to Mr. Metcalfe."

" Very public spirited of you," said Colonel Hodge.

" Profits, the cancer of the age . . ."

" I am perfectly willing," said Mr. Metcalfe, " to bear my share of the burden . . ." At the word ' share' his hearers stiffened perceptibly. " My suggestion is that we make a common fund proportionate to our present land holdings. By a rough calculation I work that out as being in the ratio of one to Mr. Hornbeam, two to Colonel Hodge, two to myself, and five to our hostess here. The figures could be adjusted," he added as he noted that his suggestion was falling a little flat.

" You can count me out," said Colonel Hodge. " Couldn't possibly run to it."

" And me," said Mr. Hornbeam.

Lady Peabury was left in, with a difficult hand to stake. Delicacy forbade recognition of the vital fact that Mr. Metcalfe was very much the richer—delicacy tempered with pride. The field must be saved, but there seemed no system of joint purchase by which she could honourably fail to bear the largest part. Duty called, clearly and unmistakably, to Mr. Metcalfe alone. She held her cards and passed the bidding. " Surely," she said, " as a business man you must see a great many objections to joint ownership. Do you propose to partition the field, or are we all to share the rent, the tithe and the tax? It would be highly inconvenient. I doubt if it is even legal."

" Certainly, certainly. I merely wished to assure you of my readiness to co-operate. The field, as such, is of no interest to me, I can assure you. I would willingly stand down."

There was a threat, almost a lack of politeness, in his tone. Colonel Hodge scented danger.

" Wouldn't it be best," he said, " to find out first if this fellow is willing to re-sell? Then you can decide which of you keep it."

" I am sure Mr. Metcalfe's commercial experience will show him where his best interests lie," said Lady Peabury.

She should not have said that. She would gladly have recalled the words the moment after they were uttered. She had vaguely wanted to say something disagreeable, to punish Mr. Metcalfe for the discomfort in which she found herself. She had not meant to antagonise him and this she had unmistakably done.

Mr. Metcalfe left The House abruptly, almost precipitately, and all that evening he chafed. For fifteen years Mr. Metcalfe had been president of the British Chamber of Commerce. He had been greatly respected by the whole business community. No one could put anything across him and he would not touch anything that was not above board. Egyptian and Levantine merchants who tried to interest Metcalfe in shady business went away with a flea in the ear. It was no good trying to squeeze him. That was his reputation in the Union Club, and here, at home in his own village, an old woman was trying to browbeat him into a bad bargain. There was a sudden change. He was no longer the public-spirited countryman; he was cards-on-the-table, brass-tacks and twenty-shillings-in-the-pound, treat-him-fair-or-mind-your-step Metcalfe, Metcalfe with his back up, fighting Metcalfe once again, Metcalfe who would cut off his nose any day to spite his face, sink any ship for a ha'p'orth of tar that was not legally due, Metcalfe the lion of the Rotarians.

" She should not have said that," said Colonel Hodge, reporting the incident to his wife over their horrible dinner. " Metcalfe won't do anything now."

" Why don't *you* go and talk to the man who's bought the field? " said Mrs. Hodge.

An Englishman's Home

"I might . . . I think I will . . . Tell you what, I'll go now."

He went.

He found the man without difficulty, since there was no other visitor staying at the Brakehurst Arms. An enquiry from the landlord elicited his name—Mr. Hargood-Hood. He was sitting alone in the parlour, sipping whisky and soda and working at *The Times'* crossword.

The Colonel said, " Evening. My name is Hodge."

" Yes? "

" I daresay you know who I am."

" I'm very sorry, I'm afraid . . ."

" I own The Manor. My garden backs on to Westmacott's field—the one you've bought."

" Oh," said Mr. Hargood-Hood, " was he called Westmacott? I didn't know. I leave all these things to my lawyer. I simply told him to find me a suitable, secluded site for my work. He told me last week he had found one here. It seems very suitable. But he didn't tell me anyone's name."

" You didn't pick this village for any particular reason? "

" No, no. But I think it perfectly charming," he added politely.

There was a pause.

" I wanted to talk to you," said Colonel Hodge superfluously. " Have a drink? "

" Thank you."

Another pause.

" I'm afraid you won't find it a very healthy site," said the Colonel. " Down in the hollow there."

" I never mind things like that. All I need is seclusion."

" Ah, a writer no doubt? "

" No."

" A painter? "

" No, no. I suppose you would call me a scientist."

" I see. And you would be using your house for week-ends? "

" No, no, quite the reverse. I and my staff will be working here all the week. And it's not exactly a house I'm building, although, of course, there will be living quarters attached. Perhaps, since we are going to be such close neighbours, you would like to see the plans . . ."

" . . . You never saw such a thing," said Colonel Hodge next morning to Mr. Metcalfe. " An experimental industrial laboratory he called it. Two great chimneys—have to have those, he said, by law, because of poison fumes, a water tower to get high pressures, six bungalows for his staff . . . ghastly. The odd thing was he seemed quite a decent sort of fellow. Said it hadn't occurred to him anyone would find it objectionable. Thought we should all be interested. When I brought up the subject of re-selling—tactfully, you know—he just said he left all that to his lawyer . . ."

Much Malcock Hall.
Dear Lady Peabury,

In pursuance of our conversation of three days ago, I beg to inform you that I have been in communication with Mr. Hargood-Hood, the purchaser of the field which separates our two properties, and his legal representative. As Col. Hodge has already informed you, Mr. Hargood-Hood proposes to erect an experimental industrial laboratory fatal to the amenities of the village. As you are doubtless aware, work has not yet been commenced, and Mr. Hargood-Hood is willing to re-sell the property if duly compensated. The price proposed is to include re-purchase of the field, legal fees and compensation for the architect's work. *The young blackguard has us in a cleft stick. He wants £500. It is excessive, but I am prepared to pay half of this, if you will pay the other half. Should you not accede to this generous offer I shall take steps to safeguard my own interests* at whatever cost to the neighbourhood.

Yours sincerely,
Beverley Metcalfe.

P.S.—I mean I shall sell The Hall and develop the property as building lots.

Much Malcock House.
Lady Peabury begs to inform Mr. Metcalfe that she has received his note of this morning, the tone of which I am unable to account for. She further begs to inform you that she has no wish to increase my already extensive responsibilities in the district. She cannot accept the principal of equal obligation with Mr. Metcalfe as he has far less land to look after and the field in question should rightly form part of your property. She does not think that the scheme for developing your garden as a housing estate is likely to be a success if Mr. Hargood-Hood's laboratory is as unsightly as is represented, which I rather doubt.

" All right," said Mr. Metcalfe. " That's that and be damned to her."

It was ten days later. The lovely valley, so soon to be defiled, lay resplendent in the sunset. Another year, thought Mr. Metcalfe, and this fresh green foliage would be choked with soot, withered with fumes; these mellow roofs and chimneys, which for two hundred years or more had enriched the landscape below the terrace, would be hidden by functional monstrosities in steel and glass and concrete. In the doomed field Mr. Westmacott, almost for the last time, was calling his cattle; next week building was to begin and they must seek other pastures. So, in a manner of speaking, must Mr. Metcalfe. Already his desk was littered with house agents' notices. All for £750, he told himself. There would be re-decorations; the cost and loss of moving. The speculative builders to whom he had viciously appealed showed no interest in the site. He was going to lose much more than £500 on the move. But so, he grimly assured himself, was Lady Peabury. She would learn that no one could put a fast one over on Beverley Metcalfe.

And she, on the opposite slope, surveyed the scene with corresponding melancholy. The great shadows of the cedars lay across the lawn; they had scarcely altered during her long tenancy, but the box hedges had been of her planting; it was she who had planned the lily pond and glorified it with lead flamingos; she had reared the irregular heap of stones under the west wall and stocked it with Alpines; the flowering shrubs were hers; she could not take them with her where she was going. Where? She was too old now to begin another garden, to make other friends. She would move, like so many of her contemporaries, from hotel to hotel, at home and abroad, cruise a little, settle for prolonged, rather unwelcome visits, on her relatives. All this for half £750, for £15 a year, for less than she gave to charity. It was not the money; it was Principle. She would not compromise with Wrong; with that ill-bred fellow on the hill opposite.

Despite the splendour of the evening an unhappy spirit obsessed Much Malcock. The Hornbeams moped and drooped;

Colonel Hodge fretted. He paced the threadbare carpet of his smoking-room. " It's enough to make a fellow turn Bolshie, like that parson," he said. " What does Metcalfe care? He's rich. He can move anywhere. What does Lady Peabury care? It's the small man, trying to make ends meet, who suffers."

Even Mr. Hargood-Hood seemed affected by the general gloom. His lawyer was visiting him at the Brakehurst. All day they had been in intermittent, rather anxious consultation. " I think I might go and talk to that Colonel again," he said, and set off up the village street, under the deepening shadows, for the Manor House. And from this dramatic, last-minute move for conciliation sprang the great Hodge Plan for appeasement and peace-in-our-time.

" . . . the Scouts are badly in need of a new hut," said Colonel Hodge.

" No use coming to me," said Mr. Metcalfe. " I'm leaving the neighbourhood."

" I was thinking," said Colonel Hodge, " that Westmacott's field would be just the place for it . . ."

And so it was arranged. Mr. Hornbeam gave a pound, Colonel Hodge a guinea, Lady Peabury £250. A jumble sale, a white elephant tea, a raffle, a pageant, and a house-to-house collection produced a further 30s. Mr. Metcalfe found the rest. It cost him, all told, a little over £800. He gave with a good heart. There was no question now of jockeying him into a raw deal. In the rôle of public benefactor he gave with positive relish, and when Lady Peabury suggested that the field should be reserved for a camping site and the building of the hut postponed, it was Mr. Metcalfe who pressed on with the building and secured the old stone tiles from the roof of a dismantled barn. In the circumstances Lady Peabury could not protest when the building was named the Metcalfe-Peabury Hall. Mr. Metcalfe found the title invigorating and was soon in negotiation with the brewery for a change of name at the Brakehurst Arms. It is true that Burns still speaks of it as " the Brakehurst," but the new name is plainly lettered for all to read: The Metcalfe Arms.

And so Mr. Hargood-Hood passed out of the history of Much Malcock. He and his lawyer drove away to their home beyond the hills. The lawyer was Mr. Hargood-Hood's brother.

" We cut that pretty fine, Jock. I thought, for once, we were going to be left with the baby."

They drove to Mr. Hargood-Hood's home, a double-quadrangle of mellow brick that was famous far beyond the county. On the days when the gardens were open to the public, record crowds came to admire the topiary work, yews and boxes of prodigious size and fantastic shape which gave perpetual employment to three gardeners. Mr. Hargood-Hood's ancestors had built the house and planted the gardens in a happier time, before the days of property tax and imported grain. A sterner age demanded more strenuous efforts for their preservation.

" Well, that has settled schedule A for another year and left something over for cleaning the fish-ponds. But it was an anxious month. I shouldn't care to go through it again. We must be more careful next time, Jock. How about moving east? "

Together the two brothers unfolded the inch ordnance map of Norfolk, spread it on the table of the Great Hall and began their preliminary, expert search for a likely, unspoilt, well-loved village.

THE
30's

191

THE
30's

PRAYER
for a New Home

by Virginia Eaton

Illustration by John R. Flanagan

WE BOUGHT a house to-day !   A great oak spreading
Its branches wide to all wild things and shy ;
Six slender birch trees with their frail leaves threading
A patterned lace across an oval sky.
Stout beams and rafters overlaid with shingles ;
Two tall red chimneys and a carven door ;
And honeysuckle with barberry mingles
Beside a shaded porch with red-tiled floor.

SO MUCH of beauty !   We would ask Thy guiding ;
Let all who cross the threshold of this place
Find hope and courage, friendliness abiding ;
And added to these, grant Thy gift of grace ;
Let peace that passes understanding rest
Upon this house, and us, and every guest.

Good Housekeeping

SEPTEMBER 1931

ONE SHILLING NETT

Beginning GOOD-BYE, SUMMER
By Fanny Heaslip Lea

John Galsworthy ~ J.E.Buckrose ~ A.Duff Cooper, M.P.

Good Housekeeping

NOVEMBER 1931

ONE SHILLING NETT

SPECIAL FURNISHING SUPPLEMENT
EARLY XMAS PRESENTS FOR ABROAD

Good Housekeeping

DECEMBER 1931

1/- nett Double Christmas Number
New Novel by O. Douglas
Virginia Woolf - Marguerite Steen - Coningsby Dawson

Good Housekeeping

FEBRUARY 1933
ONE SHILLING
NETT

MEMORIES OF A ROYAL FRIENDSHIP
by Clare Sheridan

*Mariel Brady - L.A.G. Strong - Kathleen Norris
Mary Borden - William Armstrong - E.M.Delafield*

Good Housekeeping

SEPTEMBER 1934   ONE SHILLING NETT

THE INSTITUTE'S TENTH BIRTHDAY
Beginning Mary Queen of Scots by Esmé Whittaker
Stella Gibbons · Marion Cran · Lorna Rea

Good Housekeeping

OCTOBER 1934   ONE SHILLING NETT

AUTUMN FURNISHING NUMBER

*Rafael Sabatini · Marion Cran · Princess Troubetzkoy
Helena Normanton · St. John Ervine · Winifred Holtby
Ethel Smyth · Christine Jope-Slade · Lorna Rea*

Good Housekeeping

MARCH 1935   ONE SHILLING NETT

SPRING CLEANING NUMBER

"I Wish I Had Been a Man" by | New Short Story Series by
THE COUNTESS of OXFORD AND ASQUITH | SHEILA KAYE-SMITH

Good Housekeeping

APRIL 1935   ONE SHILLING NETT

SPRING FASHIONS FOR EASTER
Sheila Kaye-Smith : Florence White : Dr. Maude Royden
Victoria Sackville-West : Countess of Oxford and Asquith

Good Housekeeping

In This Issue
Millicent
Duchess of Sutherlan
F. Brett Young
The Countess o
Oxford and Asqu
Sheila Kaye-Sm
Kathleen Wal'

MAY 1935

1/-

SPECIAL JUBILEE NUMBE